A FIELD GUIDE TO THE

Birds of Mexico and
Central America

NUMBER ONE

The John Fielding and Lois Lasater Maher Series

A FIELD GUIDE TO THE
Birds of Mexico
and Central America

By L. IRBY DAVIS

COLOR PLATES BY F. P. BENNETT, JR.

UNIVERSITY OF TEXAS PRESS
AUSTIN AND LONDON

International Standard Book Number 0-292-70700-2
Library of Congress Catalog Card Number 76-178695
© 1972 by L. Irby Davis
Composition by The William Byrd Press, Richmond, Virginia
Printing by Steck-Warlick Company, Austin, Texas
Binding by Universal Bookbindery, Inc., San Antonio, Texas

CONTENTS

Contents   vii

ACKNOWLEDGMENTS

Throughout the thirty-five years of my personal field work in Middle America I have had much help and encouragement from the many camping companions and from the numerous field students who worked with me on the bird censuses conducted in various states of the Republic of Mexico, in British Honduras, Nicaragua, Costa Rica, and Panama (the names of these companions, which include my wife, Anna May, are listed in the published reports in Audubon Field Notes, the *Condor,* or the *Newsletter* of the Texas Ornithological Society). Richard Zusi of the United States National Museum, Dean Amadon of the American Museum of Natural History, George Lowery of the Museum of Zoology at Louisiana State University, and William Hardy of the Moore Laboratory of Zoology at Occidental College all kindly helped by supplying study skins to aid F. P. Bennett, Jr. in the painting of the plates. Over the years various museum ornithologists have advised me on taxonomic points, speciation, or population problems. These include Frank Chapman, Ludlow Griscom, Charles Nichols, Alex Wetmore, Paul Slud, Robert Newman, John Aldrich, Lester Short, Ernst Mayr, and Eugene Eisenmann. The names used in the text were largely derived from those in standard reference works, such as *The Birds of North and Middle America* by Ridgway, *Catalogue of Birds of the Americas* by Hellmayr and others, and *Birds of the Ocean* by Alexander; however, some were necessarily changed or modified in order to indicate different relationships that were discovered in the field studies or to conform with new views suggested by names in recent scientific books by Slud (*The Birds of Costa Rica*) and Wetmore (*The Birds of the Republic of Panama*). Paul Schwartz, Carl Kauffeld, George Reynard, Joe Marshall, John O'Neill, and Donald Borror have supplied tape recordings that were valuable in describing vocalizations; Carl Aiken, Eddie Chalif, Dick Herbert, Roger Peterson, Harry Darrow, John Morony, Pauline James, Marshall Johnston, and Edgar Kincaid helped with the voice studies and supplied much useful reference material. Arthur Allen, Elsa Allen, and David Allen assisted in accumulating voice recordings while on joint field expeditions in Mexico. Byrl and Paul Kellogg, Sally Hoyt, and Randolph Little helped with the bioacoustical studies. Leslie Holdridge, Marion Goode, Monty Cook, Alexander Skutch, John Ernest, Robert Wilson, Darrell Cole,

Jack Ozanne, and Jorge Zeledon provided me with bases for field work in typical ecological habitats in Costa Rica and gave advice and assistance on many occasions. Paul Schwartz and Orville Crowder made it possible for me to visit typical habitats in Venezuela and Colombia respectively. To all of these people and to many more I am indebted for the assistance that each has given.

INTRODUCTION

It is the purpose of this guide to serve birders and field students who make occasional trips to the North American tropics. Accordingly, the taxonomy adopted is intended to be useful to those having little knowledge of the technical classification presently in vogue among museum systematists. A name is provided for each distinct population in order to make taxonomy useful rather than confusing to the student. Thus, some populations, which are frequently classed as "races," are treated as "species" in order to emphasize differences. No "races" are recognized as such, and gradual or clinal-type changes in plumage are ignored taxonomically—although they are mentioned in the discussion of the species. Some old or discarded genera are necessarily revived in order to make groupings more nearly "natural," that is, to emphasize similarities. The result is a classification rather like that of Ridgway. However, various taxonomic views are mentioned in each case and hence are available to those who wish to use them.

In the field it is frequently observed that color patterns may have little or nothing to do with species recognition by the birds in some groups and that behavior traits and voice structure may be important in both species and individual recognition. Since little is known about these characteristics in many groups, some populations must still be separated by color patterns until we find out definitely that other characters are available. On the other hand, since color patterns may be useless in species recognition, we should hesitate to lump distant populations that appear somewhat similar until we find that the vocal patterns and behavior traits support such lumping.

In this guide, wherever possible, voice is used as a taxonomic character. In groups in which there are a number of species that look very much alike, the voice is probably the most important "Field Mark," especially in groups that inherit the pattern as well as the quality of the voice. There are cases in which slight variations in color markings are likely to be more misleading than useful in recognizing species, whereas typical vocalizations may readily identify species and sometimes genera. In a few cases, a typical call is common to a whole genus, and additional calls are peculiar to different species within that genus.

VOICE. Whenever possible, vocalizations are described or indicated by man-made sounds. The approximate pitch is given when known, the timing is shown as exactly as possible, and accent or stress in parts of a figure or motif is indicated by the use of capital letters. We are told by those working in physiology and anatomy that the bird's inner ear is constructed in such a manner that the bird can discriminate between sound segments on the time scale at least ten times more accurately than man. This discriminatory ability suggests that the timing of the sound segments within a motif may be the most important character to a bird. A bird may respond to imitations of a motif if the pitch is off quite a bit but not at all if the timing is appreciably changed. Accordingly, a small tape recorder may be used to attract birds even though its fidelity is poor. The birder will be able to add much to the enjoyment of his field studies if he uses a battery-operated tape recorder, and he will likely be able to identify many more species by use of playback. He may even get a good idea of what the vocalization sounds like to the bird by playing back a recording at one-half or one-fourth speed. In this case the pitch, which will be lowered one or two octaves, must be ignored while one studies the more important relative spacing and form of the components. A widespread study of bird voice recordings could add much to our understanding of speciation in tropical America.

In the descriptions of vocalizations, standard international, biological-acoustical terms are used as far as possible. Definitions of the main terms are as follows:

Noise: Sound composed of random frequencies—unorganized sound.

Tone: A sound sensation having pitch. A simple, or "pure," tone has a single frequency. A "complex tone" is made up of more than one frequency. The fundamental is the component of lowest frequency. An overtone is a component having a frequency higher than the fundamental. A harmonic is a component that is an integral multiple of the fundamental—an overtone harmonically related to the fundamental.

Pitch: The subjective interpretation of frequency, but slightly dependent upon the intensity of the sound.

Figure: Sound that produces a single, complete, and distinct impression. A "note" may be said to be a special case—a figure of a single pitch; but note should not be used ordinarily in describing the vocalization of a bird, since we seldom know that a figure really has only one pitch.

Segment: A part of a figure.

Motif: A group of sound units or figures that has a special rhythmic or melodic character (may be a phrase or part of a phrase).

Phrase: One or more motifs terminated as a unit by some form of cadence.

Period: A group of phrases forming a cycle.

Pattern: Arrangement of groups of sounds in time.

Rhythm: A repetition of groups of sounds at regular intervals. A musical composition has both pattern and rhythm. Song is vocal music. This term has been used carelessly or unscientifically so frequently that it is almost impossible to avoid confusion in discussions where it is used.

Repercussion (Roll; Buzz): Continuous repetition of one unit of sound, where the single elements are not readily distinguished by the unaided ear (17 or more per sec.).

Rattle: Similar to a repercussion, but slower.

Click: A single short noise sound.

Drum: A series of clicks—a special case of a rattle or repercussion.

Warble: A continuous alternating change of frequencies.

Vibrato: Frequency modulation—a periodic frequency-intensity fluctuation in pitch.

Tremolo: Amplitude modulation—a regular variation in amplitude.

Trill: Rapid alternations (17 or more per sec.) of two sound units (figures or segments) that cause a rhythmical alternation of pitch.

Formant: A resonance pattern within a sound spectrum in which the amplitude reaches a peak. The frequencies within this pattern are called formant frequencies. A formant is usually described or named by the frequency at the peak amplitude; however, the quality of the sound may also be affected by the width of the base of the formant.

The use of some of the terms may be illustrated by discussing the song phrases of three members of a "Species Group," the Eastern Whip-poor-will, the Western Whip-poor-will, and Dusky Cheer-for-will. This illustration will also serve to demonstrate ways of showing evidence of evolutionary connection in groups that inherit their vocal structures.

(See Table 1 on following page.)

As described by man, with his poor discrimination of sound segments in time, the motif of the usual vocalization (song) of the E. Whip-poor-will is composed of three figures, the last of which is divided into two segments: *chuck, whip,* and *poor-will.* These are represented in the first diagram of Table 1 by figures (a), (b), and (c), (d), (e). Man then divides the last figure into two segments, (c) and (d-e), which he calls *poor* and *will.* These birds inherit their vocal patterns, and the timing is very important; therefore, we should try to think of them as the birds hear them. The middle diagram of Table 1 shows the corresponding motif of the Western Whip-poor-will, and the third diagram that of the Dusky Cheer-for-will. The evolutionary connection in these three inherited patterns is apparent. Each has three figures in the motif, each has the three figures in a comparable form and in the same order; however, each has elements that are markedly different on the time scale. The overall range of pitch is about the same— from about 800 Hz (cycles per sec.) to 2400 Hz in the first two cases, and from about 1700 Hz to 3000 Hz in the third case. The third case,

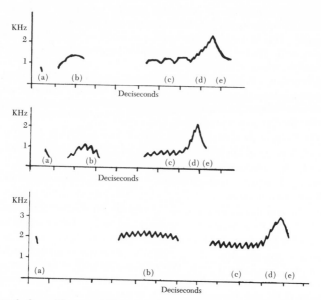

TABLE 1. Song Phrases of Eastern Whip-poor-will, Western Whip-poor-will, and Dusky Cheer-for-will

however, has a noticeably higher average pitch. The fundamental frequencies are strongly resonated, and harmonics do not appear on the usual sound spectrograms; hence, only the fundamentals are shown in the diagrams. This lack of noticeable harmonics gives the "whistled" quality to the songs of these birds. That is, the tones are almost pure. In overall length, the motif of the second example (Western Whip-poor-will) is about 0.75 sec.; of the first barely over 0.9 sec.; and of the third (Cheer-for-will) about 1.2 sec. Although this difference is likely noticeable to the birds, it is probable that the time relationship among the different figures of the motif is more important. We have from the start of figure (b) in the first example to the start of the last figure a time lapse of about 0.4 sec.; in the second example this distance is about 0.35 sec.; and in the last example the distance is about 0.43 sec. We come to some really big differences in timing when we compare such things as the rest between the first and second figures (it varies from about 0.07 sec. in the first diagram to about 0.4 sc. in the last) and the structure of the last figure in each diagram. Concerning the last figure in each diagram: in the first one we have pointed out three segments (c, d, and e), the first of which (c) contains three flat-topped subsegments and occupies a space of 0.22 sec.; in the second diagram there are six subsegments in a space of 0.2 sec.; and in the last there are ten subsegments in (c) in a space of

0.25 sec. In all diagrams the last two segments, (d) and (e), of the last figure are essentially the same (biggest difference is in the slope of (e). The (d) segment is the part called *wi*, and the (e) segment is the *ll* in the phonetic rendition. We may now see how the supposed word sounds should be written to make them more nearly fit each diagram. One: *tk-whop-porororwill* (the preliminary figure, *tk*, the (a) figure, is so soft that few people hear it). Two: *tk-wirrp-prrrrrwill*. Three: *tk-cheerrrrr-ferrrrrrrwill*. In the (b) and (c) figures of the last two phrases we have pure frequency modulation (vibrato); the carrier wave in the last case is modulated with a wave of higher frequency than the other (there are 5 warble wave cycles to 4).

To indicate pitch, the notes on the piano keyboard will be used. Middle C will be shown as C^1, the octave ending at C^2, and so on to the top key of the piano, which is C^5. The octave just below middle C will begin with C; and the second octave below will begin with C_1. This range is from 65 Hz to 4200 Hz. The fundamentals in some bird voices are higher than this range but can be indicated on the same scheme up to C^6 and beyond.

Because of space limitations in this condensed guide, such diagrams as those above will not be used in the discussions of voice in the text. Those who wish to make detailed studies on the voice of a given species or on voice in general will find explanations and illustrations of terms, aids, diagrams, and disucssions of songs and calls of many species in other publications by the author.

SPECIES. Only those species not found in United States field guides are illustrated, and for nonillustrated species only the range is given herein. Short descriptions of illustrated species are usually given, but these are intended to cover only points that may not readily be seen in the paintings or to emphasize a field mark that may be useful in separating the bird from a closely related species. More detailed discussions of various species will be found in the regional Annotated Check Lists, which are booklets prepared by the author for use by birders working in a more limited area.

The length of the bird from tip of bill to end of tail is shown (in inches) just after the species name. The species accounts are given under family headings and, in the case of large families, the accounts are listed in subfamilies in the hope that the suggested closer relationship will be useful in field identification. When the birder learns one species, its shape and behavior should enable him to place other birds he encounters in the same genus by similarity. If he is unable to place a bird in its proper family at sight, he should search through the plates and, after finding a probable species, he should check such details as field marks and range in the species accounts in the text.

Birds of Mexico and Central America

TINAMOUS: Tinamidae

The Tinamous are plump, short-legged land birds, with narrow bills, slender necks, rounded wings, and very short tails; colored varying shades of brown; distinguished from Rails, which are sometimes similar in color, by their short legs and plump bodies, and from Quails and Partridges by their more slender bills and longer necks. They nest on the ground. Vocal patterns apparently inherited.

GREAT TINAMOU, *Tinamus major.* 16   Plate 1
VOICE: As usually given, the song phrase is composed of a series of three closely joined couplets that may be recognized by their similarity to a tremulous, dragging whistling that could be phrased as *howoh-nowoh* and that is delivered at such a tempo that the three couplets will require a total time of five sec. Average pitch is about B^1.
RANGE: Mexico (humid tropical forests of s. Veracruz and adjacent e. Oaxaca to Chiapas, Campeche, and Quintana Roo; from sea level up to 2000 ft.) to Brazil and Bolivia. (Not reported in El Salvador.)

LITTLE TINAMOU, *Crypturellus soui.* 8   Plate 1
VOICE: There are several different motifs, one of which is a single figure pitched about C^4 and lasting one sec.; it usually rises a quarter to a half tone or more and then falls a half tone or more at the end and becomes tremulous shortly after the start. This motif is frequently repeated after a short pause. There is also a motif of three or four shorter figures. This last might be mistaken for a call of the Great Tinamou if the listener were careless in noticing quality and form.
RANGE: Mexico (humid tropical woods below 2000 ft. in s. Veracruz, Oaxaca, Chiapas, and Campeche) to Brazil and Bolivia.

BOUCARD TINAMOU, *Crypturellus boucardi.* 10   Plate 1
VOICE: The call is a two-figure motif with a far-way quality that makes it almost impossible to estimate the location of the bird. It may be represented as *uh-wuh* or *aah-waah.* This is drawled out, so that it requires about two sec. The pitch is near F^2.
RANGE: Mexico (humid forests from sea level up to over 4000 ft. in s. Veracruz, Oaxaca, Tabasco, and Chiapas) to s.e. Costa Rica.

RUFESCENT TINAMOU, *Crypturellus cinnamomeus.* 11   Plate 1
VOICE: A loud, plaintive, "whistled" call represented by *ee-o-oo* (the *oo* having a soft *u* sound), which almost fits the name "Tin-a-mou."

The first part is usually higher in pitch, and all parts are slurred together, so that a total time of one sec. is required. In some areas the call may be so hurried that it sounds more like *eeoo*.

RANGE: Mexico (woods and brush thickets from sea level up to 4500 ft.; on Pacific slope from Nayarit south to Chiapas; on Atlantic slope from s.e. Nuevo León to Chiapas and Yucatán) to Costa Rica.

BONAPARTE TINAMOU, *Nothocercus bonapartei.* 14   Plate 1
VOICE: A loud, hollow call represented as *cu-la*, repeated in series so that six will be delivered in five sec.
RANGE: Costa Rica to Venezuela and Ecuador; humid highlands from about 5000 ft. to above timber line.

LOONS: Gaviidae

RED-THROATED LOON, *Gavia stellata.*   19
RANGE: Arctic circumpolar regions; winters to Pacific coast of Mexico (Baja California and Sonora; rare).

ARCTIC LOON, *Gavia arctica.*   20
RANGE: Arctic regions; winters to Pacific coast of Mexico (Baja California and Sonora; common).

COMMON LOON, *Gavia immer.*   26
RANGE: N. North America, winters to coasts of Mexico (Baja California, Sonora, and Tamaulipas; uncommon).

GREBES: Podicipedidae

LEAST GREBE, *Podiceps dominicus.*   8
VOICE: There is a short, sharp call, *queek or kerk*, and a much softer, lower-pitched roll or repercussion in which some twenty-five or thirty figures are sounded in a space of one and a half sec. (as *ker-r-r-r-r-r-r*). The pitch of the call is about D^3; the quality is reedy or slightly nasal. The roll is pitched approximately four tones lower than the call.
RANGE: S. Texas, Mexico (Baja California across to Tamaulipas and south to Chiapas and Yucatán; in fresh water ponds and rivers), and south to Tierra del Fuego.

EARED GREBE, *Podiceps caspicus.*   10
RANGE: W. North America to n. Mexico; in winter south to Guatemala.

HORNED GREBE, *Podiceps auritus.* 11
RANGE: N. North America and n. Eurasia; in winter to n. Mexico where rare.

WESTERN GREBE, *Aechmophorus occidentalis.* 20
RANGE: W. North America to Mexico (Jalisco and Zacatecas; in winter in various northern states and south to Puebla.

PIED-BILLED GREBE, *Podilymbus podiceps.* 9
RANGE: North America south to Argentina.

ATITLAN GREBE, *Podilymbus gigas.* 12 Plate 9
FIELD MARKS: Head and neck almost black; bill white.
RANGE: Lake Atitlán in Guatemala.

ALBATROSSES: Diomedeidae

Large birds of the open ocean, with very long, slender wings (wing spread seven feet or more), large heads, and stout, straight bills that have a hook at the end of the upper mandible.

WANDERING ALBATROSS, *Diomedea exulans.* 44
FIELD MARKS: White with black wing tips; bill yellow; immatures mottled with black.
RANGE: Antarctic regions; wanders north to Panama.

GALAPAGOS ALBATROSS, *Diomedea irrorata.* 32 Plate 3
RANGE: Galápagos Islands; wanders to Panama and Peru.

BLACK-FOOTED ALBATROSS, *Diomedea nigripes.* 28
RANGE: Pacific Ocean; wanders along North American coast, usually well off shore from Alaska to Baja California.

LAYSAN ALBATROSS, *Diomedea immutabilis.* 28
RANGE: Is. of c.s. Pacific and occasionally off Baja California.

GRAY-HEADED ALBATROSS, *Diomedea chrysostoma.* 38
FIELD MARKS: Bill yellow with black along side; gray of nape shades into blackish brown on back and wings; underparts white.
RANGE: S. Pacific; wanders as far as Panama.

SHEARWATERS: Procellariidae

NORTHERN FULMER, *Fulmarus glacialis.* 18
RANGE: Arctic regions; wanders south to Pacific coast of Mexico.

ANTARCTIC FULMER, *Fulmarus antarcticus.*   17   Plate 3
RANGE: Antarctic regions; wanders off Pacific coast at times as far
   north as Mexico.

PINK-FOOTED SHEARWATER, *Puffinus creatopus.*   18
RANGE: E. Pacific Ocean to Baja California.

PACIFIC SHEARWATER, *Puffinus pacificus.*   15   Plate 3
RANGE: Indian and Pacific oceans to coast of Mexico and Panama.

SOOTY SHEARWATER, *Puffinus griseus.*   16
RANGE: S. Pacific and Atlantic oceans; wanders north after breeding
   season as far as coast of Baja California and rarely near coast in
   Gulf of Mexico.

SLENDER-BILLED SHEARWATER, *Puffinus tenuirostris.*   15
RANGE: Pacific Ocean; rarely off coast of Baja California.

BLACK-VENTED SHEARWATER, *Puffinus opisthomelas.*   11 Plate 3
   (Considered a race of *P. puffinus* by some.)
FIELD MARKS: Similar to Manx Shearwater but smaller and with different manner of flight (flaps wings frequently, whereas the Manx
   seldom does), and has a quite different range. (The Townsend
   Shearwater, *P. auricularis*, is similar but lacks the black flanks and
   under tail-coverts and has black cheek areas just below the eye.
   The Dusky Shearwater, *P. assimilis*, is similar in pattern, but area
   below eye is white. The Variable Petrel, *Pterodroma neglecta*, is
   brown above and may be either brown or white below, but the
   under surface of the wing is dark, except for a white patch toward
   the tip. The Dark-rumped Petrel is rather similar in pattern but has
   a white forehead. The White-necked Petrel, *P. externa*, has a black
   crown and a gray back and a collar that is almost white.)
RANGE: W. coast of Mexico (Baja California and Sonora).

AUDUBON SHEARWATER, *Puffinus lherminieri.*   11   Plate 3
RANGE: Spreads out from the Bahamas to the Gulf and Caribbean
   coast of Middle America and from the Galápagos to the coast of
   Panama and South America; breeds on coast of Bocas del Toro,
   Panama.

COOK PETREL, *Pterodroma cookii.*   11   Plate 3
FIELD MARKS: In flight shows a dark zigzag (**M**) pattern across the
   wings and back. (The New Zealand Shearwater also shows an **M**
   pattern in flight but has a quite dark cap; it is *Puffinus bulleri*
   and is sometimes known as the Gray-backed Shearwater.)
RANGE: Pacific Ocean from New Zealand to Chile; wanders north to
   Mexico.

DARK-RUMPED PETREL, *Pterodroma phaeopygia*. 16
FIELD MARKS: Forehead and underparts white; back sooty brown; spot around eye and top of wings black; tail wedge-shaped.
RANGE: Nests in Galápagos Islands; wanders at times off Pacific coast of Panama.

STORM-PETRELS: Hydrobatidae

Small swallow-like sea birds of erratic flight that seldom are seen close to shore. When skimming close over the water they frequently strike the surface with their feet as though to help their progress.

WILSON'S STORM-PETREL, *Oceanites oceanicus*. 6½
FIELD MARKS: Sooty above with white rump; tail almost straight across the end; secondaries tipped white, causing white band across wing in flight.
RANGE: Is. of Antarctic Ocean; north at times into n. Atlantic and into n. Pacific; reported off coast of Veracruz, Mexico.

GRACEFUL STORM-PETREL, *Oceanites gracilis*. 6
FIELD MARKS: Similar to last-named species but middle of belly is white.
RANGE: Pacific off South America and Galápagos Islands; wanders to Gulf of Panama.

GALAPAGOS STORM-PETREL, *Oceanodroma tethys*. 6½ Plate 3
FIELD MARKS: Similar to Leach's Storm-Petrel, but tail is less deeply forked and the rump patch triangular in shape.
RANGE: Galápagos Islands; wanders along American coast from Baja California to Chile.

LEACH'S STORM-PETREL, *Oceanodroma leucorhoa*. 7½
RANGE: N. Pacific and Atlantic oceans; breeds on Is. off Baja California coast and wanders south by sea.

SOCORRO STORM-PETREL, *Oeanodroma socorrensis*. 6½ Plate 3
(Considered a race of *O. leucorhoa* by some and of *O. monorhis* by others.)
FIELD MARKS: Similar to Leach's Storm-Petrel but has gray rump instead of white one, with dark notch at the bottom; the lateral upper tail-coverts are almost white, which gives the effect of a light line along side of rump.
RANGE: Is. off coast of California and Baja California.

HARCOURT'S STORM-PETREL, *Oceanodroma castro*. 8½
FIELD MARKS: Similar to Leach's storm-Petrel but with less deeply

forked tail and with white rump patch straight across the bottom
(almost rectangular in shape).
RANGE: E. Pacific and e. Atlantic; at times into the Gulf of Mexico as
far as the Mexican coast; rare off Pacific coast of Central America.

ASHY STORM-PETREL, *Oceanodroma homochroa.*   7
FIELD MARKS: Shows a pattern of white lines on under side of wings.
(The Sooty Storm-Petrel, *O. markhami*, is similar but is a bit larger—
8½ inches—and lacks white under wings.)
RANGE: Is. off coast of California and Baja California.

BLACK STORM-PETREL, *Oceanodroma melania.*   8½
FIELD MARKS: Has noticeably longer legs than either the Ashy Storm-
Petrel or the Sooty Storm-Petrel.
RANGE: Is. off Baja California coast; wanders south to Peru.

LEAST STORM-PETREL, *Halocyptena microsoma.*   5½
RANGE: Pacific off coast of Baja California to Ecuador.

TROPICBIRDS: Phaëthontidae

Sea birds (largely white) with heavy, straight bills and very long
central tail feathers.

RED-BILLED TROPICBIRD, *Phaethon aethereus.*   34
RANGE: Is. of Atlantic and Pacific oceans; coast of Baja California
south to Panama; Caribbean coast of Honduras to Panama.

WHITE-TAILED TROPICBIRD, *Phaethon lepturus.*   26
RANGE: Tropical oceans; occasional in the w. Caribbean as far as the
coast of Guatemala.

RED-TAILED TROPICBIRD, *Phaethon rubricauda.*   30   Plate 3
RANGE: C. Pacific and Indian oceans; occasional off coast of Baja
California.

PELICANS: Pelecanidae

WHITE PELICAN, *Pelecanus erythrorhynchus.*   50
RANGE: North America, winters to Mexico and Guatemala.

BROWN PELICAN, *Pelicanus occidentalis.*   41
RANGE: North America and South America to Tierra del Fuego.

GANNETS: Sulidae

Large sea birds with long wings, pointed bills, and pointed, wedge-shaped tails. While fishing, various species may show different styles of diving.

NORTHERN GANNET, *Morus bassanus.* 31
RANGE: N. Atlantic coasts; winters south as far as Veracruz.

BLUE-FOOTED BOOBY, *Sula nebouxii.* 26
RANGE: Is. of Pacific; off Pacific shore of Mexico to Peru.

MASKED BOOBY, *Sula dactylatra.* 27
FIELD MARKS: In adults the mask, flight feathers, and tail are black; other parts white except for bill, which is yellow, red, or gray.
RANGE: Tropical oceans; coasts of Mexico (Baja California, Tamaulipas, Yucatán) and south to Panama.

RED-FOOTED BOOBY, *Sula sula.* 22   Plate 3
FIELD MARKS: Similar to last species but lacks mask, and tail and secondaries are white.
RANGE: Tropical seas; Pacific coast of Mexico; Caribbean coast of Nicaragua and Panama.

BROWN BOOBY, *Sula leucogaster.* 23
RANGE: Tropical oceans; coasts of Mexico (Baja California to Colima; Yucatán) and south to Argentina.

CORMORANTS: Phalacrocoracidae

DOUBLE-CRESTED CORMORANT, *Phalacrocorax auritus.* 27
RANGE: North America; south in winter along Pacific as far as Guerrero, Mexico, and along Atlantic as far south as British Honduras.

OLIVACEOUS CORMORANT, *Phalacrocorax olivaceus.* 22
FIELD MARKS: In breeding plumage there is a white tuft on the side of the neck and a white edging to the orange throat patch.
VOICE: A low-pitched grunt.
RANGE: S. United States, Mexico (Sonora to Tamaulipas and south to Chiapas and Yucatán; mostly in coastal lowlands but also in inland lakes and rivers), and south to Tierra del Fuego.

BRANDT CORMORANT, *Phalacrocorax penicillatus.* 29
RANGE: Pacific coast of North America to Baja California; in winter and spring sometimes along coast of Sonora.

PELAGIC CORMORANT, *Phalacrocorax pelagicus.* 22
RANGE: Pacific coast of North America and Asia; Baja California.

ANHINGAS: Anhingidae

AMERICAN ANHINGA, *Anhinga anhinga.* 28
RANGE: S.e. United States to Argentina.

FRIGATEBIRDS: Fregatidae

MAGNIFICENT FRIGATEBIRD, *Fregata magnificens.* 35
RANGE: E. Pacific from California to Peru; Atlantic from s. United
States to Brazil (soars inland some distance at times).

MINOR FRIGATEBIRD, *Fregata minor.* 34   Plate 3
FIELD MARKS: The male cannot usually be distinguished in the field
from the male of the previous species, but the females and immatures can. The adult female has black crown and white or light
gray throat. The immature does not have a black belly (only the
tail is black); underparts tinged rusty.
RANGE: Tropical oceans; at times off Pacific coast of Mexico.

HERONS: Ardeidae

GREAT BLUE HERON, *Ardea herodias.* 38
FIELD MARKS: Crest feathers and side of crown black.
RANGE: North America to Mexico; south in winter to n. South Amer-
ica.

GREAT WHITE HERON, *Ardea occidentalis.* 38
FIELD MARKS: The blue phase of this species is called the Wunder-
mann Heron; it resembles a Great Blue Heron, but the whole crown
and crest feathers are white.
RANGE: S. Florida to the Greater Antilles; Yucatán and Quintana Roo,
Mexico (rare).

COCOI HERON, *Ardea cocoi.* 41   Plate 2
FIELD MARKS: Crown black; neck and thighs white.
RANGE: E. Panama to Argentina; tropical rivers and marshes.

CAPPED HERON, *Pilherodius pileatus.* 19   Plate 2
FIELD MARKS: White; cap black; bill and legs gray.
RANGE: Panama to Brazil and Bolivia.

GREEN HERON, *Butorides virescens.* 14
RANGE: North America to c. Panama; winters to Colombia.

STRIATED HERON, *Butorides striatus.* 12   Plate 2
FIELD MARKS: Similar to Green Heron, but sides of face, neck, and breast are gray instead of chestnut or rufous.
RANGE: Costa Rica to Argentina; also other continents.

LITTLE BLUE HERON, *Florida caerulea.* 22
RANGE: S. United States to Argentina.

REDDISH EGRET, *Dichromanassa rufescens.* 25
RANGE: Gulf coast of United States, Mexico (Baja California to Chiapas; Tamaulipas to Yucatán; mostly in salt water areas), and south to Venezuela.

AMERICAN EGRET, *Egretta egretta.* 32
(Considered conspecific with *Casmerodius albus* by many.)
RANGE: United States and south to Argentina.

SNOWY EGRET, *Egretta thula.* 20
RANGE: S. United States to Argentina.

CATTLE EGRET, *Bubulcus ibis.* 17
RANGE: United States to n. South America; also Africa, Asia, and E. Indies.

LOUISIANA HERON, *Hydranassa tricolor.* 22
RANGE: S. United States to Brazil and Ecuador.

AGAMI HERON, *Agamia agami.* 25   Plate 2
FIELD MARKS: Something like a Little Blue Heron but with more varied coloration; usually cinnamon-rufous below and greenish gray to slate above; grayish white plumes may appear on the head, tail, and lower throat; center line down throat chestnut bordered by white. Immatures have top of head black; back brown; below buffy white, more or less streaked brown.
RANGE: Mexico (s. Veracruz to Chiapas; rare) to Bolivia.

BLACK-CROWNED NIGHT-HERON, *Nycticorax nycticorax.* 20
RANGE: All continents except Australia.

YELLOW-CROWNED NIGHT-HERON, *Nyctanassa violacea.* 21
RANGE: United States to Brazil and Peru; migratory in north.

LINEATED TIGER-BITTERN, *Tigrisoma lineatum.* 23   Plate 2
RANGE: Mexico (Chiapas; rare) to Argentina; wooded streams.

SALMON'S TIGER-BITTERN, *Tigrisoma salmoni.* 22   Plate 2
FIELD MARKS: Similar to Lineated Tiger-Bittern, but has heavier and
    shorter bill; crown is black; back black, marked with narrow buff
    bands.
RANGE: Costa Rica (humid woods of Caribbean slope) to Venezuela
    and Bolivia.

MEXICAN TIGER-BITTERN, *Tigrisoma mexicanum.* 26   Plate 2
VOICE: Alarm call is a loud, throaty *wahg or ahaak;* also does a hoarse
    "booming."
RANGE: Mexico (Sonora to Chiapas; Tamaulipas to Chiapas and Yu-
    catán) to n.w. Colombia; favors boggy inland streams or mangrove
    areas.

LEAST BITTERN, *Ixobrychus exilis.* 11
RANGE: North America to Brazil.

AMERICAN BITTERN, *Botaurus lentiginosus.* 23
RANGE: North America; in winter south to Panama.

PINNATED BITTERN, *Botaurus pinnatus.* 22   Plate 2
RANGE: E. Mexico (s. Tamaulipas to Quintana Roo) to Argentina.

BOAT-BILLED HERONS: Cochleariidae

NORTHERN BOAT-BILLED HERON, *Cochlearius zeledoni.* 20
                                                    Plate 2
    (Considered a race of *C. cochlearius* by others.)
VOICE: Something like the voice of a Black-crowned Night-Heron but
    a bit more like a croak; frequently a series of figures given after the
    fashion of a laugh.
RANGE: Mexico (Sinaloa to Chiapas; s. Tamaulipas to Yucatán) to
    Panama and w. Colombia; sluggish inland streams or mangroves.

SOUTHERN BOAT-BILLED HERON, *Cochlearius cochlearius.* 20
                                                    Plate 2
RANGE: E. Panama to Argentina and e. Peru.

STORKS: Ciconiidae

WOOD STORK, *Mycteria americana.* 35
RANGE: S. United States and south to Argentina.

JABIRU STORK, *Jabiru mycteria.* 48   Plate 2
RANGE: S. Mexico to Argentina; marshy areas along streams.

IBISES: Threskiornithidae

CAYENNE IBIS, *Mesembrinibis cayennensis.* 20   Plate 2
RANGE: E. Costa Rica and south to Argentina and Bolivia; in swampy woods.

WHITE IBIS, *Eudocimus albus.* 22
RANGE: S. United States to Venezuela and Peru.

GLOSSY IBIS, *Plegadis falcinellus.* 19
RANGE: Old World; s.e. United States; Greater Antilles; Costa Rica, Panama, and n. Colombia.

WHITE-FACED IBIS, *Plegadis chihi.* 19
RANGE: S. and w. United States to s. Mexico (in winter south to Costa Rica); from Brazil and Peru south to Argentina and Chile.

WHITE-THROATED IBIS, *Theristicus caudatus.* 28   Plate 2
RANGE: E. Panama to Argentina and Bolivia.

ROSEATE SPOONBILL, *Ajaia ajaja.* 28
RANGE: S. United States to Argentina.

FLAMINGOS: Phoenicopteridae

AMERICAN FLAMINGO, *Phoenicopterus ruber.*
RANGE: Bahamas, Greater Antilles, Mexico (tip of Yucatán peninsula), Venezuela, Guianas, and Galápagos Islands.

DUCKS: Anatidae

WHISTLING SWAN, *Cygnus columbianus.* 36
RANGE: North America, in winter south to n. Mexico.

TRUMPETER SWAN, *Cygnus buccinator.* 45
RANGE: W. North America; at least one winter record as far south as Tamaulipas.

BLUE GOOSE, *Chen caerulescens.* 19
RANGE: Arctic North America; winters to n. Mexico.

SNOW GOOSE, *Chen hyperborea.* 19
(Considered a race of *C. caerulescens* by some.)
RANGE: Arctic North America; in winter to c. and s. Mexico.

ROSS GOOSE, *Chen rossii.* 16
RANGE: N.e. Canada; winters to Chihuahua and Tamaulipas.

WHITE-FRONTED GOOSE, *Anser albifrons.* 20
RANGE: Arctic regions; in winter as far south as s. Mexico.

BLACK BRANT, *Branta nigricans.* 17
   (Considered a race of *B. bernicla* by some.)
RANGE: Arctic coast of Siberia and North America; winters to Baja California.

CANADA GOOSE, *Branta canadensis.* 21
RANGE: N. North America; winters to Chihuahua and Veracruz, Mexico.

TUNDRA GOOSE, *Branta leucopareia.* 21
   (Considered a race of *B. canadensis* by some.)
FIELD MARKS: Similar to Canada Goose, but has a browner breast and usually a white collar at base of the black neck "stocking" (separating the black of the neck from the grayish brown of the breast); usually has a black area on the throat that separates the cheek patches. Bill is shorter and higher than in Canada Goose.
RANGE: N.w. North America; winters occasionally in n. Mexico.

CACKLING GOOSE, *Branta minima.* 16
   (Considered a race of *B. canadensis* by some.)
FIELD MARKS: Similar to Tundra Goose but is much smaller and darker; there is a still darker brown collar at base of black stocking of neck (just below the white collar when that is present) that may be observed under good lighting conditions.
RANGE: W. Alaska; south in winter as far as Baja California.

RICHARDSON'S GOOSE, *Branta hutchinsii.* 17
   (Considered a race of *B. canadensis* by some.)
FIELD MARKS: A small edition of the Canada Goose, with a light breast, without white or dark brown collar at base of black neck stocking, and without black area on the throat separating the white cheek patches.
RANGE: Arctic coast of Hudson Bay; south in winter to n. Mexico.

WHITE-FACED TREE-DUCK, *Dendrocygna viduata.* 12   Plate 9
RANGE: Costa Rica south through tropical South America; also Africa.

FULVOUS TREE-DUCK, *Dendrocygna bicolor.* 13
RANGE: S.w. United States to Argentina; also Asia and Africa.

BLACK-BELLIED TREE-DUCK, *Dendrocygna autumnalis.* 14
RANGE: S. Texas to Argentina.

AMERICAN COMB-DUCK, *Sarkidiornis sylvicola.* 24   Plate 9
FIELD MARKS: Upper back and underparts white; lower back, wings, and tail greenish black; bill black and bearing a "comb" (in male).
RANGE: E. Panama and n. and e. South America; in swampy woods.

MUSCOVY DUCK, *Cairina moschata.* 26   Plate 9
RANGE: Mexico and south to Argentina.

MALLARD DUCK, *Anas platyrhynchos.* 16
RANGE: Eurasia and North America; winters south to Veracruz, Mexico.

MEXICAN DUCK, *Anas diazi.* 15
FIELD MARKS: Both sexes are similar to a female Mallard Duck but have a plain grayish brown tail instead of having outer feathers edged with white; bill of male is greenish yellow and that of female yellowish orange with dusky line along ridge (not mottled with black as is frequently the case in female Mallard); the speculum is bordered with narrow white bars (the fore white bar may be partly dusky or buff and at times may be wanting, in which case the bird's appearance is almost identical with the Mottled Duck). The Mottled Duck is a bird of the coastal lowlands and has a tiny black spot on each side of the bill at the base, similar to, but smaller than, the one at the tip.
RANGE: S.w. United States and c. Mexico (highlands of Chihuahua and Durango; south to Puebla).

MOTTLED DUCK, *Anas fulvigula.* 15
RANGE: Gulf coast lowlands of Florida, Louisiana, Texas, and Tamaulipas; wanders into e. San Luis Potosí at times.

NORTHERN PINTAIL, *Anas acuta.* 18½
RANGE: Northern parts of N. Hemisphere; south in winter to Colombia.

GADWALL DUCK, *Anas strepera.* 14½
RANGE: Eurasia and w. North America; south in winter to n. Mexico.

GREEN-WINGED TEAL, *Anas carolinensis.* 10½
RANGE: N. North America; south in winter to Colombia.

BLUE-WINGED TEAL, *Anas discors.* 11
RANGE: North America; south in winter to Brazil and Peru.

CINNAMON TEAL, *Anas cyanoptera.*   11
RANGE: W. North America to n. Mexico; rarely in Central America; also Colombia, Paraguay, and Argentina; northern birds winter to Panama.

AMERICAN WIDGEON, *Mareca americana.*   14
RANGE: W. North America; south in winter to Colombia and West Indies.

NORTHERN SHOVELLER, *Spatula clypeata.*   13
RANGE: North America, Europe, and Asia; south in winter to n. South America.

WOOD DUCK, *Aix sponsa.*   13½
RANGE: North America; in winter south to Mexico (Sinaloa, Distrito Federal, San Luis Potosí, and Tamaulipas).

CANVASBACK DUCK, *Aythya valisineria.*   15
RANGE: N. w. North America; south in winter as far as Guatemala.

REDHEAD DUCK, *Aythya americana.*   14½
RANGE: N.w. North America; south in winter to Mexico and Guatemala.

RING-NECKED DUCK, *Aythya collaris.*   12
RANGE: N. North America; south in winter as far as Panama.

GREATER SCAUP, *Aythya marila.*   13
RANGE: North America and Eurasia; south in winter to n. Mexico.

LESSER SCAUP, *Aythya affinis.*   12
RANGE: N.w. North America; winters south to Colombia and the West Indies; a few stragglers remain through the summer in Mexico.

WHITE-WINGED SCOTER, *Melanitta deglandi.*   16
(Considered a race of *M. fusca* by some.)
RANGE: N.w. North America; south in winter as far as Baja California.

SURF SCOTER, *Melanitta perspicillata.*   14
RANGE: N. North America; south in winter to n.w. Mexico.

AMERICAN SCOTER, *Melanitta americana.*   14
(Considered a race of *M. nigra* by some.)
RANGE: N. North America; south in winter to coast of Baja California.

AMERICAN GOLDENEYE, *Bucephala americana.*   13
(Considered a race of *B. clangula* by some.)
RANGE: N. North America; winters to w. Mexico.

BUFFLEHEAD DUCK, *Bucephala albeola.* 10
RANGE: N.w. North America; winters south to Mexico.

MASKED DUCK, *Oxyura dominica.* 10
RANGE: S. Texas to Argentina and Chile; rare and local.

RUDDY DUCK, *Oxyura jamaicensis.* 11
RANGE: W. Canada, United States, Mexico (local and irregular in summer; more widespread in winter), Guatemala, British Honduras, and West Indies.

HOODED MERGANSER, *Lophodytes cucullatus.* 13
RANGE: N. North America; in winter south to c. Mexico.

AMERICAN MERGANSER, *Mergus americana.* 18
(Considered a race of *M. merganser* by some.)
RANGE: N. North America; winters south as far as Mexico at times.

RED-BREASTED MERGANSER, *Mergus serrator.* 16
RANGE: Arctic regions; winters in America south to n. Mexico (coasts of Baja California, Sonora, and Tamaulipas).

AMERICAN VULTURES: Cathartidae

KING VULTURE, *Sarcoramphus papa.* 27   Plate 4
FIELD MARKS: The juveniles are brownish black and have a brown instead of a white iris; immature birds are variously intermediate between the juvenile and adult plumage. In flight, this species shows a silhouette against the sky that looks more nearly like that of a Black Vulture than that of a Turkey Vulture (the wings are broad with rather short primaries, and the tail is slightly rounded).
RANGE: Mexico (Sinaloa to Chiapas; Veracruz to Quintana Roo; from sea level up to 3000 ft.; most likely to be seen below the Isthmus of Tehuantepec) to n. Argentina.

BLACK VULTURE, *Coragyps atratus.* 22
RANGE: S. United States and south through most of South America.

TURKEY VULTURE, *Cathartes aura.* 25
RANGE: North and South America.

LESSER YELLOWHEAD, *Cathartes burrovianus.* 22   Plate 4
FIELD MARKS: Similar to Turkey Vulture but has black instead of brownish black feathers (belly may be browner—even browner than that of Turkey Vulture, which may have belly blacker than back); forehead

red; crown blue; face and neck orange yellow; tiny wartlike pimples on wrinkles at side of neck.

RANGE: Mexico (marshy areas in lowlands from Tamaulipas s.; rare and local) to n.w. Venezuela and N. Colombia.

HAWKS: Accipitridae

WHITE-TAILED KITE, *Elanus leucurus.* 14½
RANGE: S. Texas and California, south to Argentina and Chile; favors savannahs with some good perching and nesting trees (rare and local in Central America).

PEARL KITE, *Gampsonyx swainsonii.* 8½   Plate 5
FIELD MARKS: Narrow band across nape, wing-coverts, tips of secondaries, and under parts are white. Immatures show buff or brown wash.
RANGE: W. Nicaragua; Guiana and Colombia to Argentina.

SWALLOW-TAILED KITE, *Elanoides forficatus.* 21
RANGE: S.e. United States, Mexico (breeds in cloud forests or mixed pine and sweet gum woods of c. and s. Chiapas; migratory), and south to Argentina and Bolivia.

CAYENNE KITE, *Leptodon cayanensis.* 18   Plate 4
FIELD MARKS: Tail is black with two white or pale gray bars; axillars either black or white; under side of primaries barred black and white; bend of wing white (this may show as a tiny wrist mirror in flight). Immatures (light phase): Head and under parts white; spot on back of crown, line over eye, line back of eye, back, wings and tail black; tail barred with brown and tipped white; primaries barred with brown. Or (dark phase): the head, back, and throat brownish black.
VOICE: Something like that of a small falcon but lower in pitch; a series of staccato figures of even pitch and tempo, as *ca-ca-ca-ca*. Twenty figures may be sounded in ten sec., but the rate will vary at times from one and a half to three figures per sec. The pitch is about G³.
RANGE: Mexico (s. Tamaulipas and south to Yucatán) to Argentina.

HOOK-BILLED KITE, *Chondrohierax uncinatus.* 15   Plate 5
FIELD MARKS: A broad-winged species with slightly rounded tail. The iris in adult is white but is brown in immatures. There is a gray and a dark phase. The latter is glossy brownish black with white band across white-tipped tail.
RANGE: Extreme s. Texas, Mexico (Sinaloa to Guerrero and Oaxaca; Tamaulipas to Yucatán; in forests or savannah regions—humid or dry—from sea level up to 3000 ft; uncommon) and south to Argentina and Bolivia.

DOUBLE-TOOTHED KITE, *Harpagus bidentatus.* 13 Plate 5
FIELD MARKS: Throat creamy-white with dark line down center.
RANGE: Mexico (Mexico to Veracruz; s. Oaxaca and Chiapas) to Brazil
and Bolivia.

MISSISSIPPI KITE, *Ictinia misisippiensis.* 12½
RANGE: S. United States; migrates south to Guatemala and occasionally
stragglers reach parts of South America.

PLUMBEOUS KITE, *Ictinia plumbea.* 12½ Plate 5
FIELD MARKS: Tail black with inner webs of all except two central feathers marked with two white bands (appears as three narrow bars
across tail when viewed from below); inner web of primaries rufous
(shows in flight only).
RANGE: Mexico (s. Tamaulipas and south to Chiapas and Yucatán; migratory) to Argentina and Bolivia.

EVERGLADE KITE, *Rostrhamus sociabilis.* 15
RANGE: Florida and Mexico (Veracruz to Campeche), south to Argentina and Bolivia.

SLENDER-BILLED KITE, *Helicolestes hamatus.* 14 Plate 5
FIELD MARKS: Similar to Everglade Kite but tail shorter and without
white. The immature has two white bands across tail.
RANGE: Panama (Darien) to Brazil and Peru; favors forest over open
marsh.

NORTHERN GOSHAWK, *Accipiter gentilis.* 19
RANGE: N. Eurasia and n. North America; south to n.w. Mexico (Sonora, Sinaloa, Durango, and Chihuahua; rare).

BICOLORED HAWK, *Accipiter bicolor.* 15½ Plate 5
RANGE: Mexico (s. Tamaulipas, e. San Luis Potosí, and south to Yucatán) to Brazil and Peru.

COOPER'S HAWK, *Accipiter cooperii.* 15½
RANGE: North America to n. Mexico (Baja California across to Nuevo
León); in winter south to Guatemala (straggler found in Colombia).

TINY HAWK, *Accipiter superciliosus.* 8 Plate 5
RANGE: Nicaragua to Argentina; in humid areas and rare in Central
America.

SHARP-SHINNED HAWK, *Accipiter striatus.* 11
RANGE: North America to mts. of Mexico; in winter to w. Panama.

WHITE-BELLIED HAWK, *Accipiter chionogaster.* 12   Plate 5
(Considered a race of *A. striatus* by some and a race of *A. ery-
thronemius* of South America by others.)
RANGE: Mts. of Chiapas to Nicaragua; the habitat is pine woods.

SAVANNA HAWK, *Heterospizias meridionalis.* 19   Plate 4
RANGE: Panama to Argentina and Bolivia.

WHITE-TAILED HAWK, *Buteo albicaudatus.* 21
RANGE: S.w. United States to Argentina and Chile.

ROUGH-LEGGED HAWK, *Buteo lagopus.* 19
RANGE: N. North America; in winter rarely straggles to n. Mexico.

FERRUGINOUS HAWK, *Buteo regalis.* 20
RANGE: W. North America; south in winter as far as c. Mexico.

RED-TAILED HAWK, *Buteo jamaicensis.* 22
RANGE: North America to w. Panama (Mexico south in mts.); in winter
northern birds range in the lowlands to Nicaragua.

ZONE-TAILED HAWK, *Buteo albonotatus.* 20
RANGE: S.w. United States to Paraguay and Bolivia.

RED-SHOULDERED HAWK, *Buteo lineatus.* 16
RANGE: North America to c. Mexico (Baja California across to Tamaulipas and south to Mexico), uncommon and local; more widespread
in winter.

SWAINSON'S HAWK, *Buteo swainsoni.* 20
RANGE: North America to n. Mexico; migrates to Argentina and
Chile.

BROAD-WINGED HAWK, *Buteo platypterus.* 16
RANGE: E. North America to Texas; migrates to Brazil and Chile.

LARGE-BILLED HAWK, *Buteo magnirostris.* 13   Plate 5
FIELD MARKS: Back grayish brown; throat and upper breast not barred;
thighs, in any plumage, more or less buff; tail light gray or rufous
and crossed by four black bars; wings show variable amount of rufous edging to the primaries. Similar in shape to Broad-winged Hawk.
VOICE: A common call is a complaining, nasal *eeyaaa*, which is drawn
out about one sec. and slurs down about a half tone; there is also a
shriller, more sharply accented *heeaaa heea*, the accent being on the
e sound in each part of the call. The first figure of this last call requires about one sec., and the last figure a half sec., with about a
half-sec. pause between the figures. The "song" is a staccato series of

figures that may be given either when perched or when soaring high overhead. It usually begins slowly with two to four figures (rated two or three per sec.), accelerates to five figures per sec., and may continue for fifteen sec. or more. The faster figures are higher in pitch; the first two may be represented by *yah* or *cah* and the faster ones by *yeh* or *keh*.

RANGE: Rio Grande Delta of Texas to Argentina and Bolivia.

SHORT-TAILED HAWK, *Buteo brachyurus.* 15
RANGE: Florida and Mexico (Michoacán to Oaxaca; Tamaulipas to Yucatán; rare and local in most states) to Argentina and Bolivia.

GRAY HAWK, *Buteo plagiatus.* 16   Plate 5
(Considered a race of *B. nitidus* by others.)
FIELD MARKS: Smooth, dark gray back (no bars); tail black with white tip and two white bars across central portion (occasionally the upper one is not complete, and at times there are three bars). Juvenile birds are dark brown above, including the head, and are almost white below with dark streaks; feathers of head may have lighter edges.
VOICE: The "song" is a series of short screams (figures) of such quality that they almost resemble a wail. A series of six figures will require about six and a half sec.; a single figure could be represented by *ah-weeeoo.* The *ah* is quite short and is pitched about C^3; the *weee* is the stressed portion and is pitched one tone higher (D^3); and the final *oo* drops to D^3 flat. There is also a call that brings to mind one of the Large-billed Hawk, but it lacks the complaining quality.
RANGE: S.w. United States to n.w. Costa Rica; favors open woods in lowlands.

SHINING HAWK, *Buteo nitidus.* 15   Plate 5
FIELD MARKS: Back and head light gray, barred with dark gray; tail black with white tip and broad white bar not far above end (occasionally there is a second narrow, incomplete band higher up). Immature birds have the crown and sides of head buff streaked with brown.
RANGE: S.w. Costa Rica to Argentina and Bolivia.

HARRIS' HAWK, *Parabuteo harrisi.* 19
(Considered a race of *P. unicinctus* by others.)
FIELD MARKS: Black of under parts not streaked with white.
RANGE: S.w. United States to w. Ecuador.

WHITE HAWK, *Leucopternis ghiesbreghti.* 18   Plate 4
(Considered a race of *L. albicollis* by others.
RANGE: S. Mexico (c. Oaxaca to Chiapas in west and Veracruz south-

ward in east; favors humid forest edges but is sometimes found in relatively dry pine woods) to w. Colombia.

SEMIPLUMBEOUS HAWK, *Leucopternis semiplumbea.* 13
Plate 5

FIELD MARKS: Tail black with white bar about one third of way up from end and sometimes second partial bar nearer the base. Immatures show narrow dark streaks below.
RANGE: Honduras to Ecuador; in tropical forest.

PLUMBEOUS HAWK, *Leucopternis plumbea.* 15   Plate 5
(Considered a race of *L. schistacea* by some authors.)
FIELD MARKS: Under wing-coverts and indistinct bars on thighs white; tail black with narrow white tip and white band about one third of way up from end. Immatures have the belly mottled with white.
RANGE: E. Panama and Pacific slope in Colombia and Ecuador.

PRINCE HAWK, *Leucopternis princeps.* 17   Plate 5
FIELD MARKS: Throat dark slate; tail black with white bar across middle and some incomplete bars above this; barred below.
RANGE: Costa Rica to Ecuador.

BLACK-COLLARED HAWK, *Busarellus nigricollis.* 18   Plate 5
RANGE: Mexico (Sinaloa to Chiapas; e. San Luis Potosí and Veracruz to Campeche; favors marshes or savanna ponds) to Argentina.

BLACK CRAB-HAWK, *Buteogallus anthracinus.* 19   Plate 4
(Called Mexican Crab Hawk, Mexican Black Hawk, and Lesser Black Hawk by other authors.)
RANGE: S.w. United States to Guiana and Peru; favors swamps, ponds, and streams.

PACIFIC CRAB-HAWK, *Buteogallus subtilis.* 18
(Considered a race of *B. anthracinus* by others.)
FIELD MARKS: Similar to Black Crab-Hawk but smaller. In s.w. Colombia, Ecuador, and Peru these birds show considerable rufous edging to wing feathers (primaries and secondaries), which may even appear as a patch on the folded wing; however, such marks are so restricted in more northern birds that they are not likely to be noticed.
RANGE: Mexico (Chiapas) to n.w. Peru; confined to Pacific coastal mangrove swamps for the most part, but sometimes wanders up rivers for some distance inland.

RIDGWAY'S BLACK-HAWK, *Hypomorphnus ridgwayi.* 22

Plate 4

(Listed as a race of *H. urubitinga* by others; sometimes placed in the genus *Urubitinga* and, more recently, in *Buteogallus.*)

FIELD MARKS: Tail is white with a broad black subterminal bar and a second narrower one higher up; thighs of adult are narrowly barred with white (Black Crab-Hawks show this only in immature plumage).

VOICE: The song phrase is a series of short motifs, one of which may be represented as *ca-ca-ca-keeeo* (there may be only two of the *ca* figures). About five motifs will be delivered in ten sec. Pitch of the *ca* is about B^3, and the *keeeo* is C^4 in the main, although there is a slight terminal downward slur. At times a simple *keeeoo* may be given as a loud scream.

RANGE: Mexico (Sonora to Chiapas; Tamaulipas to Yucatán; mostly in wooded lowlands but at times up to 3000 ft. or more) to Panama.

BRAZILIAN BLACK-HAWK, *Hypomorphnus urubitinga.* 22

Plate 4

(Listed in the genus *Buteogallus* by some.)

FIELD MARKS: Similar to previous species but only one black bar on tail; no white bars on thighs of adult; legs pale greenish yellow instead of orange yellow.

RANGE: Extreme e. Panama to Brazil and Bolivia.

SOLITARY EAGLE, *Urubitornis solitaria.* 27

Plate 4

(Placed in genus *Harpyhaliaetus* by some and listed as a race of *Harpyhaliaetus coronatus* by others.)

RANGE: Mexico (Sonora, Chihuahua, Durango, and south to Jalisco and Oaxaca; usually in the pine region of the mountains; rare) to Peru.

GUIANA CRESTED-EAGLE, *Morphnus guianensis.* 32

Plate 4

FIELD MARKS: Throat white; breast gray; belly barred with very pale rufous. Immatures have the whole under parts white, the breast flecked with gray.

RANGE: Honduras to Colombia and Guiana to Argentina; humid forests.

BANDED CRESTED-EAGLE, *Morphnus taeniatus.* 32

Plate 4

(Considered a color phase of *M. guianensis* by some.)

FIELD MARKS: Belly barred with black. Immatures are paler and have black barring restricted to lower belly or to under tail-coverts.

RANGE: Panama to Bolivia; in "rain forests"; very rare.

HARPY EAGLE, *Harpia harpyja.* 35

Plate 4

RANGE: S. Mexico (Veracruz and Oaxaca and south) to Argentina and Bolivia; in heavy tropical forests.

BLACK-AND-WHITE HAWK-EAGLE, *Spizastur melanoleucus.* 23
Plate 4

FIELD MARKS: Under side of primaries pale, almost white; legs feathered down to yellow feet. Immatures are browner above than adults and have some white on the wings.

RANGE: Mexico (Oaxaca to Chiapas and Veracruz to Yucatán), Guatemala, Honduras, Nicaragua, Costa Rica, and Panama and on to Argentina and Peru.

ORNATE HAWK-EAGLE, *Spizaetus ornatus.* 24
Plate 4

FIELD MARKS: Tail grayish brown, crossed by four black bars; legs feathered to the yellow feet. Immature has head largely buffy white.

RANGE: Mexico (Tamaulipas south to Yucatán; favors forests) to Argentina and Peru.

TYRANT HAWK-EAGLE, *Spizaetus tyrannus.* 26
Plate 4

FIELD MARKS: Tail black, crossed by four bands that appear gray from above and white from below; legs feathered to orange yellow feet. Immature has top of head buffy white, streaked with brownish black; thighs barred as in adult.

RANGE: Mexico (Oaxaca to Chiapas; e. San Luis Potosí to Yucatán; rare) and Central America (except El Salvador) to Brazil and Bolivia.

GOLDEN EAGLE, *Aquila chrysaetos.* 32

RANGE: Eurasia and North America to Mexico (Baja California across to Nuevo León and south to Guanajuato and Hidalgo; chiefly in the mountains but occasionally down to sea level).

BALD EAGLE, *Haliaeetus leucocephalus.* 32

RANGE: North America to n. Mexico (Baja California); winters as far south as Veracruz at rare intervals.

MARSH HAWK, *Circus cyaneus.* 20

RANGE: North America to Baja California; also Eurasia; in winter south as far as Colombia.

BLACK CRANE-HAWK, *Geranospiza nigra.* 18
Plate 4

(Considered a race of *G. caerulescens* by some authors.)

RANGE: Mexico (Sonora to Chiapas; Tamaulipas and e. San Luis Potosí to Yucatán; usually along wooded streams or wet savannas) to Ecuador.

OSPREYS: Pandionidae

OSPREY, *Pandion haliaetus.* 22
RANGE: Almost cosmopolitan but favors temperate zone regions in North America; northern birds migrate in winter.

FALCONS: Falconidae

LAUGHING FALCON, *Herpetotheres cachinnans.* 20 Plate 4
FIELD MARKS: A short-billed, large-headed, almost owl-like bird, with elongated feathers on the crown that may be erected into a bushy crest. Feeds largely on snakes.
VOICE: A series of soft calls rapidly delivered so that it resembles a soft laugh, *ha-ha-ha-ha-ha*, that can be heard only a short distance. A louder series of figures (each represented by *haw*) may be spaced at about one-sec. intervals. This last resembles the call of the Collared Forest-Falcon, but that bird spaces the *haw* figures so widely that one is more likely to consider them single calls. The song (most frequently given in the early morning or in the evening) is composed of loud but fairly mellow motifs, represented by *woo-oo ka-woo*. There is sometimes an elaborate series of varied calls leading up to the song, and frequently the mate joins in and makes a duet by giving a *coo* or some similar sound just before or just after the motif.
RANGE: Mexico (Sonora to Chiapas and Tamaulipas to Yucatán; mostly in lowland forests and savannahs) to Argentina and Bolivia.

COLLARED FOREST-FALCON, *Micrastur semitorquatus.* 21
Plate 4
FIELD MARKS: A fast-flying bird with rounded wings and a long tail marked with four narrow white bands. Dark above in any color phase. Light phase is white below and has white collar across hindneck; tawny phase has collar and under parts pinkish buff or darker; dark phase has no collar and may be quite dark below, sometimes barred or spotted on the belly with white. Immatures are barred below. (The immature Bicolored Hawk lacks the dark "falcon mark" running from ear region toward jaw or throat.)
VOICE: A loud, sonorous *haaw* or *haah* (the Indians say it is *gua*). Frequently, only one call is given, but at times there may be a series, in which case each figure is deliberate and evenly spaced and not varied in tempo as in the Laughing Falcon. Rarely there is a series of figures that could be said to form a "laugh," but this phrase is different in quality from the laugh of the other species.
RANGE: Mexico (Sinaloa to Chiapas; Tamaulipas to Yucatán) to Argentina and Bolivia; in tropical woods.

BARRED FOREST-FALCON, *Micrastur ruficollis.* 14 Plate 5
FIELD MARKS: The immature frequently has a buffy white nuchal collar, which is, however, less distinct than in the case of the Collared Forest-Falcon.
VOICE: A sharp *eeow* or *wow,* usually continued as a series with the figures spaced at about one-sec. intervals. Pitch about E^2, slurring down about two tones.
RANGE: Mexico (Puebla to Oaxaca and Chiapas; e. San Luis Potosí and Veracruz to Yucatán; in humid woods; rare) to Argentina and Ecuador.

MIRANDOLLE'S FOREST-FALCON, *Micrastur mirandollei.* 13
Plate 5
FIELD MARKS: Similar to Collared Forest-Falcon but smaller and lacks collar across hindneck. Immatures are marked below with mixture of gray and buffy white.
RANGE: Costa Rica to Brazil and Peru. (Rare.)

RED-THROATED CARACARA, *Daptrius americanus.* 20 Plate 4
FIELD MARKS: Named "Ca-cao" by natives because of the raucous call.
RANGE: Mexico (Veracruz to Chiapas; rare) to Brazil and Peru; in humid woods.

YELLOW-HEADED CARACARA, *Milvago chimachima.* 17
Plate 5
RANGE: Pacific slope savannas of Panama to Argentina and Bolivia.

CRESTED CARACARA, *Caracara cheriway.* 22
(Considered a race of *C. plancus* by some authors.)
FIELD MARKS: Distinguished from other species of same genus in South America by lack of white barring on scapulars and upper wing-coverts (these parts are solid brown or black).
RANGE: S.w. United States and Florida, southward on continent to Peru.

PRAIRIE FALCON, *Falco mexicanus.* 16
RANGE: W. North America to Baja California; winters to Oaxaca, Hidalgo, and Tamaulipas, Mexico.

PEREGRINE FALCON, *Falco peregrinus.* 18
RANGE: Nearly world-wide. In North America breeds from Alaska to Baja California; migrates to Argentina and Chile.

ORANGE-BREASTED FALCON, *Falco deiroleucus.* 14 Plate 5
VOICE: Similar to White-throated Falcon but lower in pitch.
RANGE: Mexico (Veracruz; very rare) to Argentina and Peru.

WHITE-THROATED FALCON, *Falco petoensis.* 10   Plate 5
(Considered a race of *F. rufigularis* by some.)
voice: A series of calls, such as *ke* or *kee,* given at a rate of about
twenty figures in ten sec. (varies somewhat) and at a pitch of about
D^4. The figures are sometimes longer and become more like *keeee.*
This last is sometimes delivered with a decided vibrato.
range: Mexico (from Sonora and Durango to Chiapas; from Nuevo
León and Tamaulipas to Yucatán; from sea level up to about 4000
ft., but more common below 2000 ft.) to Colombia west of e. Andes
and w. Peru.

APLOMADO FALCON, *Falco femoralis.* 16
range: S.w. United States (possibly now exterminated) to Argentina.

PIGEON HAWK, *Falco columbarius.* 11
range: N. North America; n. Eurasia; migrates in America to Venezuela and Peru.

SPARROW HAWK, *Falco sparverius.* 10
range: North and South America in "temperate zone" savannas; northern birds migrate as far south as the lowlands of Panama.

CURASSOWS: Cracidae

Medium-sized to large, forest-dwelling, gallinaceous birds, with feet
adapted for tree habitat (the hind toe is long and placed at the same
level as the others); feathers of crown more or less elongated.

CENTRAL AMERICAN CURASSOW, *Crax rubra.* 32   Plate 9
field marks: Male has black body while that of female is rufous
brown to chestnut with some black markings and white bars.
voice: The male does at times a very thin "whistle" that can probably
be heard no more than fifty feet. It rises from about G^3 to C^4 in one
and a half sec. and, after a short pause, is frequently followed by
two short figures at the pitch on which the "whistle" ends, as *quee
quee.* The "song" is a slow series of widely spaced phrases of three
motifs each, and it does not sound as though there is any voiced
sound involved (it is a kind of "booming," as when air is expelled
from an inflated sac). Many natives think this a growl of some large
cat. The phrase may be represented as *ah-oo ahoo-ahahoo ah-oo.*
The first and last *ah* are drawn out more than the others (at least
twice as long), and the first and last *oo* are strongly accented and
shut off abruptly so that the sound is more like *oot.* The phrase requires about seven sec., including pauses. The female gives numerous
little *querk* calls that at times bring to mind the "small talk" of a
chicken; some of these are drawled out to *querrrk.*

RANGE: Mexico (central Tamaulipas southward to Oaxaca, Chiapas, and Yucatán; mostly in tropical forests but up into cloud forest occasionally when the acorns are ripe; increasingly uncommon (rapidly being eliminated by forest destruction and hunting), south to w. Ecuador.

CRESTED GUAN, *Penelope purpurascens.*   31   Plate 9

VOICE: There is a low, hoarse call that might be likened to a moan, growl, or snore. It may be indicated as *ahooh*. It is usually given from a tree top at dawn and resembles somewhat the "boom" of the Central American Curassow but is not accented or phrased in the same way. There are also some low grunting calls that develop into a kind of honk by suddenly jumping one or two octaves, as *uh uh oo-uh oo-uh*. The first two *uh* figures are pitched about F and the *oo* is F^2; the final *uh* may be either F or F^1; or the *oo* may sound as though F^1 and F^2 were being sounded simultaneously or almost so. Several birds may give this type of call more or less together so that quite a jumble is produced. This phrase may be the "song" of the species, but there is another phrase that is frequently called a song. This is a series of some fourteen figures (*coa*) delivered in about four sec. It begins rather fast and slows down a bit at the end. The figures might be said to be whistled but are loud and of an almost "hollow" quality. There is also an alarm call that is a loud, sharp *querk*.

RANGE: Mexico (Sinaloa to Chiapas; Tamaulipas to Yucatán; forests from sea level up to cloud forest and at times on up into the edge of the pines; rapidly being eliminated by hunting and forest destruction) to Venezuela and w. Ecuador.

LITTLE GUAN, *Penelopina nigra.*   21   Plate 9

VOICE: The call is a shrill ascending "whistle," as *oooeeeeeeee*, that begins about B^2 and goes up at least two octaves, smoothly (after the fashion of a siren gaining speed), in about two sec. There is also a reedy, vibratory call. It could be likened to a fast rattle or a roll. It seems to begin at about the same pitch as the "whistle," holds steady or sometimes rises somewhat, and then drops three or four tones below the starting point in a total time of two sec.

RANGE: Mexico (cloud forests of s. Oaxaca and Chiapas), Guatemala, El Salvador, Honduras, and Nicaragua.

BLACK GUAN, *Chamaepetes unicolor.*   28   Plate 9

RANGE: Mts. of Costa Rica and w. Panama; cloud forests at 5000 to 6000 ft. elevation.

HORNED GUAN, *Oreophasis derbianus.*   31   Plate 9

RANGE: Mts. of extreme s.w. Chiapas and n.w. Guatemala; in humid forests above 7000 ft.

WAGLER CHACHALACA, *Ortalis wagleri.*   20   Plate 9

(Considered a race of *O. poliocephala* by some.)

voice: The loud, hoarse (almost gutteral) song of the male (delivered from a tree top) is usually introduced by one or more preliminary figures. The song phrase with preliminaries may be represented by *cuv cuv cuv er-it up*. The *cuv er-it up* phrase is then repeated a number of times without preliminaries. The *er-it* is really a four-figure motif, but the tempo is so fast that the sound segments cannot be distinguished as separate figures; nevertheless, *e-r-r-it* would be a more accurate description of the motif. The song of the female (the birds sing duets) is similar but of slightly higher pitch. The female song phrase may be likened to, *Make a-h-i-g-h hill.* In the female the middle motif is, as indicated, made up of five figures, but again the tempo is such that words can not be used to really suggest the sounds. If one merely suggests the middle motif by *ah-high*, it will serve as a reminder.

range: N.w. Mexico (Sonora and Chihuahua south to Nayarit and n.w. Jalisco; from sea level up to 5000 ft. in woods or tall brush).

WESTERN CHACHALACA, *Ortalis poliocephala.*   20   Plate 9

(Considered a race of *O. vetula* by some.)

voice: The song phrase is similar to that of the Wagler Chachalaca, but the accent, or rising inflection, at the terminal figure is lacking; there are more sound segments or figures in the middle motif, which causes it to sound more rolling.

range: Mexico (Colima and s. Jalisco south to Chiapas where it is found along the Pacific coast as far south as Tonalá and then over the continental divide near Arriaga and north to Cintalapa and thence into the mts. a bit to the north; from arid brushland at sea level up to 9000 ft. in the pine-fir association).

WHITE-BELLIED CHACHALACA, *Ortalis leucogastra.*   18
Plate 9

(Considered a race of *O. vetula* by some.)

field marks: Similar to the Western Chachalaca but much smaller. Whole belly is quite white; tip of tail white. This species might well be called the Short-tailed Chachalaca, since it is the only species with the tail shorter than the wing.

voice: The song phrase is similar to that of the Western Chachalaca but is accented differently, is fractionally longer, and the rolling segments seem more crowded together. At a distance, groups of the crowded figures or segments may seem to fuse together and appear to some observers to make up three simple motifs, as in the Eastern Chachalaca; when near at hand, however, the rolling character of the song readily separates it from the eastern bird. The song phrase of the male may be kept in mind by using the words *Come-to-the-woods* (the phrase requires 0.8 sec.); for the female one might say, *Run-for-the-hills*. The first phrase in a song period may be irregular or atypical and may even be a simple *cha-cha-lac-ah*. Preliminary figures similar to those of the preceding species are frequently used, but they may be shortened to *cu* or changed to *chuc*. As with other species, alarm calls and cackles are given.

RANGE: Mexico (Pacific slope of Chiapas south of Tonalá up to 1000 ft. or more) and Pacific slope in Guatemala, El Salvador, and n.w. Nicaragua.

EASTERN CHACHALACA, *Ortalis vetula.*   18

VOICE: The song phrase of this species shows none of the rattle or the rolling effect that is prominent in the previous species; it sounds as though it were composed of three distinct figures that may be represented in the male by *Slap er back* and, in the female by *Keep it up*. As with other species, it is often difficult to distinguish elements of a single motif when several birds are singing in chorus. The preliminary figure occasionally used at the start of a song period is *cha*. In addition to the song, many other phrases, cackles, and alarm calls are given at times. Some sound like snorts and some are heavy purring sounds which, after being repreated for some time, may swell into a loud clatter or cackle not unlike the noise a chicken makes when frightened. There is a loud, explosive alarm call and a very thin "whistle." The last is sometimes heard amidst a chorus of song. It sounds as though one of the birds were gasping for breath.

RANGE: The Rio Grande Delta in Texas, Mexico (the east side of the continental divide from the Rio Grande Delta in Tamaulipas and Nuevo León to Chiapas and Yucatán), and south to n.w. Costa Rica where it reaches the Pacific coast.

GRAY-HEADED CHACHALACA, *Ortalis cinereiceps.*   18   Plate 9
(Considered a race of *O. garrula* by some.)

FIELD MARKS: Head mouse-gray; back and breast olive-brown; belly light brown; tail tipped white or pale gray.

VOICE: Cackles, rattles, and cries bring to mind those of other species, but the "song phrase" seems to be used differently since there is no record of any tree-top chorus. The "song phrase" is made up of what sounds like four figures that are accented so as to suggest the pattern *chac-cha-lac-ah*. This is delivered in a rather soft, quick manner and repeated to form a hurried period of three phrases with the accent in each phrase being on the *lac*.

RANGE: S.e. Honduras, e. Nicaragua, e. and s. Costa Rica to Panama, and extreme n.w. Colombia; humid regions mostly in lowlands.

PARTRIDGES: Phasianidae

BEARDED WOOD-PARTRIDGE, *Dendrortyx barbatus.* 8 Plate 6
FIELD MARKS: Crown feathers slightly elongated and capable of being erected into low, bushy crest; tail more than three inches long; throat gray.
VOICE: The song is a series of identical motifs delivered hurriedly. The motif may be indicated by *weel-pitcher*.
RANGE: Mts. of e. San Luis Potosí and Veracruz, Mexico; in cloud forests and pine woods with grassy ground cover at 4000 to 5000 ft.

LONG-TAILED WOOD-PARTRIDGE, *Dendrortyx macroura.* 11
Plate 6
FIELD MARKS: Line over eye and line along jaw white, brownish white, or brown (if brown it may not be noticed); breast gray (sometimes streaked with rufous); throat black.
VOICE: A loud but rather hollow *coa qup.* There is also a rapid *co co co co co*, the figures being spaced about a half sec. apart. This last is likely to be heard before dawn.
RANGE: Highland forests in Mexico (Jalisco, Mexico, Puebla, Morelos, Guerrero, Oaxaca, and Veracruz) mostly above 8000 ft.

HIGHLAND WOOD-PARTRIDGE, *Dendrortyx leucophrys.* 9
Plate 6
FIELD MARKS: Throat white.
RANGE: Highland forests in Mexico (pine woods of c. and s. Chiapas), Guatemala, Honduras, El Salvador, Nicaragua, and Costa Rica.

LONG-TOED PARTRIDGE, *Dactylortyx thoracicus.* 8 Plate 6
FIELD MARKS: The female is similar to the male, but the facial markings are purplish gray instead of tawny, and the throat is grayish white.
VOICE: The song is usually introduced by four preliminary calls. These are short, loud, almost explosive figures, and the tempo speeds up as they are given, so that the rest between the first two is probably almost twice as long as that between the last two. The total time required by the preliminary motif is about four sec.; the pitch is about A^2. A single figure brings to mind some of the shorter, more hurried "whistles" of the Rufescent Tinamou (which are frequently heard in Chiapas). The last of the preliminary figures is followed immediately by some three to six motifs that may be represented as *pitch-will-weeler*. These may vary to *chu-will-a-weeler*, or *chu-will-weeler*, and sometimes the motif may sound as though it were a simple *chu-weeler*. The song is so hurried that five of the motifs may be delivered in five sec.

RANGE: Mexico (on the Pacific slope from Jalisco to Chiapas; on the Atlantic slope from Tamaulipas to Chiapas and Yucatán; in most regions favors moderately humid oak forests from 3000 to 4000 ft. elevation) to El Salvador and Honduras.

MARBLED WOOD-QUAIL, *Odontophorus gujanensis.* 9   Plate 6
RANGE: S.w. Costa Rica to Brazil and Boliva; in tropical woods.

BLACK-EARED WOOD-QUAIL, *Odontophorus melanotis.* 9
Plate 6
(Considered a race of *O. erythrops* by others.)
RANGE: E. Honduras to w. Panama; tropical forests.

WHITE-THROATED WOOD-QUAIL, *Odontophorus leucolaemus.*
8   Plate 6
FIELD MARKS: Center of throat is white, but at times this area is almost crowded out by the surrounding black; the black feathers have light bases that may show through as white blotches.
RANGE: Subtropical forests of Costa Rica and w. Panama.

TACARCUNA WOOD-QUAIL, *Odontophorus dialeucos.* 9   Plate 6
RANGE: Panama (subtropical woods on mts. of Darien).

SPOTTED WOOD-QUAIL, *Odontophorus guttatus.* 9   Plate 6
VOICE: The song is loud and mellow. A motif, which may be represented as *Come-with-me-now*, is repeated at such a rate that twenty will be delivered in eighteen sec. The pitch of the figures is about G^1-B^1-A^1-A^1 flat. The *with* is louder and accented more than the other parts; at times it seems to be stressed more in every other motif, which gives the song a slight swinging effect.
RANGE: S.e. Mexico (humid forests from sea level up to 5000 ft. in Veracruz, Puebla, Oaxaca, Tabasco, Chiapas, and Campeche) to Panama.

MOUNTAIN QUAIL, *Oreortyx picta.* 9
RANGE: W. United States and south to Baja California.

SCALED QUAIL, *Callipepla squamata.* 8
RANGE: S.w. United States and Mexico (Sonora across to Tamaulipas and south to Morelos and Hidalgo; in semi-desert regions).

CALIFORNIA QUAIL, *Lophortyx californica.* 8
RANGE: Pacific coast of United States, south to Baja California.

GAMBEL QUAIL, *Lophortyx gambelii.* 8½
RANGE: Arid regions of s.w. United States and n.w. Mexico (Baja California, Sonora, and Sinaloa).

DOUGLAS QUAIL, *Lophortyx douglasii.* 8   Plate 6
VOICE: The call is a loud *quirk,* something like the rallying call of a Bobwhite.
RANGE: W. Mexico (from Sonora and Chihuahua south to Nayarit and Jalisco).

BARRED QUAIL, *Philortyx fasciatus.* 7   Plate 6
FIELD MARKS: Crest straight and slender. Immatures have black throat.
RANGE: C.w. Mexico (Colima, Michoacán, Mexico, Morelos, Guerrero, and Puebla; semi-desert areas).

MONTEZUMA QUAIL, *Cyrtonyx montezumae.* 7
RANGE: S.w. United States and Mexico (in the w. mts. from Sonora and Chihuahua south to Puebla; in the e. mts. from Coahuila, Nuevo León, and Tamaulipas south to Veracruz).

SALLE'S QUAIL, *Cyrtonyx sallei.* 7   Plate 6
(Considered a race of *C. montezumae* by some.)
FIELD MARKS: Intermediate in appearance between the preceding species and the following species.
RANGE: Mexico (Guerrero and w. Oaxaca).

OCELLATED QUAIL, *Cyrtonyx ocellatus.* 7   Plate 6
FIELD MARKS: The male is similar to Salle's Quail, but breast is tawny buff; spots on sides of breast are buffy white to buff; spots on sides opposite upper belly are tawny and larger; spots on lower sides are rufous and so large that they tend to run together, leaving almost no gray areas.
RANGE: S. Mexico (relatively dry pine forests of e. Oaxaca and Chiapas) and south to Honduras and Nicaragua.

TAWNY-FACED QUAIL, *Rhynchortyx cinctus.* 6   Plate 6
RANGE: Tropical forests on Caribbean slope of Honduras, Nicaragua, and Costa Rica; on both slopes of Panama; south to w. Ecuador.

GENUS *COLINUS*: Since all species of the genus whistle *BobWhite,* it seems reasonable that there would be some hybridization between any two populations that were brought together. Many "species" have been lumped by museum workers when hybrids have been found;

however, some other cases in which hybrids have been found have not been lumped as yet by anyone. The treatment below divides the genus into "species," which should prove more useful to birders.

NORTHERN BOBWHITE, *Colinus virginianus.*   8
RANGE: United States and n.e. Mexico (Coahuila, Nuevo León, and Tamaulipas).

RUFOUS-BELLIED BOBWHITE, *Colinus pectoralis.*   8   Plate 6
  (Considered a race of *C. virginianus* by others.)
FIELD MARKS: Throat of male white, bordered below by black area of variable width; belly and sides rufous to chestnut; thighs and under tail-coverts at times streaked or edged with black.
RANGE: Mexico (s. Nayarit, Jalisco, Guanajuato, Mexico, Morelos, Queretaro, c. and w. San Luis Potosí, Hidalgo, Puebla n. and s.e. Oaxaca, the Atlantic coastal plains of Veracruz, Tabasco and Chiapas, and possibly adjacent Guatemala. In extreme s. Tamaulipas and adjacent e. San Luis Potosí and n. Veracruz, some birds show mixed characters, being more rufous below than the Northern Bobwhite, but showing white streaks on the belly and flanks. The area in which the hybrids are found is not wide in relation to the total range of the species.).

MASKED BOBWHITE, *Colinus ridgwayi.*   8   Plate 6
  (Considered a race of *C. virginianus* by others.)
RANGE: Mexico (c. Sonora); formerly s. Arizona, but now eliminated.

BLACK-HEADED BOBWHITE, *Colinus atriceps.*   8   Plate 6
  (Considered a race of *C. virginianus* by others.)
FIELD MARKS: Similar to previous species, but male has whole head and neck black. Some birds have a partial white line over the eye. "Intergrades": In w. Oaxaca and extreme w. Chiapas the Black-headed Bobwhite and the Rufous-bellied Bobwhite are found together at times. They hybridize, and a single covey may contain several males with solid black throats, several with entirely white throats, and some with white throats that are variously speckled, spotted, or striped with black.
RANGE: S. Oaxaca, c. and s. Chiapas, and a small adjacent area in Guatemala.

BLACK-THROATED BOBWHITE, *Colinus nigrogularis.*   8   Plate 6
RANGE: Mexico (Yucatán, Campeche, and Quintana Roo), British Honduras and adjacent Guatemala, and e. Honduras. (Near the Tabasco border some birds show characters suggesting hybridization with the Rufous-bellied Bobwhite.)

WHITE-FACED BOBWHITE, *Colinus leucopogon.* 8   Plate 6
(Considered a race of *C. cristatus* by some.)
RANGE: Arid tropical zone of s.e. El Salvador east of Rio Lempa.

WHITE-BREASTED BOBWHITE, *Colinus hypoleucus.* 8 Plate 6
(Considered a race of *C. leucopogon* by others.)
RANGE: S. Guatemala and the grasslands of El Salvador west of the Rio Lempa.

SCLATER'S BOBWHITE, *Colinus sclateri.* 8   Plate 6
(Considered a race of *C. leucopogon* by some and *cristatus* by others.)
FIELD MARKS: Similar to following species, but male has solid brownish black throat.
RANGE: Central plateau and Pacific slope of Honduras and n.w. Nicaragua.

DICKEY'S BOBWHITE, *Colinus dickeyi.* 8   Plate 6
(Considered a race of *C. leucopogon* by some.)
RANGE: S.w. Nicaragua and n.w. Costa Rica.

CRESTED BOBWHITE, *Colinus cristatus.* 9   Plate 6
RANGE: Semi-arid plains of n.w. Panama; Colombia, Venezuela, Guiana, and n.e. Brazil.

TURKEYS: Meleagrididae

BRONZE TURKEY, *Meleagris gallopavo.* 36
RANGE: E. and s.w. United States and Mexico (from Sonora south to Guerrero and Oaxaca; from Coahuila, Nuevo León, and Tamaulipas south to Veracruz; mostly in the transition zone on the mts.).

OCELLATED TURKEY, *Agriocharis ocellata.* 30   Plate 9
RANGE: S.e. Mexico (Tabasco, extreme e. Chiapas, Campeche, Yucatán, and Quintana Roo) and the Peten region of British Honduras and Guatamela; mostly in second-growth woods and abandoned fields.

CRANES: Gruidae

WHOOPING CRANE, *Grus americana.* 45
RANGE: N.c. Canada; winters on Texas Gulf coast; rarely one wanders into Tamaulipas.

SANDHILL CRANE, *Grus canadensis.*   37
RANGE: N.e. Siberia, w. and s.e. North America, and Cuba; south in
   winter to Mexico (Baja California across to Tamaulipas and south
   to Quintana Roo).

LIMPKINS: Aramidae

LIMPKIN, *Aramus guarauna.*   24
RANGE: S.e. United States and Mexico to Argentina and Bolivia.

RAILS: Rallidae

KING RAIL, *Rallus elegans.*   14
RANGE: E. United States; in winter to Mexico (as far south as Veracruz).

WESTERN RAIL, *Rallus obsoletus.*   15
   (Considered a race of *R. elegans* by some and a race of *R. longirostris* by others.)
FIELD MARKS: These birds are from two to three inches larger than
   Clapper Rails and from one to two inches larger than King Rails;
   being rather brown above they look more like King Rails in the field
   than Clapper Rails. The lesser upper wing-coverts (areas near bend
   of wing) are bright brown (sometimes somewhat rufous brown)
   instead of bright rufous or chestnut as in the King Rail; they lack
   the dark olive-gray wash that is usually so pronounced in the
   Clapper Rail. The breast is buff, varying from pinkish buff or
   salmon buff to light brownish buff. The face is usually brown or
   brownish gray but sometimes mouse-gray, although not likely to be
   a decided blue gray as in the Clapper Rail.
RANGE: Salt marshes and mangrove swamps from California south to
   Nayarit.

MEXICAN RAIL, *Rallus tenuirostris.*   14   Plate 1
   (Considered a race of *R. elegans* by some authors, a race of *R.
   obsoletus* by some, and a race of *R. longirostris* by others.)
FIELD MARKS: Similar to the Western Rail but with rufescent flanks and
   a rufous breast; jaw pinkish cinnamon.
RANGE: Isolated in fresh water marshes of central Mexico in the
   Distrito Federal, Mexico (Rio Lerma), and Tlaxcala.

CLAPPER RAIL, *Rallus longirostris.*   12
FIELD MARKS: These birds never have the lesser upper wing-coverts
   bright rufous or chestnut; the cheeks are bluish gray or grayish
   olive.

RANGE: Salt and brackish water marshes of e. United States, the West Indies, e. Mexico (Tamaulipas to Yucatán and Quintana Roo), and British Honduras; also South America from Guiana and Colombia to Brazil and Peru.

VIRGINIA RAIL, *Rallus limicola.* 7½
RANGE: North America to c. Mexico (Baja California, Sonora, and Distrito Federal; elsewhere in winter) and Guatemala; also marshes in mts. of Colombia, Ecuador, Chile, and Argentina.

SPOTTED RAIL, *Pardirallus maculatus.* 9½   Plate 1
RANGE: Cuba, Mexico (marshes in Veracruz and Chiapas), British Honduras, Costa Rica, and South America (Venezuela and Colombia to Argentina).

UNIFORM RAIL, *Amaurolimnas concolor.* 8   Plate 1
RANGE: Mexico (swampy woods of Veracruz and Oaxaca and south) and south to Brazil and Bolivia.

CAYENNE WOOD-RAIL, *Aramides cajanea.* 15   Plate 1
RANGE: S.w. and extreme s. Costa Rica to Argentina and Bolivia.

WHITE-BANDED WOOD-RAIL, *Aramides albiventris.* 15   Plate 1
(Considered a race of *A. cajanea* by others.)
VOICE: A loud cackle usually given in the early morning or in the evening. The song (which is different in structure from that of the previous species) may be represented by a series of motifs, such as *cuac-cuack-cu-cu-cuack-cuack-cuack-cuack cu-cu-cu-cu-cuack-cuack cu-cu-cu-cu-cuack-cuack*, etc., continuing for five sec. or more. The *cu* is pitched at about C^2. The first motif of a series may be irregular, but succeeding ones are usually regular with four *cu* figures and two *cuacks*; there may be a slight *ah* sound at the end of the fourth *cu* in a series. About ten of these motifs will be delivered in fifteen sec. The longer figures may sound more like *queack*.
RANGE: Mexico (Oaxaca to Chiapas; s. Tamaulipas, Hidalgo, Distrito Federal to Chiapas and Yucatán; near water holes, ponds, or marshy stream sides in woods or savannahs (may remain in a habitat in the dry season after a pond has dried up); to n. and e. Costa Rica.

RUFOUS-HEADED WOOD-RAIL, *Aramides axillaris.* 12   Plate 1
RANGE: Mexico (coastal lagoons and marshes from Sinaloa to Guerrero; also Yucatán) to Guiana and Ecuador.

SORA RAIL, *Porzana carolina.* 8
RANGE: North America to Baja California; in winter to Brazil and Peru.

YELLOW-BREASTED RAIL, *Porzana flaviventer.*   5   Plate 1
RANGE: Mexico (grassy marshes in Veracruz) to Argentina.

BLACK RAIL, *Laterallus jamaicensis.*   4½
RANGE: United States, Mexico (Veracruz and Baja California), Guatemala, British Honduras, Panama, Jamaica, Peru, and Chile (range
not well known).

GRAY-BREASTED RAIL, *Laterallus exilis.*   5½   Plate 1
RANGE: Caribbean slope in Honduras and Nicaragua; also n. South
America to Brazil and Peru.

WHITE-THROATED RAIL, *Laterallus albigularis.*   6½   Plate 1
  (Considered a race of *L. melanophaius* by some authors.)
FIELD MARKS: Forehead and crown bright brown; cheeks russet;
  nape, sides of neck, and breast chestnut; chin and throat white;
  belly, flanks, and thighs black, narrowly barred with white; bill
  greenish black with green spot at base.
RANGE: S.w. Costa Rica, Pacific slope of Panama, Caribbean slope of
  e. Panama (from Colón to Colombia border), w. Colombia, and
  w. Ecuador.

GRAY-HEADED RAIL, *Laterallus cinereiceps.*   6   Plate 1
  (Considered a race of *L. albigularis* by most authors.)
FIELD MARKS: Forehead, crown, and cheeks gray; nape, sides of neck,
  and breast chestnut; back brown; chin pale buff; center part of
  upper throat buffy white to pale buff; lower throat, sides of neck,
  and breast orange cinnamon; lower belly, flanks, and thighs black,
  narrowly barred with white. A light phase has middle of throat
  and breast and most of belly white and is generally lighter in color.
VOICE: The usual call is a reedy roll similar to Least Grebe roll. (This
  call sounds the same as that of the previous species.)
RANGE: Nicaragua, e. Costa Rica, and w. Panama (largely confined to
  the Caribbean slope but possibly extending across the divide in
  river valleys for a short distance); found in grassy spots along rivers,
  roadside ditches, or flats, where rain puddles are likely to form, in
  the tropical zone, and up to 4000 ft. or so.

RUDDY RAIL, *Laterallus ruber.*   6   Plate 1
RANGE: Marshes in tropical zone from Mexico (Tamaulipas to Yucatán)
  to Nicaragua.

YELLOW RAIL, *Coturnicops noveboracensis.*   6
RANGE: North America to Mexico (marshes of Rio Lerma in state of
  Mexico).

FLORIDA GALLINULE, *Gallinula cachinnans.* 13
(Considered a race of the Common Gallinule of Europe, *G. chloropus,* by some authors.)
RANGE: S. Canada to Panama.

PURPLE GALLINULE, *Porphyrula martinica.* 12
RANGE: S. United States to Argentina and Bolivia.

AMERICAN COOT, *Fulica americana.* 14
RANGE: North America south to w. Argentina and Chile.

SUNGREBES: Heliornithidae

Slender-necked water birds with Rail-like bills, rounded tails with stiff feathers, and lobed or scolloped toes.

AMERICAN FINFOOT, *Heliornis fulica.* 14   Plate 1
RANGE: Mexico (e. San Luis Potosí and Veracruz south to Chiapas and Campeche; on quiet lowland rivers) to Argentina and Bolivia.

SUNBITTERNS: Eurypygidae

Fan-tailed wading birds with long slender necks, straight, Rail-like bills that are hardly longer than the head; broad wings; soft Bittern-like plumage; tibias largely bare of feathers.

GREATER SUNBITTERN, *Eurypyga major.* 19   Plate 1
(Considered a race of *E. helias* by some authors.)
RANGE: S. Mexico (Tabasco and Chiapas) southward to w. Columbia and w. Ecuador (not found in El Salvador).

JACANAS: Jacanidae

Rail-like birds that have very long toes adapted for walking on floating aquatic vegetation and a spur at bend of the wing.

NORTHERN JACANA, *Jacana spinosa.* 8   Plate 1
RANGE: Rio Grande Delta of Texas to Panama.

BLACK JACANA, *Jacana hypomelaena.* 8   Plate 1
(Considered a race of *J. spinosa* by some authors, and of *J. jacana,* the Wattled Jacana, by others.)

FIELD MARKS: Similar to previous species, but with red wattles and greenish black body coloration in adults. (There may be a few hybrids in Panama.)

RANGE: Panama and n. Colombia.

OYSTERCATCHERS: Haematopodidae

AMERICAN OYSTERCATCHER, *Haematopus palliatus.*   17
(Considered a race of *H. ostralegus* of Europe by some authors.)
RANGE: North America, West Indies, Mexico, Guatemala, Costa Rica, Panama; also Brazil and Argentina on the Atlantic and Colombia to Chile on the Pacific; favors sand or shell beaches.

BLACK OYSTERCATCHER, *Haematopus bachmani.*   17
(Considered a race of *H. ostralegus* by some.)
RANGE: Pacific coast of North America to n. Baja California; favors rocky beaches.

PLOVERS: Charadriidae

CAYENNE LAPWING, *Belonopterus cayennensis.*   12   Plate 1
(Sometimes listed as *B. chilensis,* sometimes as *Vanellus chilensis.*)
RANGE: Panama and South America east of Andes; also s. Chile.

BLACK-BELLIED PLOVER, *Squatarola squatarola.*   11
(Listed as *Pluvialis squatarola* by some.)
RANGE: Circumpolar in Arctic region; migrates in America as far south as Brazil.

AMERICAN GOLDEN PLOVER, *Pluvialis dominica.*   10
RANGE: Arctic America, south on migration to Argentina.

SEMIPALMATED PLOVER, *Charadrius semipalmatus.*   7
(Listed as a race of *C. hiaticula* by some.)
RANGE: N. North America; migrates south to Patagonia.

PIPING PLOVER, *Charadrius melodus.*   6
RANGE: E. North America; winters to Mexico (Tamaulipas) and West Indies.

SNOWY PLOVER, *Charadrius nivosus.*   6
(Considered a race of *C. alexandrinus* by some.)
RANGE: W. and s. United States to Mexico (Baja California and Tamaulipas); further south in winter.

COLLARED PLOVER, *Charadrius collaris.* 6   Plate 1
RANGE: Mexico (Sinaloa to Chiapas; e. San Luis Potosí and Veracruz to Tabasco; coastal plains and beaches) to Argentina and Bolivia.

KILLDEER, *Charadrius vociferus.* 9
RANGE: North America to Mexico (Baja California to Chihuahua and south to Guerrero; Tamaulipas; elsewhere in winter); also Greater Antilles and coast of Peru.

WILSON PLOVER, *Charadrius wilsonia.* 7
RANGE: S. United States on both coasts, West Indies and south to Peru and Venezuela; northern birds winter to Peru and Brazil.

MOUNTAIN PLOVER, *Eupoda montana.* 8
RANGE: Plains of w. United States; in winter south to Mexico (Baja California across to Tamaulipas).

SNIPES: Scolopacidae

UPLAND PLOVER, *Bartramia longicauda.* 11
RANGE: S. Canada and n. United States; winters to Argentina.

HUDSONIAN CURLEW, *Numenius hudsonicus.* 15
(Listed as race of *N. phaeopus* of Europe by some.)
RANGE: Arctic America; winters to Brazil and Chile.

LONG-BILLED CURLEW, *Numenius americanus.* 20
RANGE: W. North America to Texas; winters south to Guatemala.

HUDSONIAN GODWIT, *Limosa haemastica.* 14
RANGE: Arctic North America; winters to Argentina and Chile.

MARBLED GODWIT, *Limosa fedoa.* 17
RANGE: Plains of Canada and n. United States; winters to Chile.

LESSER YELLOWLEGS, *Totanus flavipes.* 10
RANGE: N. North America; winters to Argentina and Chile.

GREATER YELLOWLEGS, *Totanus melanoleucus.* 13
RANGE: N. North America; winters to Tierra del Fuego.

SOLITARY SANDPIPER, *Tringa solitaria.* 8
RANGE: Canada; winters to Argentina.

SPOTTED SANDPIPER, *Actitis macularia.* 7
RANGE: North America through United States; winters to Argentina and Chile.

WILLET, *Catoptrophorus semipalmatus.* 15
RANGE: North America to n.e. Mexico; winters to Brazil and Peru.

WANDERING TATTLER, *Heteroscelus incanus.* 11
RANGE: Alaska and British Columbia; in winter along Pacific coast to Ecuador and various islands of Pacific.

SURFBIRD, *Aphriza virgata.* 10
RANGE: Alaska; winters south to Chile.

RUDDY TURNSTONE, *Arenaria interpres.* 8
RANGE: Arctic regions; in America winters to Brazil and Chile.

BLACK TURNSTONE, *Arenaria melanocephala.* 8
RANGE: N.w. North America; winters south to Baja California.

SHORT-BILLED DOWITCHER, *Limnodromus griseus.* 11
RANGE: N. North America; winters to Brazil.

LONG-BILLED DOWITCHER, *Limnodromus scolopaceus.* 12
  (Considered a race of *L. griseus* by some.)
RANGE: N.e. Siberia to n.w. Canada; winters to Argentina.

WILSON'S SNIPE, *Capella delicata.* 11
  (Considered a race of *C. gallinago* by many.)
RANGE: N. North America; winters to Venezuela and Colombia.

AMERICAN KNOT, *Calidris rufa.* 10
  (Considered a race of *C. canutus* by others.)
RANGE: N. North America; winters to Tierra del Fuego.

SANDERLING, *Crocethia alba.* 7
RANGE: Arctic regions; winters to Argentina and Chile.

SEMIPALMATED SANDPIPER, *Ereunetes pusillus.* 6
RANGE: Arctic-America; winters to Chile.

WESTERN SANDPIPER, *Ereunetes mauri.* 6½
RANGE: Alaska; winters to Venezuela and Peru.

LEAST SANDPIPER, *Erolia minutilla.* 5
RANGE: Arctic America; winters to Brazil and Peru.

WHITE-RUMPED SANDPIPER, *Erolia fuscicollis.* 7
RANGE: Arctic America; winters to Brazil.

BAIRD SANDPIPER, *Erolia bairdii.* 7
RANGE: N.e. Siberia and n. North America; winters to Argentina.

PECTORAL SANDPIPER, *Erolia melanotos.* 8
RANGE: E. Siberia and arctic America; winters to Argentina.

RED-BACKED SANDPIPER, *Erolia pacifica.* 8
   (Considered a race of *E. alpina* by others.)
RANGE: Alaska and n.w. Canada; migrates to Nicaragua.

STILT SANDPIPER, *Micropalama himantopus.* 8
RANGE: Arctic North America; winters to Argentina and Bolivia.

BUFF-BREASTED SANDPIPER, *Tryngites subruficollis.* 8
RANGE: Arctic America; winters to Argentina and Peru.

S T I L T S : Recurvirostridae

BLACK-NECKED STILT, *Himantopus mexicanus.* 14
   (Considered a race of *H. himantopus* of Europe by some.)
RANGE: United States to Peru.

AMERICAN AVOCET, *Recurvirostra americana.* 14
RANGE: W. North America to Texas and Mexico (to San Luis Potosí);
   winters south to Guatemala.

P H A L A R O P E S : Phalaropodidae

RED PHALAROPE, *Phalaropus fulicarius.* 8
RANGE: Arctic regions; winters to Argentina.

WILSON'S PHALAROPE, *Steganopus tricolor.* 9
RANGE: W. Canada and w. United States; winters to Argentina.

NORTHERN PHALAROPE, *Lobipes lobatus.* 7
RANGE: Arctic regions; winters to Peru.

THICK-KNEES: Burhinidae

DOUBLE-STRIPED THICK-KNEE, *Burhinus bistriatus.* 18 Plate 1
RANGE: Mexico (Oaxaca, Chiapas, Veracruz, and Tabasco; savannas)
to n.w. Costa Rica; also Hispaniola, n.e. Colombia, Venezuela,
Guiana and n. Brazil. One Texas record.

JAEGERS: Stercorariidae

CHILEAN SKUA, *Catharacta chilensis.* 19   Plate 3
(Considered a race of the Northern Skua, *C. skua,* by many.)
FIELD MARKS: Similar to Northern Skua but cinnamon-rufous below.
RANGE: S. South America; wanders off Pacific coast as far as Canada.

POMERINE JAEGER, *Stercorarius pomarinus.* 20
RANGE: Arctic regions; winters south to coast of Peru.

PARASITIC JAEGER, *Stercorarius parasiticus.* 18
RANGE: N. North America; winters to Straits of Magellan.

LONG-TAILED JAEGER, *Stercorarius longicaudus.* 20
RANGE: Arctic; winters to Argentina and Chile.

GULLS: Laridae

GRAY GULL, *Larus modestus.* 15   Plate 3
FIELD MARKS: Head white (brown in winter plumage); other parts
gray except for white band in wing and black tip to tail; bill and
feet black.
RANGE: Arid regions of Peru and Chile; feeds in Humboldt Current;
wanders to coast of Panama.

BAND-TAILED GULL, *Larus belcheri.* 17
FIELD MARKS: Head white in summer and brownish black in winter;
back black; rump white; tail white with black band across middle;
below white; bill yellow with red tip and black crossband.
RANGE: W. coast of South America from Peru to Chile; wanders off
Pacific coast of Panama occasionally.

HEERMANN GULL, *Larus heermanni.* 18
RANGE: N. Northern Hemisphere; winters in America to Panama.

RING-BILLED GULL, *Larus delawarensis.* 18
RANGE: N. North America; winters to Mexico, rarely to Panama.

HERRING GULL, *Larus argentatus.* 22
RANGE: N. Northern Hemisphere; winters in America, South to Panama.

CALIFORNIA GULL, *Larus californicus.* 20
RANGE: W. North America to Nevada; winters to Guatemala.

WESTERN GULL, *Larus occidentalis.* 24
RANGE: Pacific coast of United States and n. Mexico (Baja California); winters south to Nayarit.

GLAUCOUS-WINGED GULL, *Larus glaucescens.* 24
RANGE: N. Pacific coasts; winters south to China and Mexico (Baja California and Sonora).

LAUGHING GULL, *Larus atricilla.* 15
RANGE: Atlantic and Gulf coast of North America to Yucatán; also s.w. California and south to Sinaloa; winters south to Brazil and Peru (birds in winter plumage remain all year in winter range).

FRANKLIN GULL, *Larus pipixcan.* 13
RANGE: Canada and w. United States; winters to Chile.

BONAPARTE GULL, *Larus philadelphia.* 12
RANGE: Alaska and w. Canada; winters south to Mexico.

SABINE GULL, *Xema sabini.* 12
RANGE: Arctic regions; winters to coast of Peru.

BLACK-LEGGED KITTIWAKE, *Rissa tridactyla.* 16
RANGE: Arctic regions; winters at sea south to Baja California.

BLACK TERN, *Chlidonias niger.* 9
RANGE: Northern Hemisphere, temperate zone; winters in America to Chile.

GULL-BILLED TERN, *Gelochelidon nilotica.* 13
RANGE: Local but almost world-wide in temperate areas; winters in America to Brazil and Ecuador.

CASPIAN TERN, *Hydroprogne caspia.* 19
RANGE: Northern Hemisphere; in America to s. Texas, Baja California, and Sinaloa; winters south to Colombia.

COMMON TERN, *Sterna hirundo.* 13
RANGE: Northern Hemisphere, temperate zone; winters to Argentina.

FORSTER'S TERN, *Sterna forsteri.* 14
RANGE: North America to Veracruz; winters to Guatemala (both coasts).

ROSEATE TERN, *Sterna dougallii.* 14
RANGE: Old World; Atlantic coast of North America; British Honduras; winters in America to Venezuela.

BRIDLED TERN, *Sterna anaethetus.* 13
RANGE: Islets in tropical seas; British Honduras, Mexico (Guerrero), Nicaragua, Panama; Guiana, Venezuela; Colombia (on Pacific).

SOOTY TERN, *Sterna fuscata.* 15
RANGE: Islands of tropical seas; Mexico (Baja California to Nayarit; Yucatán and Quintana Roo), Honduras, Panama; wanders off coast of Venezuela and Brazil; also Peru and Chile.

LEAST TERN, *Sterna albifrons.* 8
RANGE: Temperate and tropical regions of world; in America along Atlantic from Massachusetts to British Honduras, the Lesser Antilles, and Venezuela, and along the Pacific from California to Guatemala; winters south to Brazil and Peru.

ROYAL TERN, *Thalasseus maximus.* 18
RANGE: S.e. North America to Mexico (Baja California to Oaxaca; Tamaulipas to Yucatán and Quintana Roo); winters to Argentina and Peru.

ELEGANT TERN, *Thalasseus elegans.* 16
(Listed as *T. comatus* by some; placed in genus *Sterna* by some.)
RANGE: Pacific coast of Mexico (Baja California to Oaxaca); winters south to Chile.

CABOT'S TERN, *Thalasseus acuflavidus.* 14
(Considered a race of *T. sandvicensis* by others.)
RANGE: United States (s. Atlantic and Gulf states) to West Indies, Mexico (Yucatán and Quintana Roo; Tamaulipas and Veracruz birds possibly not breeding), and British Honduras; winters to Brazil and Colombia.

BROWN NODDY, *Anous stolidus.* 14
FIELD MARKS: Top of head pale gray, fading to grayish white (almost pure white) on forehead; back dark brown; tail almost black; below dark brown, the throat grayer.
RANGE: Islands of Gulf of Mexico, Caribbean, tropical Atlantic and tropical Pacific oceans; off coast of Mexico (Nayarit to Guerrero;

Quintana Roo) to Panama (both coasts), Venezuela, and Colombia.

WHITE-CAPPED NODDY, *Anous minutus.* 12½
(Listed as a race of *A. tenuirostris* of Indian Ocean by some.)
FIELD MARKS: Similar to previous species but top of head whiter and rest of plumage darker (almost pure black).
RANGE: Islands in tropical Atlantic and Pacific; off coast of Honduras; Clipperton and Cocos Islands. (Not in Hawaiian Islands, where the Hawaiian Noddy with the light gray tail is found.)

WHITE TERN, *Gygis alba.* 11½
FIELD MARKS: White; ring around eye black; tail deeply forked.
RANGE: Tropical oceans; Socorro Island off w. coast of Mexico, Cocos and Galápagos Islands.

SKIMMERS: Rynchopidae

BLACK SKIMMER, *Rynchops nigra.* 17
RANGE: E. United States; Mexico (Sonora to Chiapas; Tamaulipas to Yucatán) to Panama; Venezuela to Argentina and Colombia to Chile; may range far up from coast on wide rivers.

AUKS: Alcidae

XANTUS MURRELET, *Endomychura hypoleuca.* 8
RANGE: Coast and islands off s. California and w. Baja California.

CRAVERI'S MURRELET, *Endomychura craveri.* 8
(Listed as a race of *E. hypoleuca* by some.)
FIELD MARKS: Similar to preceding species but is darker above (the back is blackish slate instead of slate gray) and has decidedly darker under wing-coverts (gray instead of pure white).
RANGE: Islands in Gulf of California off coast of Sonora; wanders along Pacific coast after breeding season.

ANCIENT MURRELET, *Synthliboramphus antiquus.* 9
RANGE: Islands and coast of n. Pacific; in winter straggles south as far as Baja California.

CASSIN AUKLET, *Ptychoramphus aleuticus.* 8
RANGE: Pacific coast of North America to n. Baja California.

RHINOCEROS AUKLET, *Cerorhinca monocerata.* 14
RANGE: N. Pacific; winters occasionally to Baja California.

PIGEONS: Columbidae

DOMESTIC PIGEON, *Columba livia.*   13
RANGE: In North America found in a semi-feral condition about ranches and towns to s. Mexico.

WHITE-CROWNED PIGEON, *Columba leucocephala.*   13   Plate 10
RANGE: Florida Keys to islands off coast of Yucatán and Quintana Roo, Nicaragua, and w. Panama.

BAND-TAILED PIGEON, *Columba fasciata.*   13
RANGE: S.w. British Columbia and w. United States to n. Nicaragua.

WHITE-NAPED PIGEON, *Columba albilinea.*   13   Plate 10
(Considered a race of *C. fasciata* by most.)
FIELD MARKS: Similar to Band-tailed Pigeon but darker, the white of the underparts being replaced by pale gray and confined to the under tail-coverts; the bill is entirely yellow (no black tip).
RANGE: Highlands of Costa Rica to Venezuela, n.w. Argentina and Peru.

SCALED PIGEON, *Columba speciosa.*   12   Plate 10
(Listed in genus *Patagioenas* by some.)
RANGE: S. Mexico (s. Veracruz and e. Oaxaca to Yucatán and Campeche; in humid tropical forests) to Paraguay and Bolivia.

RED-BILLED PIGEON, *Columba flavirostris.*   13
(Listed in genus *Patagioenas* by some.)
RANGE: S. Texas to Costa Rica where confined to the northwest and to the central highlands and Caribbean lowlands in the northeast.

CAYENNE PIGEON, *Columba cayennensis.*   12   Plate 10
(Listed in genus *Patagioenas* by some.)
RANGE: Mexico (c. Veracruz to e. Chiapas and Quintana Roo) to Argentina and Peru.

SHORT-BILLED PIGEON, *Columba nigrirostris.*   11   Plate 10
(Listed in genus *Oenoenas* by some.)
RANGE: S. Mexico (s. Veracruz and e. Oaxaca to e. Chiapas and Yucatán) to Panama; favors humid lowlands.

RUDDY PIGEON, *Columba subvinacea.*   12   Plate 10
(Listed in genus *Oenoenas* by some.)
RANGE: Mts. of Costa Rica and w. Panama.

BERLEPSCH'S PIGEON, *Columba berlepschi.* 11   Plate 10
(Listed as a race of *C. subvinacea* by others and in genus *Oenoenas* by some.)
FIELD MARKS: Similar to previous species but with shorter wings and tail and much shorter bill; colors duller; underparts lighter and shading to a gray wash; the rump more purple.
RANGE: Lowlands of extreme s.e. Panama to w. Colombia and Eucador.

MOURNING DOVE, *Zenaidura macroura.* 11
(Placed in genus *Zenaida* by some.)
RANGE: Alaska to Panama; occasionally migrates to Colombia.

SOCORRO DOVE, *Zenaidura graysoni.* 12   Plate 10
RANGE: Socorro Island off west coast of Mexico.

YUCATAN DOVE, *Zenaida yucatanensis.* 10   Plate 10
(Considered a race of *Z. aurita* by others.)
FIELD MARKS: Looks like a cross between a White-winged Dove and a Mourning Dove; tail short and feathers white-tipped except for middle two; less white on wing than on White-winged Dove.
RANGE: Mexico (Yucatán, Quintana Roo, and nearby islands).

WHITE-WINGED DOVE, *Zenaida asiatica.* 11
RANGE: S.w. United States to Chile.

INCA DOVE, *Scardafella inca.* 7
(Considered a race of *S. squamata* of South America by some.)
RANGE: S.w. United States to n.w. Costa Rica.

SCALY GROUND-DOVE, *Columbina passerina.* 6
RANGE: S. United States to Costa Rica; n. South America to Brazil and Ecuador.

LITTLE GROUND-DOVE, *Columbina minuta.* 5½   Plate 10
RANGE: S. Mexico (Veracruz to Campeche and Chiapas; tropical areas) to c. Panama; also Venezuela and Colombia to Paraguay and Peru.

RUDDY GROUND-DOVE, *Columbina rufipennis.* 6½   Plate 10
(Considered a race of *C. talpacoti* by some.)
RANGE: Mexico (s. Sinaloa to Guerrero; s. Tamaulipas and e. San Luis Potosí to Quintana Roo and Chiapas) to Guiana and Colombia.

BLUE GROUND-DOVE, *Claravis pretiosa.* 8   Plate 10
RANGE: E. Mexico (cloud forests in w. Tamaulipas and e. San Luis

Potosí to humid lowlands in Yucatán, Quintana Roo, and Chiapas) to Argentina and Bolivia; favors edge or open second growth.

MONDETOUR GROUND-DOVE, *Claravis mondetoura.*   8   Plate 10
RANGE: Mexico (cloud forests or wet mountain woods in Veracruz and Chiapas) to Venezuela and Bolivia.

WHITE-FRONTED DOVE, *Leptotila verreauxi.*   11
RANGE: S. Texas, Mexico (s. Sonora to Tamaulipas and south to Chiapas, Yucatán, and Quintana Roo; in dense brush in semi-arid or humid regions), and south to Argentina and Bolivia.

GAUMER DOVE, *Leptotila gaumeri.*   10   Plate 10
  (Considered a race of *L. jamaicensis* by others.)
VOICE: The plaintive song phrase lasts about two sec. and may be suggested by *My-nose-is-cold.*
RANGE: Mexico (Campeche, Yucatán, and Quintana Roo; also nearby islands; favors underbrush habitats used by previous species).

GRAY-HEADED DOVE, *Leptotila plumbeiceps.*   10   Plate 10
FIELD MARKS: Head bluish gray to slate gray, becoming almost white on forehead and contrasting distinctly with the brown back. Juveniles have scapulars and wing-coverts margined with tawny.
VOICE: A rather loud but low-pitched *boo, moo,* or *oooo.* It sounds very much like a child imitating a cow.
RANGE: E. Mexico (s. Tamaulipas and e. San Luis Potosí to Chiapas; in humid woods from sea level up to 2000 ft. or more) to w. Panama and w. Colombia (not found in El Salvador).

BATTY'S DOVE, *Leptotila battyi.*   10   Plate 10
  (Considered a race of *L. plumbeiceps* by some.)
FIELD MARKS: Similar to Gray-headed Dove, but back is chestnut brown, the pink wash on breast is stronger, and the cheeks are brownish gray; has less white at tip of tail than White-fronted Dove.
VOICE: According to Alex Wetmore the call is a two-figure motif likened to a slowly delivered *hoo-hoo* (sometimes three figures) that has a quality somewhat like the call of the White-fronted Dove, but weaker.
RANGE: Panama (heavy mt. forests of Veraguas at about 2000 ft. and islands off the Pacific coast).

CASSIN DOVE, *Leptotila cassinii.*   10   Plate 10
FIELD MARKS: Juveniles have the feathers of the wing-coverts, neck, and breast more or less margined with cinnamon.
RANGE: S.e. Mexico (humid forests of Tabasco and Chiapas) to Colombia (not found in El Salvador).

VERAGUA QUAIL-DOVE, *Geotrygon veraguensis.* 9   Plate 10
FIELD MARKS: There is no rufous tint on tail, but some rufous on inner webs of primaries. Juveniles are spotted and barred.
RANGE: E. Costa Rica to c. Panama in wet forests up to about 1000 ft.; w. Colombia and Ecuador.

LAWRENCE QUAIL-DOVE, *Geotrygon lawrencii.* 10   Plate 10
RANGE: E. Mexico (cloud forest on Tuxtla mts. of s. Veracruz) to w. Panama (wet forests on Caribbean slope above 2000 ft. in subtropical zone).

GOLDMAN QUAIL-DOVE, *Geotrygon goldmani.* 10   Plate 10
RANGE: Mts. of e. Panama and adjacent Colombia.

COSTA RICAN QUAIL-DOVE, *Geotrygon costaricensis.* 10
Plate 10
FIELD MARKS: Middle tail feathers reddish brown; no rufous on inner web of primaries.
RANGE: Mts. of Costa Rica and w. Panama.

WHITE-BELLIED QUAIL-DOVE, *Geotrygon albiventer.* 9
Plate 10
(Considered a race of *G. violacea* by others.)
FIELD MARKS: Foreneck and chest light lavender pink; upper throat, lower breast, belly, and under tail-coverts white (the only Quail-Dove in our range with white belly and under tail-coverts).
RANGE: Tropical forests (usually at 1000 to 2000 ft.) from Nicaragua to w. Venezuela and n. Colombia.

RUDDY QUAIL-DOVE, *Geotrygon montana.* 9   Plate 10
RANGE: Mexico (s. Sinaloa to Chiapas; w. Tamaulipas to Yucatán; usually found on or near ground in heavy woods below 3000 ft.) to South America.

WHITE-FACED QUAIL-DOVE, *Geotrygon albifacies.* 11 Plate 10
(Considered a race of *G. linearis* by some.)
RANGE: Mts. of Mexico (cloud forests and humid mountain forests of Guerrero, e. San Luis Potosí, Veracruz, and Chiapas; from 4000 to 9000 ft.) to n. Nicaragua.

CHIRIQUI QUAIL-DOVE, *Geotrygon chiriquensis.* 11   Plate 10
(Considered a race of *G. linearis* by some.)
RANGE: Mts. of Costa Rica and w. Panama.

PARROTS: Psittacidae

Short-necked birds with a strong hook to the upper bill and with two
toes directed backwards. Most of them nest in hollow trees or old
woodpecker holes, but a few use holes in cliffs. Although many of
them have some brightly colored feathers, the birds usually appear almost black when flying high overhead with a light sky as background.
The family contains a number of distinct subgroups. The Macaws are
large birds with heavy bills and long pointed tails; they fly with relatively slow wing beats, somewhat after the fashion of Herons. The
genus *Rhynchopsitta* is made up of birds that resemble Macaws in
shape, type of bill, habits, and manner of flight but that are much
smaller and, hence, will be called Macawlets. The Parakeets are
smaller still, have pointed tails and pointed wings and fly with quick,
Swallow-like wing beats. The Parrots have relatively short and straight
or slightly rounded tails; they fly with quick, shallow wing beats after
the fashion of Ducks.

BLUE-AND-YELLOW MACAW, *Ara ararauna.*   30   Plate 7
RANGE: E. Panama (Darien) to Brazil and Bolivia; like most species
of the genus, this Macaw is found in "remote" areas.

MILITARY MACAW, *Ara militaris.*   27   Plate 7
RANGE: Mexico (s. Sonora to Oaxaca; Nuevo León and s.w. Tamaulipas to Zacatecas and Guanajuato; mostly in the mts. [from 3000 to
8000 ft.] but sometimes wanders into lowlands in semi-arid regions);
also in the Andes from w. Venezuela to Argentina and Colombia
to Ecuador, Peru, and Bolivia.

GREEN MACAW, *Ara ambigua.*   30   Plate 7
RANGE: Nicaragua to w. Colombia and adjacent Ecuador.

SCARLET MACAW, *Ara macao.*   32   Plate 7
RANGE: Mexico (lowland forests from s. Veracruz to Chiapas [both
slopes] and Campeche; usually below 3000 ft.; rare) to Brazil and
Bolivia.

RED-AND-GREEN MACAW, *Ara chloroptera.*   30   Plate 7
RANGE: E. Panama to Argentina and Bolivia.

SEVERA MACAW, *Ara severa.*   17   Plate 7
RANGE: E. Panama to Brazil and Bolivia.

THICK-BILLED MACAWLET, *Rhynchopsitta pachyrhyncha.*   15
                                                          Plate 7
RANGE: Mexico (pine forests in mts. of Sonora, Sinaloa, Chihuahua,

and Durango; wanders widely, at times as far as Michoacán and Veracruz); occasionally appears in s. Arizona.

MAROON-FRONTED MACAWLET, *Rhynchopsitta terrisi.* 16
Plate 7
RANGE: Mexico (pine forests in mts. of Coahuila, Nuevo León, and w. Tamaulipas); rare, or largely exterminated.

GREEN PARAKEET, Aratinga holochlora. 9½ Plate 7
RANGE: E. Mexico (Chihuahua to Tamaulipas and south to Chiapas) to Caribbean slope of n. Guatemala; semi-arid regions at 2000 to 6000 ft.

PACIFIC PARAKEET, *Aratinga strenua.* 11 Plate 7
(Considered a race of *A. holochlora* by some.)
FIELD MARKS: Similar to last-named species but much larger and with relatively larger bill and feet; also ecologically different.
RANGE: Pacific lowlands from s.w. Mexico (Oaxaca) to Nicaragua.

RED-THROATED PARAKEET, *Aratinga rubritorquis.* 10 Plate 7
(Considered a race of *A. holochlora* by others.)
RANGE: E. Guatemala to n. Nicaragua.

FINSCH'S PARAKEET, *Aratinga finschi.* 10 Plate 7
RANGE: S. Nicaragua to w. Panama; mostly on Caribbean slope foot-hills.

AZTEC PARAKEET, *Aratinga astec.* 8 Plate 7
RANGE: E. Mexico (s. Tamaulipas and e. San Luis Potosí to Chiapas and Quintana Roo) south in Caribbean tropical lowlands to w. Panama.

ORANGE-FRONTED PARAKEET, *Aratinga canicularis.* 8 Plate 7
RANGE: Pacific slope from Mexico (Sinaloa and Durango to Chiapas) to n.w. Costa Rica; favors dry tropical woods.

VERAGUA PARAKEET, *Aratinga ocularis.* 8½ Plate 7
(Considered a race of *A. pertinax* by some.)
RANGE: Pacific lowlands of w. Panama (Chiriqui and Veragua).

HOFFMANN PARAKEET, *Pyrrhura hoffmanni.* 9 Plate 8
RANGE: Highlands of c. and s. Costa Rica and w. Panama.

BARRED PARAKEET, *Bolborhynchus lineola.* 6 Plate 8
RANGE: Mexico (Guerrero, Veracruz, and Chiapas; subtropical zone in mts.) to Venezuela and Peru.

TOVI PARAKEET, *Brotogeris jugularis.* 6½   Plate 8
RANGE: Mexico (Pacific lowlands from Guerrero to Chiapas) to Venezuela and Colombia.

MEXICAN PARROTLET, *Forpus cyanopygius.* 5   Plate 8
RANGE: W. Mexico (arid tropical zone up to 3000 ft. in s. Sonora and Durango and south to Colima and Jalisco).

SPECTACLED PARROTLET, *Forpus conspicillatus.* 4½   Plate 8
RANGE: E. Panama (Darien) to w. Colombia.

BLUE-FRONTED PARROTLET, *Touit dilectissima.* 5½   Plate 8
RANGE: E. Panama (Darien) to n.w. Venezuela, n. and w. Colombia, and n.w. Ecuador.

COSTA RICAN PARROTLET, *Touit costaricensis.* 5½   Plate 8
(Considered a race of *T. dilectissima* by some.)
RANGE: E. Costa Rica to w. Panama; humid, subtropical foothills on Caribbean slope; rare.

RED-EARED PARROT, *Pionopsitta haematotis.* 7½   Plate 8
RANGE: Mexico (Veracruz to Campeche) to w. Panama.

RED-NECKLACED PARROT, *Pionopsitta coccinicollaris.* 8 Plate 8
(Considered a race of *P. haematotis* by some.)
RANGE: E. Panama to n.w. Colombia.

BONAPARTE PARROT, *Pionopsitta pyrilia.* 8   Plate 8
RANGE: E. Panama to w. Venezuela and n. Colombia.

BLUE-HEADED PARROT, *Pionus menstruus.* 9   Plate 8
RANGE: S. Costa Rica to Brazil and Bolivia.

WHITE-CROWNED PARROT, *Pionus senilis.* 9   Plate 8
RANGE: E. Mexico (humid tropical zone and cloud forests in s.w. Tamaulipas and e. San Luis Potosí to Chiapas and Quintana Roo) to w. Panama.

WHITE-FRONTED PARROT, *Amazona albifrons.* 9½   Plate 8
RANGE: Mexico (s. Sonora to Chiapas along Pacific slope; s. Veracruz to Chiapas and Yucatán) to n.w. Costa Rica.

YELLOW-LORED PARROT, *Amazona xantholora.* 9½   Plate 8
RANGE: Yucatán Peninsula of Mexico and n. British Honduras.

RED-CROWNED PARROT, *Amazona viridigenalis.* 11   Plate 8
RANGE: N.e. Mexico (Nuevo León, Tamaulipas, e. San Luis Potosí, and extreme n. Veracruz); more or less a temperate zone bird.

FINSCH PARROT, *Amazona finschi.* 11   Plate 8
RANGE: W. Mexico (s.e. Sonora and s.w. Chihuahua to Oaxaca); mostly in the mts. from 2000 to 7000 ft.

YELLOW-CHEEKED PARROT, *Amazona autumnalis.* 11½ Plate 8
RANGE: E. Mexico (s. Tamaulipas and e. San Luis Potosí to Chiapas and Campeche) to n.e. Honduras; favors humid tropics.

RED-FRONTED PARROT, *Amazona salvini.* 11½   Plate 8
(Considered a race of *A. autumnalis* by others.)
RANGE: S. Honduras to w. Venezuela and n.w. Ecuador.

YELLOW-HEADED PARROT, *Amazona oratrix.* 12½   Plate 8
(Considered a race of *A. ochrocephala* by others.)
RANGE: Mexico (Colima and Guerrero; Nuevo León and Tamaulipas to e. Oaxaca and Yucatán) to British Honduras.

YELLOW-NAPED PARROT, *Amazona auropalliata.* 12½   Plate 8
(Considered a race of *A. ochrocephala* by others.)
RANGE: S.w. Mexico (Pacific slope of Oaxaca and Chiapas) to n.w. Costa Rica; favors semi-arid savannas or dry woods; crosses over onto Caribbean slope to some extent from Honduras southward.

YELLOW-CROWNED PARROT, *Amazona ochrocephala.* 12
Plate 8
FIELD MARKS: A yellow spot in center of crown (may extend forward over forehead).
RANGE: Panama to Venzuela and Peru.

BLUE-CROWNED PARROT, *Amazona guatemalae.* 14   Plate 8
Considered a race of *A. farinosa* by others.)
FIELD MARKS: No yellow on crown; crown bluish green to azure blue, color sometimes running down over nape.
RANGE: S. Mexico (rain forests in Veracruz and e. Oaxaca to Chiapas); south to w. Colombia, Ecuador, and w. Peru; humid lowlands.

CUCKOOS: Cuculidae

BLACK-BILLED CUCKOO, *Coccyzus erythropthalmus.* 11
RANGE: Temperate North America to n. Florida and Kansas; winters to Peru.

YELLOW-BILLED CUCKOO, *Coccyzus americanus.* 11
RANGE: North America to n. Mexico (Baja California to Tamaulipas
and south to Sinaloa and Veracruz; occasionally further south);
winters to Argentina and Bolivia.

MANGROVE CUCKOO, *Coccyzus minor.* 12   Plate 12
RANGE: S. Florida and Mexico (Sinaloa to Chiapas; Rio Grande Delta
region of Tamaulipas to Quintana Roo; in mangroves or inland in
semi-arid brushland up to 1500 ft. or more) to Brazil and n. Colombia.

CAYENNE SQUIRREL-CUCKOO, *Piaya cayana.* 16   Plate 12
RANGE: E. Mexico (Tamaulipas and e. San Luis Potosí to e. Oaxaca,
Chiapas, and Quintana Roo; from sea level up to 4500 ft.) to
Argentina and Bolivia.

MEXICAN SQUIRREL-CUCKOO, *Piaya mexicana.* 17   Plate 12
(Considered a race of *P. cayana* by others.)
RANGE: Mexico in s. Sonora and Chihuahua south to w. Puebla and
Oaxaca (above the Isthmus of Tehuantepec).

LITTLE SQUIRREL-CUCKOO, *Piaya minuta.* 9   Plate 12
RANGE: E. Panama (from Canal Zone to border of Colombia) to Brazil
and Bolivia.

GREATER ANI, *Crotophaga major.* 16   Plate 12
RANGE: E. Panama to Argentina.

SMOOTH-BILLED ANI, *Crotophaga ani.* 13   Plate 12
RANGE: S. Florida, Mexico (Holbox and Cozumel islands), islands off
Caribbean coast of Honduras and Nicaragua, s.w. Costa Rica,
the lowlands of Panama (not in Bocas del Toro), and south to
Argentina and Ecuador; favors savannas or open areas.

GROOVE-BILLED ANI, *Crotophaga sulcirostris.* 12   Plate 12
RANGE: S. Texas, Mexico (s. Sonora to Tamaulipas and south to
Chiapas and Yucatán; mostly in the lowlands but at times up to 5000
ft.) and south to Guiana and Peru.

STRIPED CUCKOO, *Tapera naevia.* 11   Plate 12
VOICE: The commonest "song" is made up of a series of two-figure
motifs. It may be represented as *peep peep* or *chee chee;* this motif
is repeated at about two-sec. intervals. The pitch is about E[4]; the
quality is that of a clear whistle. Another song phrase may be
likened to *chee chee pee-dee;* this requires about one and a half
sec. and is repeated in about two sec.; the pitch is about the same
as the previous example, except that the *pee* is a bit higher (F[4]).

RANGE: Mexico (s. Veracruz to Chiapas; crosses over to Pacific coast of Oaxaca and Chiapas below Isthmus of Tehuantepec; from sea level to 3000 ft. or more but more common in lowlands; favors low brush regions or thickets in savannas) to Argentina and Peru.

RUFOUS-RUMPED CUCKOO, *Morococcyx erythropygus.* 10

Plate 12

VOICE: The call is a short burry "whistle" lasting about a half sec. and is repeated at five- to seven-sec. intervals. It may be represented as *churrr*. The pitch is about A³. The song is made from this same figure, given in series so that there is a speed-up and slow-down pattern of about twenty-nine figures in the space of seventeen sec. This works up to about one or two tones higher in pitch than the call. It begins with about two-sec. spacing between the first three figures, then only one sec., then a half sec.; after this the figures are so hurried that they seem more like *chur* and about four are sounded in a sec. for a few seconds; then there is a gradual slow-down to the end with the volume dwindling away also (something like a spring-wound machine running down).

RANGE: Mexico (Pacific slope from s. Sinaloa to Chiapas; from sea level up to about 4000 ft. but more common in the arid or semi-arid lowlands) to w. Costa Rica (not found in British Honduras).

PHEASANT CUCKOO, *Dromococcyx phasianellus.* 14 Plate 12

VOICE: The quality is the same as that of the Striped Cuckoo, but the phrasing is different. The commonest song phrase is made up of three figures that may be shown as *dont-see-surrrr*. The last figure is vibrato; the pitch is about A¹-A¹ sharp-A¹; the total time required is about two sec. Another song phrase is composed of four figures and has no vibrato. There is no couplet at the end as in the Striped Cuckoo.

RANGE: Mexico (s. Veracruz and e. Oaxaca to Chiapas and Yucatán; in semi-arid regions, humid woods, or cloud forests from sea level up to 5000 ft.; local) to Argentina and Bolivia.

GREATER ROADRUNNER, *Geococcyx californianus.* 20

RANGE: s.w. United States to c. Mexico (Baja California across to Tamaulipas and south to Michoacán, Mexico, Hidalgo, and Veracruz; mostly in arid or semi-arid regions from sea level to 7000 or more).

LESSER ROADRUNNER, *Geococcyx viaticus.* 19 Plate 12

(Listed as *G. velox* by some.)

FIELD MARKS: Pale buff below with dusky under tail-coverts; median portion of throat and chest unstreaked.

VOICE: A series of very soft figures (*cooc*), delivered about one per sec. Instead of being loud as a Trogon, like the Greater Roadrunner, the

calls of this species are softer than those of a White-fronted Dove. A
"song" phrase similar to the call of the White-fronted Dove may be
indicated by *uh-woo uh-oo uh-oo uh-oo;* it begins quite softly and
fades rapidly, so that it can scarcely be heard after the third motif.
RANGE: Mexico (extreme s. Sonora to Chiapas; Durango and San Luis
   Potosí to Mexico and Morelos; Veracruz to Yucatán; from sea level
   up to 8000 ft.) to n. Nicaragua.

SALVIN'S GROUND-CUCKOO, *Neomorphus salvini.*   19   Plate 12
   (Considered a race of *N. geoffreyi* by others.)
RANGE: Nicaragua to n.w. Colombia; favors heavily forested hill
   country up to the lower slopes of the mountains.

BARN OWLS: Tytonidae

BARN OWL, *Tyto alba.*   15
RANGE: Almost cosmopolitan.

OWLS: Strigidae

FLAMMULATED SCREECH-OWL, *Otus flammeolus.*   6
   (Considered a race of *O. scops* by some.)
FIELD MARKS: All members of this genus have ear tufts, but in this
   species they are unusually short. The eyes are brown (only one
   other species in North America has brown eyes; all others have
   yellow).
RANGE: Mts. of w. North America to Mexico and Guatemala; above
   7000 ft.

EASTERN SCREECH-OWL, *Otus asio.*   7
RANGE: E. North America to n.e. Mexico (Tamaulipas and e. Nuevo
   León).

WESTERN SCREECH-OWL, *Otus kennicotti.*   7
   (Considered a race of *O. asio* by others.)
FIELD MARKS: Separated from other Screech-Owls by vocal patterns.
   Birds in n.w. Mexico sometimes listed as the Vinaceous Screech-
   Owl have to be included here since we cannot distinguish a differ-
   ence in voice.
RANGE: W. North America to n.w. Mexico (Baja California, Sonora,
   Sinaloa, and w. Chihuahua).

RIO BALSAS SCREECH-OWL, *Otus seductus.*   8   Plate 11
   (Considered a race of *O. asio* by some and of *O. vinaceus* by
   others.)

FIELD MARKS: Eyes brown.

RANGE: Confined to the drainage system of the Rio Balsas from e. Colima to central Guerrero.

SPOTTED SCREECH-OWL, *Otus trichopsis*. 6½

VOICE: The "song" phrase consists of a series of six to ten soft, mellow hoots that are of about equal length and evenly spaced so that ten may be sounded in one and a half sec. The pitch is about F^2 (female, G^2). In this song phrase the length of the individual figures may increase very slightly (also the volume) throughout the duration. When bothered or excited, a different phrase may be given, which starts with a couplet, and the other figures are of somewhat greater length, as *hoo-hoo hooo hooo hoo-hoo hooo hooo hooo*. The usual "song" phrase is from 1.2 to 1.5 sec. in length.

RANGE: Mts. of Arizona, Mexico (n.e. Sonora and Chihuahua, south through Nayarit and Guanajuato to Oaxaca; Nuevo León to Chiapas; in pine-oak association, mostly from 6000 to 8000 ft.), and south to Honduras.

BEARDED SCREECH-OWL, *Otus barbarus*. 6¼   Plate 11

FIELD MARKS: Similar to Spotted Screech-Owl, but bottom of tarsus and toes are bare.

RANGE: Mts. of s. Chiapas and Guatemala at about the same elevation as frequented by the Guatemalan Screech-Owl.

GUATEMALAN SCREECH-OWL, *Otus guatemalae*. 7½   Plate 11

FIELD MARKS: Similar to Bearded Screech-Owl, but lacks "whiskers" on face and bare area at bottom of tarsus (only toes are bare).

VOICE: The "song" phrase begins so softly that it can scarcely be heard but builds rather quickly to a steady volume and holds for some five or ten sec. It is very even and steady, and holds to one effective pitch. There are about 14 figures per sec. Since the figures are identical, the phrase is a soft rattle. The pause between the phrases is several times longer than a single phrase. There seems to be much less individual variation and greater uniformity in this case than in any other species in the genus.

RANGE: Mexico (upper arid tropical and transitional zones in s.e. Sonora, Sinaloa, and Durango; lower arid tropical zone in s.w. Sinaloa and Jalisco; humid mts. of s.w. Tamaulipas to c. Veracruz and e. Oaxaca to Chiapas; arid lowlands of Campeche, Yucatán and Quintana Roo; apparently always below the range of the Spotted Screech-Owl) and south to Nicaragua.

VERMICULATED SCREECH-OWL, *Otus vermiculatus*. 7 Plate 11
(Considered a race of *O. guatemalae* by some.)

FIELD MARKS: Similar to Guatemalan Screech-Owl, but lower part of tarsus is naked instead of feathered to toes; underparts more densely vermiculated and black stripes so narrow that they are almost unnoticed; "eyebrows" are brown or rufous instead of lighter than the face to almost white.

VOICE: Similar to that of Guatemalan Screech-Owl but higher in pitch; the song phrases shorter.

RANGE: Costa Rica to w. Ecuador; tropical forests up to subtropics.

COOPER SCREECH-OWL, *Otus cooperi*. 8 Plate 11
(Considered a race of *O. choliba* by some.)

VOICE: A straight rattle holds to one effective pitch and tempo throughout; about twelve figures are sounded in a sec. and a half; the rests between the figures are constant and about the same length as the figures. Each rattle figure is inflected upward a short distance and then inflected downward at least twice as far, causing a "rougher" effect than that found in the Western Screech-Owl. There is also a two-motif phrase. In it the first motif has the figures so close together that the effect approaches that of a roll (six figures are sounded in about four-tenths of a sec., and yet the individual figures are of near-normal length and hence almost fused together). The second motif has about ten figures in one sec. The immature bird uses the same type of whine or cry as in other species.

RANGE: Mexico (Pacific lowlands from s. Oaxaca to Chiapas) to n.w. Costa Rica; from sea level up to about 3000 ft.

CHOLIBA SCREECH-OWL, *Otus choliba*. 8 Plate 11
VOICE: The usual song phrase is a rattle of nine or ten short figures followed by two accented figures of greater duration and volume; the whole phrase requires about one sec. The pitch is the same throughout; the effect may be suggested by *hu-hu-hu-hu-hu-hu-hu-hu-hu-Cu Hoo*. There is another phrase of about twelve figures that are equally spaced and of about the same volume, except for the first and last figures, which are softer.

RANGE: Costa Rica to Argentina and Peru; in relatively humid regions as compared to Cooper Screech-Owl.

CLARK SCREECH-OWL, *Otus clarkii*. 9 Plate 11
FIELD MARKS: Above brown, vermiculated, mottled, or spotted with black; eyebrows usually tawny but occasionally almost white; no well-defined facial rim; some white spots on wing; below mixed tawny brown and buffy white, the brown more or less barred with black; lower one-third of tarsus and toes naked; iris yellow.

RANGE: Mts. of c. Costa Rica to w. Panama.

CRESTED OWL, *Lophostrix cristata*. 16 Plate 11
RANGE: S. Mexico (Veracruz, e. Oaxaca, and Chiapas) to Guiana and Ecuador; favors tropical and subtropical woods.

HORNED OWL, *Bubo virginianus.* 20
RANGE: W. Hemisphere; a rare highland bird in Central America.

SPECTACLED OWL, *Pulsatrix perspicillata.* 18   Plate 11
VOICE: Calls of two quite different pitches are used, but it is not known
   if they are used by the same sex. The "song" phrase, however, is
   used by both sexes, and the pitch is not decidedly different in the
   two. It is a short, rapid series of low hoots that sounds something
   like a chuckle, as *hoo-hoo-hoo-hoo-hoo-hoo-hoo.* Such a series of
   seven or eight hoots will be given in about one and a quarter sec.;
   the pitch is about B. Another common call is more like a hunting
   call and is frequently given in flight. It is a short "whistle" of about
   a half-sec. duration and is pitched about B^1. It may be represented
   as *wer.* After a pause of five to ten sec., this may be repeated.
   When disturbed, the high-pitched voice may give out some loud
   complaining phrases, or the low-pitched one a single low hoot that is
   suggestive of a growl.
RANGE: S. Mexico (s. Veracruz, e. Oaxaca, and Chiapas; favors humid
   lowland woods but is sometimes found up to 5000 ft.) to Argentina and Bolivia.

FERRUGINOUS PYGMY-OWL, *Glaucidium brasilianum.*   6½
                                                          Plate 11
VOICE: The "song" phrase is a series of whistled figures (if one whistles
   wuh or *wer,* a very good imitation will result). There are usually
   from ten to sixty figures in a phrase; the tempo is fast (rate of about
   150 figures per minute—fastest of any of the genus), and the pitch
   is F^3 (the figure begins at about D^3 but builds up throughout its
   duration, which is about 0.1 sec.); each figure is clear, fairly loud,
   and mellow.
RANGE: S.w. United States to Straits of Magellan; from sea level
   up to 4000 ft.

NORTHERN PYGMY-OWL, *Glaucidium gnoma.*   6½
VOICE: Similar to last species, but pitch is a bit lower and tempo
   much slower (the figures in the "song" phrase are spaced, in
   different calls, from about 0.5 to 2.0 sec. apart; the pitch of each
   figure is almost constant at about C^3 (if there is any variation in pitch
   it is a gradual drop of about a half tone in a figure).
RANGE: W. North America to Mexico (mts. of Baja California
   across to Tamaulipas and south to Chiapas; from 6000 to 13000 ft.
   but occasionally down to 4000 ft.) and Guatemala.

LEAST PYGMY-OWL, *Glaucidium minutissimum.*   5½   Plate 11
VOICE: The song consists of a series of short motifs. The motif is usually
   composed of two, sometimes three, figures, occasionally four but

rarely more. There may be as many as thirteen of these two-figure motifs sounded in a minute. Rarely, a single figure may be repeated after a rest of several sec.

RANGE: Mexico (c. Sinaloa to Guerrero; s.w. Tamaulipas and e. San Luis Potosí to Chiapas; from sea level up to over 6000 ft.) and locally south (not reported for El Salvador or Nicaragua) to Brazil and Paraguay.

JARDINE PYGMY-OWL, *Glaucidium jardinii.* 6   Plate 11
(Considered a race of *G. brasilianum* by some.)

FIELD MARKS: Crown spotted with white (no streaks—only Ferruginous Pygmy-Owl has streaks on crown); four visible white bars on tail (three in Least Pygmy-Owl and five or six in Ferruginous Pygmy-Owl).

RANGE: Mts. of Costa Rica to Venezuela and Peru.

ELF OWL, *Micrathene whitneyi.* 5

VOICE: The "song" is made up of a series of phrases that are usually composed of about six similar figures, except for the first one, which is weaker than the others and a trifle lower in pitch; all show the same pitch range and spacing (the pitch at the start of the figure is about F^3, rises quickly to G^3, and then slurs down to C^3, all in a space of about 0.07 sec.). The rests between the figures are about 0.1 sec. long. The phrase may be likened to a fast *ya ya-ya-ya-ya-ya*. Such a six-figure phrase has a duration of about 0.9 sec.

RANGE: S.w. United States and Mexico (Baja California, Sonora, and Tamaulipas to Puebla).

BURROWING OWL, *Speotyto cunicularia.* 9

RANGE: S.w. United States and Florida and locally south to Tierra del Fuego.

MOTTLED WOOD-OWL, *Ciccaba virgata.* 13   Plate 11

VOICE: Most frequently heard is a series of five short hoots that are somewhat clipped off, so that one might be represented by *hut*. The first two hoots are spaced possibly a half sec. apart; the others are then given at shorter and shorter intervals, so that the whole motif takes no more than two sec. Answering calls (presumably a different sex) are pitched slightly differently. Immatures call with a catlike wail; this is louder and higher pitched and lasts about one sec.

RANGE: Mexico (s. Sonora and Chihuahua to Guerrero; s. Nuevo León and Tamaulipas to Chiapas and Yucatán; from sea level up to 8000 ft.; in semi-arid or humid woods) to Argentina and Ecuador.

BLACK-AND-WHITE WOOD-OWL, *Ciccaba nigrolineata.* 14

Plate 11

RANGE: Mexico (e. San Luis Potosí to Chiapas; humid tropical woods) to Venezuela and w. Ecuador.

SPOTTED OWL, *Strix occidentalis.* 19
RANGE: W. North America to Mexico (mts. of Sinaloa; Chihuahua to Michoacán).

BARRED OWL, *Strix varia.* 19
RANGE: S. Canada to Mexico (Durango to Oaxaca; Veracruz and Puebla).

FULVOUS OWL, *Strix fulvescens.* 17 Plate 11
(Considered a race of *S. varia* by some.)
RANGE: Mts. of s. Mexico (Oaxaca and Chiapas), Guatemala, El Salvador, and Honduras.

STRIPED OWL, *Rhinoptynx clamator.* 14 Plate 11
FIELD MARKS: Eyes brown (Long-eared Owl has yellow eyes).
VOICE: There is a phrase composed of a series of low-pitched, staccato hoots, *ah ah ah ah ah ah ah.* A phrase of seven such figures would likely require 1.4 sec. (the figure being less than 0.1 sec. in length, and the rests between figures about 0.15 sec.). The pitch is likely about G_1, but, since some harmonics are resonated rather strongly, it is not easy to place it. The harmonics give a slight nasal quality that brings to mind the call of a Mexican Tree-Frog, in spite of the difference in pitch. Other calls include a soft *ahooooo* lasting about 0.7 sec; a *hooo* lasting 0.4 sec; and a series of loud figures resembling "barking" (*ow* figures that become louder and a bit longer as the series progresses, varying from about 0.12 to 0.2 sec., with the interspaces about 0.3 sec.).
RANGE: E. Mexico (Veracruz to Chiapas) and south to Brazil and Uruguay.

LONG-EARED OWL, *Asio otus.* 14
RANGE: Eurasia and North America to n. Baja California; winters to c. Mexico.

STYGIAN OWL, *Asio stygius.* 15 Plate 11
RANGE: Mexico (mts. of Durango; Chiapas; 6000 to 10000 ft.), Guatemala, British Honduras, and Nicaragua to Argentina and Ecuador; rare.

SHORT-EARED OWL, *Asio flammeus.* 14
RANGE: Eurasia; North America to California and Ohio; winters to

Guatemala (rarely to Costa Rica); also resident in South America (Colombia to Chile and Venezuela to Argentina).

ACADIAN SAWWHET-OWL, *Aegolius acadicus.*   7
VOICE: The "song" is rather similar to that of the Ferruginous Pygmy-Owl, but the figures are further apart (tempo slower); each figure slurs down at the terminal end, whereas the figures in the Ferruginous Pygmy-Owl slur up. The pitch is the same as that of the Northern Pygmy-Owl (varying from C^3 to B^2, but the downward inflection is all at the extreme end rather than throughout the figure), and the spacing and length of the figures is similar; however, the phrases of the Northern Pygmy-Owl are shorter, and the spacing of the figures is likely to be more irregular.
RANGE: North America to Mexico (Chihuahua to Oaxaca and Vera-cruz).

RIDGWAY'S SAWWHET-OWL, *Aegolius ridgwayi.*   7   Plate 11
VOICE: Similar to previous species.
RANGE: Mexico (higher mts. of s. Chiapas) to Costa Rica and Panama.

OILBIRDS: Steatornithidae

OILBIRD, *Steatornis caripensis.*   16   Plate 13
RANGE: Extreme e. Panama (Darien) to Guiana and Bolivia.

POTOOS: Nyctibiidae

GRAND POTOO, *Nyctibius grandis.*   19   Plate 11
VOICE: The "song" is a loud, hoarse call (*baahoo*) delivered at intervals. When disturbed or alarmed, the bird makes loud "barking" sounds.
RANGE: Guatemala to Brazil and Peru.

GRAY POTOO, *Nyctibius griseus.*   13½   Plate 11
VOICE: The "song" phrase consists of a series of similar figures that are technically almost pure notes. These start at about C^3 and descend about an octave in four or five approximately equal steps. Each figure lasts about 0.4 sec., and the whole phrase is usually about 3 sec. in length.
RANGE: Nicaragua and Costa Rica to Panama and south to Argentina and Bolivia.

JAMAICAN POTOO, *Nyctibius jamaicensis.*   16   Plate 11
VOICE: The "song" phrase is a series of hoarse or guttural figures that

lasts about two sec. or a bit longer but is sometimes shortened or not all heard. It begins slowly, then speeds up, but becomes softer toward the end so that it somewhat resembles a slow laugh. It may be represented as *wah wah-wah-wa-wa*. At times only two figures will be heard and rarely only one. The structure of the sound is similar to that of the Grand Potoo and radically different from that of the Gray Potoo.

RANGE: Jamaica; Mexico (Sinaloa to Chiapas; s. Tamaulipas and e. San Luis Potosí to Quintana Roo; in humid or semi-desert woods from sea level up to 4000 ft. but more common below 2000 ft.) to n. Honduras and Guatemala.

NIGHTJARS : Caprimulgidae

SEMI-COLLARED NIGHTHAWK, *Lurocalis semitorquatus.* 11
Plate 13

FIELD MARKS: A dark bird with a short, truncate tail (very noticeable in flight). The narrow white band across the throat may be difficult to see in poor light. It sometimes calls in flight and circles just above treetops in openings and edge situations in lowland tropics.

RANGE: Nicaragua to Brazil and Peru; humid lowlands, up to 1500 ft.

TRILLING NIGHTHAWK, *Chordeiles acutipennis.* 7
RANGE: S.w. United States to Brazil and Bolivia; most birds seen in Central America are migrants or winter residents.

BOOMING NIGHTHAWK, *Chordeiles minor.* 8
RANGE: North America to Panama; northern birds are migratory and winter to South America.

WHITE-COLLARED CUEJO, *Nyctidromus albicollis.* 10
VOICE: The "song" consists of a series of figures that vary somewhat as the bird "works into" the "song", the first ones usually being somewhat hoarser and slower. The figure may be represented as *puwirrrr*; the first segment is a smooth "whistle," and the last half is a very fast vibrato. Only the latter part may be heard at a distance, and hence a single call might be confused with that of the next species or perhaps with others that use a *will* in the vocalization. Near at hand it can be noticed that the figure is longer than those of others (over 0.5 sec.).

RANGE: S. Texas, Mexico (Sinaloa to Chiapas; Nuevo León and Tamaulipas to Chiapas and Yucatán; in semi-arid or humid woods or savannas from sea level up to about 4000 ft.; partly migratory), and south to Argentina and Bolivia.

YUCATAN WILL, *Setochalcis badius.*   10   Plate 13
   (Listed as race of *Caprimulgus salvini* by some and in genus *An-trostomus* by others.)
VOICE: The "song" of this species is made up of a single vibrato figure repeated in series. This figure may be represented as *will*. It is not over three-tenths of a sec. long; as it rises to the high point and then falls back to the starting point, the pitch varies from about C³ to C⁴; the *wi* segment is only about half as long as *ll*, which is the downward inflection. This *will* is almost identical to that used in the motif of the next species.
RANGE: Mexico (Campeche, Yucatán, and Quintana Roo) and n. British Honduras.

RUFOUS WIT-WIT-WILL, *Setochalcis rufus.*   9   Plate 13
   (Listed in genus *Caprimulgus* by some and in *Antrostomus* by others.)
VOICE: The song consists of a series of phrases composed of four figures. The first figure may be likened to a soft *chuck*. This is followed by a three-figure motif, *wit-wit-will*. The time required for delivery of the whole phrase is about 0.8 sec., and the range of pitch is about the same as that found in the last species. The *will* figure is of the same length as that in the previous species and is formed in much the same way; again the *wi* segment is no more than half as long as the *ll*. This would seem to indicate very close relationship between these two species (the former has merely lost the preliminary figure and the two *wits* in the structure of the call). In addition to the usual song this species does at times a very low-pitched guttural repercussion arranged in a "time signal" pattern. The effect of this song may be indicated by *tk-rrrrrrrrrrrr*. This motif requires 0.2 sec. and is repeated in a long series with a 0.1-sec. rest between motifs. The pitch of the *tk* is about D³, and that of the *r* figures (which are very close together) is F². Most members of this genus and probably all members of the genus *Antrostomus* use a rather similar "time signal" song. (The closely related Cuejo uses a number of short calls of similar structure, but they lack the *tk* figure and hence the "time signal" effect.) As do other members of the genus, this bird sings while perched.
RANGE: S.e. Costa Rica to Argentina and Bolivia.

EASTERN WHIP-POOR-WILL, *Setochalcis vociferus.*   9
   (Listed as *Caprimulgus vociferus* by some and *Antrostomus vociferus* by others.)
VOICE: The usual song is discussed in the Introduction. The "time signal" song differs from that of the preceding species by having two *tk* figures and about thirty *r* figures in a motif (*tk tk-rrrrrrrr-rrrrrrrrrrrrrrrrrrrrrr*) in a total time of 0.3 sec.

RANGE: E. North America; winters to Costa Rica.

WESTERN WHIP-POOR-WILL, *Setochalcis arizonae.* 9
(Listed as a race of *Caprimulgus vociferus* by others.)

VOICE: Usual song is discussed in the Introduction. The time signal song is composed of motifs that are about 0.2 sec long; they contain two *tk* figures and about seventeen *r* figures (*tk tk-rrrrrrrrrrrrrrrr*).

RANGE: S.w. United States and Mexico (Sonora to Chihuahua, Nuevo León, and w. Tamaulipas and south to c. Chiapas; in mts. at 5000 to 10000 ft.) to w. Guatemala.

DUSKY CHEER-FOR-WILL, *Setochalcis saturatus.* 9   Plate 13
(Listed in genus *Caprimulgus* by some and in *Antrostomus* by others.)

VOICE: Discussed in Introduction. This species and the previous four represent a vocal genus: they all use a *will* structure in the song phrase, and that structure is in all cases at least partly frequency-modulated; this and the two previous species have this *will* structure as a segment of a figure (indicating a "subgenus" or "species group,"), while in the other two it is distinctly set apart and longer.

RANGE: Mts. of Costa Rica and w. Panama.

CAROLINA CHUCK-WILL'S-WIDOW, *Antrostomus carolinensis.*
11

(Listed as *Caprimulgus carolinensis* by others.)

VOICE: The song phrase is a three-figure motif that may be represented by *ll willo willa.* There is no frequency modulation; all figures are smoothly "whistled"; the pitch varies from about C^3 to C^4, and each of the three figures covers this whole range (the first figure is slurred downward the full octave in two or three centiseconds); the length of the motif is about one sec., and the rest between the first two figures is about double that between the last two. (This species sings on migration and has been heard in extreme s. Veracruz.)

RANGE: S.e. United States; winters through e. Mexico to Colombia.

SALVIN'S CHUCK-WILL, *Antrostomus salvini.* 10   Plate 13
(Listed as *Caprimulgus salvini* by others.)

VOICE: The song phrase is a two-figure motif with a quality and average pitch similar to the previous species (smooth "whistled" figures showing no frequency modulation). This may be represented as *Chuck wi'll* (the apostrophe indicates a slight momentary drop in pitch, which has the effect of a hesitation; however, this drop in pitch is very slight compared with the drop at the middle of the *willo* or *willa* of the preceding species, although the picture suggests close evolutionary connection). The motif is usually repeated at a rate of four in five sec., but there is an occasional (momentary) speed-up to a rate of six motifs in five sec.

RANGE: E. Mexico (s. Nuevo León and Tamaulipas, through e. San Luis Potosí and Veracruz to Chiapas; favors semi-arid tropics).

OCELLATED POORWILL, *Nyctiphrynus ocellatus*.   8   Plate 13
FIELD MARKS: Sooty brown (almost black) with round white spots on wings and belly and white bars on tail.
RANGE: Nicaragua to Argentina and Bolivia. Presumably rare in Central America, as only one specimen has been collected (in Nicaragua).

EARED POORWILL, *Otophanes mcleodii*.   7½   Plate 13
FIELD MARKS: Feathers at side of cap elongated and erectile, thus capable of forming "ear tufts"; feathers of chest elongated, forming an erectile lappet; tail feathers (except middle pair) tipped white.
VOICE: The call is a two-figure motif with a maximum pitch of about B^3 and a duration of 0.3 sec. It may be represented as *wirt wirrrrr*. The vibrato causes the call to resemble more nearly one of a Cuejo than some other *poorwill*.
RANGE: W. Mexico (mts. of Chihuahua to Jalisco and Colima).

YUCATAN POORWILL, *Nyctagreus yucatanicus*.   7½   Plate 13
(Listed in the genus *Otophanes* by some.)
FIELD MARKS: Chest feathers erectile as in preceding species; no erectile ear tufts.
VOICE: The song is a series of motifs that vary in length from 0.8 to 1.0 sec. The pitch varies from D^3 to B^3; there is no frequency modulation; if it were not so drawn-out, the motif would be similar to one by the Carolina Chuck-will's-widow, since the form may be represented by *up willa-well*. This effect is suggestive of close relationship with Northern Poorwill, which does a *Poorwill-up* at times.
RANGE: The Yucatán Peninsula of Mexico and n. Peten of Guatemala.

NORTHERN POORWILL, *Phalaenoptilus nuttallii*.   7
RANGE: W. North America to c. Mexico (Baja California across to Tamaulipas and South to Oaxaca and Puebla; arid regions from sea level up to 8000 ft. or more; partly migratory).

SPOTTED-TAIL PIT-SWEET, *Antiurus maculicaudus*.   7
                                                                    Plate 13
(Has been listed under the genera *Caprimulgus*, *Antrostomus*, and *Stenopsis*.)
VOICE: The males call, as they fly over the open grassland in tropical savanna regions, after the fashion of Nighthawks. (The birds perch in the woods during the day, except that the female nests on the ground in the grassy areas, behavior also similar to the Nighthawk.) The call is a very shrill, thin motif of two figures and requires a total time of about a half sec.; it may be represented as *pit sweet*. The pitch of the motif ranges from B^4 up to G^5; the first figure is in-

flected down and then up over most of the pitch range in a space of half a decisec.; the *sweet* is inflected down and then up over the whole range of pitch quite smoothly in about three decisec.

RANGE: S. Mexico (humid savannas of s. Veracruz) to Brazil and Peru. No specimens have been collected between Mexico and Colombia.

WHITE-TAILED PIT-SWEER, *Antiurus albicauda*. 8 Plate 13
(Has been listed under the genera *Caprimulgus, Antrostomus, Stenopsis*, and *Thermochalcis*, and as a race of *cayennensis*.)

VOICE: Calls in flight. The structure, quality, and pitch is similar to preceding species, but inflection is different and motif 50% longer.

RANGE: Costa Rica to Caribbean lowlands of Colombia.

RIDGWAY'S COOKACHEEA, *Setopagis ridgwayi*. 8 Plate 13
(Listed under the genus *Antrostomus* by some and *Caprimulgus* by others.)

VOICE: In this genus the song phrase is made up of a series of staccato figures. In the species there are usually from nine to seventeen figures in a phrase. The last three figures in the phrase make up a terminal motif and are indicated by *uh-chee-ah*. This *uh* figure is lower in pitch than the one preceding it, and the *chee* is the highest in pitch of any figure in the phrase; the final figure drops back to a pitch about half way between the other two. All the other figures are more or less alike, but they become progressively longer, higher in pitch, and closer together as the phrase develops. However, they are all so quick that we indicate them by the same term, *cuc*. The total effect is rather like that of the music of a Katydid or some other insect. A phrase of sixteen figures will require less than two sec; the total range in pitch is about C^3 to F^4. Occasionally the terminal motif is quickly repeated.

RANGE: W. Mexico (Sonora to Durango and South to Chiapas and w. Veracruz; favors open, semi-arid brushland) to Honduras; occasional in s.w. United States.

SWIFTS: Apodidae

WHITE-COLLARED SWIFT, *Streptoprocne zonaris*. 8 Plate 13
RANGE: Mexico (Guerrero to Chiapas; e. San Luis Potosí to Tabasco; mostly in mts.) to Argentina and Bolivia.

WHITE-NAPED SWIFT, *Streptoprocne semicollaris*. 9 Plate 13
RANGE: Mexico (Sinaloa and Chihuahua to Morelos, Mexico, and Hidalgo; favors regions at from 6000 to 9000 ft.)

CHAPMAN'S SWIFT, *Chaetura chapmani*. 4½ Plate 13
RANGE: C. Panama to Colombia and Brazil.

CHIMNEY SWIFT, *Chaetura pelagica.* 5
RANGE: E. North America; winters in e. Peru; migrates around Gulf
of Mexico.

VAUX SWIFT, *Chaetura vauxi.* 4¼
RANGE: W. North America to n.w. California; migrates through Mexico
(Baja California to Durango and south to Chiapas and Veracruz)
to Guatemala.

RICHMOND SWIFT, *Chaetura richmondi.* 4   Plate 13
(Considered a race of *C. vauxi* by others.)
RANGE: E. Mexico (Tamaulipas to Chiapas and Campeche) to Panama;
in tropical lowlands.

GAUMER SWIFT, *Chaetura gaumeri.* 4   Plate 13
(Considered a race of *C. vauxi* by others.)
RANGE: Mexico (semi-arid lowlands of Yucatán, Quintana Roo, and
Cozumel Island).

GRAY-RUMPED SWIFT, *Chaetura phaeopygos.* 4   Plate 13
(Considered a race of *C. cinereiventris* by some and of *C. sclateri*
by others.)
RANGE: Caribbean lowlands of Nicaragua, Costa Rica, and Panama.

SMOKY SWIFT, *Chaetura fumosa.* 4½   Plate 13
(Listed as a race of *C. spinicauda* by some.)
FIELD MARKS: Similar to preceding species, but rump is pale buffy
gray instead of slate gray and the upper tail-coverts are black in-
tead of gray (this causes the buffy gray area to appear as a bar
across the rump).
RANGE: S.w. Costa Rica to n. Colombia; lowlands.

ANDRE'S SWIFT, *Chaetura andrei.* 5   Plate 13
FIELD MARKS: Dark smoky brown; the throat paler, contrasting with
the dark breast; tail very short and tipped with spines.
RANGE: Panama to Argentina.

CHESTNUT-COLLARED SWIFT, *Cypseloides brunneitorques.* 5
                                                              Plate 13
(Considered a race of *C. rutilus* by some.)
RANGE: Mexico to Bolivia; highlands (above 2000 feet).

CHERRIE'S SWIFT, *Cypseloides cherriei.* 5   Plate 13
FIELD MARKS: Sooty black, somewhat paler below; a conspicuous
white spot just above the lores and a narrower one back of eye.
RANGE: Mts. of Costa Rica to w. Venezuela and Colombia.

WHITE-CHINNED SWIFT, *Cypseloides cryptus.* 5   Plate 13
RANGE: British Honduras to Guiana and Peru.

BLACK SWIFT, *Cypseloides niger.* 7
RANGE: Alaska to Costa Rica; West Indies and British Guiana; favors
mts. and cliffs; northern birds are migratory.

WHITE-THROATED SWIFT, *Aeronautes saxatalis.* 6
RANGE: Mt. regions of w. North America to Honduras; migratory.

GREATER SWALLOW-TAILED SWIFT, *Panyptila sanctihieronymi.*
7   Plate 13
RANGE: Mexico (Michoacán to c. Chiapas; mostly 4000 to 5000 ft.),
Guatemala, Honduras, and Nicaragua.

LESSER SWALLOW-TAILED SWIFT, *Panyptila cayennensis.* 5
Plate 13
RANGE: E. Mexico (s. Veracruz to Chiapas; from sea level up to 2000
ft.), Honduras, Nicaragua, Costa Rica, Panama, and south to Brazil
and Ecuador.

HUMMINGBIRDS: Trochilidae

BRONZE HERMIT, *Glaucis aenea.* 4   Plate 14
(Considered a race of *G. hirsuta* by some.)
FIELD MARKS: Bill decurved and more than twice as long as head;
under tail-coverts cinnamon.
RANGE: Nicaragua to w. Panama; w. Colombia to n.w. Ecuador; favors
tropical-zone forest edge up to 1000 ft.; scarce.

HAIRY HERMIT, *Glaucis hirsuta.* 4½   Plate 14
FIELD MARKS: Similar to previous species, but lower bill largely yellow
and under tail-coverts not cinnamon.
RANGE: E. Panama and Canal Zone to Brazil and Bolivia.

RUCKER'S HERMIT, *Threnetes ruckeri.* 4½   Plate 14
FIELD MARKS: Bill less than twice as long as head and decurved; basal
half of tail feathers (except middle pair) white.
RANGE: Honduras to w. Venezuela and w. Ecuador; tropical forest.

GREEN HERMIT, *Phaethornis coruscus.* 6   Plate 14
(Listed as a race of *P. guy* by others.)
FIELD MARKS: Females and immatures have the underparts mostly
dark gray (merely washed with bluish green toward the sides);
hence they do not glisten in the light.

RANGE: Costa Rica to n.w. Colombia; favors humid subtropical highlands.

LONG-BILLED HERMIT, *Phaethornis longirostirs.*   6   Plate 14
(Considered a race of *P. superciliosus* by some and *P. malaris* by others.)
RANGE: Mexico (Nayarit to w. Oaxaca; Veracruz to Chiapas) to w. Colombia and w. Ecuador.

BLACK-CHEEKED HERMIT, *Phaethornis anthophilus.*   5   Plate 14
RANGE: E. Panama to w. Venezuela and n. Colombia.

BOUCARD'S HERMIT, *Phaethornis adolphi.*   3½   Plate 14
(Considered a race of *P. longuemareus* by some.)
RANGE: Mexico (s. Veracruz and e. Oaxaca to Chiapas and Yucatán; found low in understory in humid woods) to n.w. Colombia.

BRONZE-TAILED SICKLEBILL, *Eutoxeres aquila.*   5   Plate 16
RANGE: Costa Rica to Peru; tropical and subtropical up to 3000 ft.

EQUATORIAL TOOTHBILL, *Androdon aequatorialis.*   5¼ Plate 14
RANGE: E. Panama and w. Colombia to w. Ecuador; tropical zone.

VERAGUAN LANCEBILL, *Doryfera veraguensis.*   4½   Plate 14
(Considered a race of *D. ludoviciae* by others.)
FIELD MARKS: Bill more than twice as long as head, black and almost straight; forehead bright metallic blue or greenish blue.
RANGE: Mts. of Costa Rica and w. Panama.

GREEN-FRONTED LANCEBILL, *Doryfera ludoviciae.*   4¼
FIELD MARKS: Similar to previous species but forehead metallic green.
RANGE: Mts. of e. Panama (Darien) to w. Venezuela and n. Boliva.

WHITE-NECKED JACOBIN, *Florisuga mellivora.*   4   Plate 14
FIELD MARKS: Bill barely longer than head, essentially straight and black. Female metallic bronze green above; tail tipped white; throat dusky, feathers broadly margined with white; sides mottled or scaled with white and bronze green; belly white.
RANGE: Mexico (humid tropical lowlands of s. Veracruz and e. Oaxaca to Chiapas) to Brazil and n. Bolivia.

WEDGE-TAILED SABREWING, *Campylopterus curvipennis.*   5½
                                                          Plate 14
FIELD MARKS: Bill one and half times as long as head, dark, and slightly decurved; underparts pale gray.
VOICE: The song is a rapid, low-pitched jumble, remindful of the "whisper song" of a Northern House-Wren.

RANGE: Mexico (s.w. Tamaulipas and e. San Luis Potosí to Chiapas and Yucatán; tropical and subtropical woods) to Guatemala.

RUFOUS SABREWING, *Campylopterus rufus.* 5   Plate 14
FIELD MARKS: Upper bill black and the lower one somewhat pink at the base; two central tail feathers bronze green.
RANGE: Mexico (mts. of s. Chiapas; mostly from 5000 to 7000 ft.), Guatemala, and El Salvador.

VIOLET SABREWING, *Campylopterus hemileucurus.* 5½   Plate 14
FIELD MARKS: Three outer tail feathers white on bottom third. Female green above and dusky greenish gray below, with a green spot or speckles on the throat; tiny white spot back of eye.
RANGE: Mexico (subtropical woods in mts. of Guerrero, Oaxaca, Veracruz, Tabasco, and Chiapas; occasionally descending into lowlands) to w. Panama.

BROWN VIOLETEAR, *Colibri delphinae.* 4¼   Plate 14
FIELD MARKS: Stripe along jaw dull white. The dull grayish brown underparts have a slightly streaked appearence because the feathers have somewhat lighter margins. Immatures may lack the blue ear spot and have the feathers of the upper parts margined rusty brown.
RANGE: Guatemala and British Honduras to Guiana and Bolivia; favors "edge" and hedgerows in tropical and subtropical zones above 2000 ft.

MEXICAN VIOLETEAR, *Colibri thalassinus.* 4½   Plate 14
FIELD MARKS: Spot on chest metallic violet blue; feathers of throat with a dark central spot. Female is duller and may lack the metallic chest spot. Immatures have many feathers margined pale gray.
RANGE: Mexico (in temperate-zone oak woods from Jalisco and San Luis Potosí south to Chiapas) to Nicaragua.

LESSER VIOLETEAR, *Colibri cyanotus.* 4   Plate 14
(Considered a race of *C. thalassinus* by some.)
FIELD MARKS: Similar to the larger Mexican Violetear but lacks the metallic violet blue chest spot.
RANGE: Costa Rica to Venezuela and Colombia; favors humid mountain areas of open woods and pastures (mostly above 5000 ft.).

PREVOST'S MANGO, *Anthracothorax prevostii.* 4½   Plate 14
FIELD MARKS: Bill decidedly longer than head, noticeably decurved and black; a black line running down center of chin and throat. Female is white below with a somewhat interrupted midline running all the way from chin to belly (bluish green on chest and black on chin and belly).
RANGE: Mexico (Caribbean slope from s. Tamaulipas to Chiapas and

Yucatán; from sea level up to 4000 ft.) to n.w. Costa Rica; also n.w. Venezuela.

VERAGUAN MANGO, *Anthracothorax veraguensis.* 4¼   Plate 14
(Considered a race of *A. prevostii* by some.)
FIELD MARKS: Similar to Prevost's Mango but with the chin and throat metallic green (no black center line).
RANGE: W. Panama on Pacific slope.

BLACK-THROATED MANGO, *Anthracothorax nigricollis.* 4¼
Plate 14
FIELD MARKS: Similar to Prevost's Mango, but throat and middle of breast and belly are black. In female the midline of underparts is all black instead of partly green.
RANGE: Panama and south to Argentina and Bolivia.

GREEN PUFFLEG, *Haplophaedia aureliae.* 4   Plate 17
RANGE: Mts. of s.e. Panama to n. Bolivia.

BUFFON'S PLUMELETEER, *Chalybura buffonii.* 4½   Plate 17
FIELD MARKS: (In this genus the under tail-coverts are plumelets.) Bill longer than head, almost straight and black. Female has the outer tail feathers tipped with pale gray; throat and breast pale gray, more or less spotted with green; belly white.
RANGE: E. Panama and Canal Zone to Colombia.

GOULD'S PLUMELETEER, *Chalybura urochrysia.* 5   Plate 17
FIELD MARKS: Female has the whole belly gray.
RANGE: E. Panama (Darien) to w. Ecuador.

ISAURA'S PLUMELETEER, *Chalybura isaurae.* 4½   Plate 17
(Considered a race of *C. urochrysia* by others.)
FIELD MARKS: Similar to previous species, but throat of male is metallic blue instead of glittering green; both sexes are darker above and have the tail more definitely bronze.
RANGE: Caribbean slope of w. Panama (crosses barely onto Pacific slope of a few mts.).

DUSKY PLUMELETEER, *Chalybura melanorrhoa.* 4½   Plate 17
(Considered a race of *C. urochrysia* by some.)
FIELD MARKS: Similar to last species but male has green throat and black under tail-coverts; female is brownish gray below.
RANGE: Caribbean slope in Nicaragua and Costa Rica; tropical.

GREEN-CROWNED BRILLIANT, *Heliodoxa jacula.* 5   Plate 17
FIELD MARKS: Bill as long as head, straight, and black. Female has

outside tail feathers tipped white; spot back of eye, short mustache line, throat and belly white.

RANGE: Highlands of Costa Rica to Ecuador.

WHITE-BELLIED MOUNTAINGEM, *Oreopyra hemileucus.*   4
Plate 15

(Listed under genus *Lampornis* by some.)

FIELD MARKS: Bill, about as long as head, straight, and black. Throat in male is purple and that of female is white.

RANGE: Subtropics in Costa Rica and w. Panama.

GREEN-THROATED MOUNTAINGEM, *Oreopyra viridipallens.*   4¼
Plate 15

(Listed under genus *Lampornis* by some.)

FIELD MARKS: Female has outer tail feathers brownish gray instead of black, white stripe back of eye is less conspicuous, and throat is pale grayish white instead of green.

RANGE: Mexico (edge in mt. forest of Chiapas) to Honduras.

SYBIL'S MOUNTAINGEM, *Oreopyra sybillae.*   4½   Plate 15
(Listed as race of previous species by some.)

FIELD MARKS: Similar to previous species but much more extensively green below; throat of female is buff, and outside tail feather on each side is white with subterminal bar of light gray.

RANGE: Highlands of n. Nicaragua.

PURPLE-THROATED MOUNTAINGEM, *Oreopyra calolaema.*   4
Plate 15

(Listed as a race of *Lampornis castaneoventris* by some.)

FIELD MARKS: Female has the tail bronze green instead of blue black, and the outer feathers are black subterminally and tipped with pale gray; underparts tawny; femoral tufts white.

RANGE: Highlands of w. Nicaragua, Costa Rica, and w. Panama.

WHITE-THROATED MOUNTAINGEM, *Oreopyra castaneoventris.*
4   Plate 15

(Listed under genus *Lampornis* by some.)

FIELD MARKS: Similar to previous species, except that the adult male has the throat white (sometimes with a few lilac-tipped feathers at edge).

RANGE: Mts. of w. Panama.

GRAY-TAILED MOUNTAINGEM, *Oreopyra cinereicauda.*   4
Plate 15

(Listed as a race of last species by some.)

FIELD MARKS: Tail in adult male is ash gray (not blue black).

RANGE: Mountains of s. Costa Rica.

DE LATTRE'S COQUETTE, *Lophornis delattrei.* 2½ Plate 16
FIELD MARKS: Bill shorter than head, straight and pink with dark tip.
Female lacks crest.
RANGE: Mexico (the record consists of two males collected in s.w.
Guerrero), s.w. Costa Rica, Panama, Colombia, Peru, and Bolivia.

HELENA'S COQUETTE, *Lophornis helenae.* 2½ Plate 16
(Placed in genus *Paphosia* by some.)
RANGE: S.e. Mexico (humid tropical and subtropical areas in s. Vera-
cruz, e. Oaxaca, and Chiapas) along Caribbean slope to c. Costa
Rica.

ADORABLE COQUETTE, *Lophornis adorabilis.* 3 Plate 16
FIELD MARKS: Crest of male white. Female has sooty black head, white
or buff band across rump, white throat flecked with dusky bronze,
and a rufous belly.
RANGE: C. and s.w. Costa Rica and w. Panama; favors open hilly
areas in tropical and subtropical zones.

VERAGUAN SNOWCAP, *Microchera albocoronata.* 2¼ Plate 16
FIELD MARKS: Bill shorter than head, straight and black; outer tail
feathers white for basal two-thirds and black terminally; face and
underparts black except for white under tail-coverts.
RANGE: W. Panama (woodlands of Veragua).

COSTA RICAN SNOWCAP, *Microchera parvirostris.* 2¼ Plate 16
(Considered a race of *M. albocoronata* by others.)
FIELD MARKS: Similar to preceding species, but male has basal portion
of outer tail feathers white and remainder bronze black, sometimes
with tiny white tip, and underparts differently marked (throat dusky-
brown; below dark coppery purple except for white under tail-
coverts).
RANGE: Woods in lowlands and subtropical zone in Costa Rica; also
Nicaragua.

CONSTANT STARTHROAT, *Anthoscenus constantii.* 4½ Plate 15
(Listed in genus *Heliomaster* by some.)
FIELD MARKS: Bill more than twice as long as head, straight and
black; rump has white spot, or streak, in center, and there are conspicuous (when displayed) white tufts on the sides between the
flanks and rump which may appear as a streamer near each side
of the tail.
RANGE: Mexico (Durango to Chiapas; mostly in semi-arid regions
from sea level up to 5000 ft.) to Costa Rica; dry woods or scrub.

LONG-BILLED STARTHROAT, *Anthocenus longirostris.* 4½
    (Listed in the genus *Heliomaster* by some.)   Plate 15
FIELD MARKS: Very similar to last species, but male has greenish blue
    crown spot; white spot back of eye is much smaller or indistinct;
    when perched, wings do not quite extend to end of tail; under
    tail-coverts are black with white edges (in Constant Starthroat they
    are dusky subterminally but have wider white margins, which give
    a generally paler appearance); when feathers are spread, basal
    half of tail viewed from beneath appears dull green, whereas that
    of the Constant Starthroat appears gray.
RANGE: S.w. Mexico (Guerrero to Chiapas; mostly in tropical zone)
    and along Pacific slope of Guatemala and El Salvador, through
    Costa Rica to Bolivia; also Trinidad.

BARROT'S FAIRY, *Heliotryx barroti.* 4½   Plate 15
    (Considered a race of *H. aurita* by some.)
RANGE: S. Mexico (Tabasco) to w. Ecuador; favors humid lowlands,
    but has been found well up into mts.

COPPER-HEADED EMERALD, *Lawrencius cupreiceps.* 3
    (Listed as *Elvira cupreiceps* by some.)   Plate 17
FIELD MARKS: The bill is distinctly decurved.
RANGE: Subtropical woods on Caribbean slope of Costa Rica.

WHITE-TAILED EMERALD, *Elvira chionura.* 3   Plate 17
    (Listed as *Eupherusa chionura* by some.)
FIELD MARKS: Bill slightly shorter than head and straight; otherwise
    rather similar to last species. Female white below, except for metallic
    green sides.
RANGE: S.w. Costa Rica and w. Panama; favors subtropical woods.

WHITE-BELLIED EMERALD, *Agyrtrina candida.* 3   Plate 16
    (Listed under genus *Amazilia* by others.)
FIELD MARKS: Bill somewhat longer than head, straight or faintly
    decurved, and pink at base of lower mandible (not always visible);
    central underparts white and speckled with tiny green spots which
    may extend all over the throat and breast; sides bronze green;
    under tail-coverts pale brownish gray.
RANGE: Mexico (Atlantic slope from e. San Luis Potosí to Chiapas
    and Yucatán; more common in lowlands, but exists up to 4000 ft)
    to Costa Rica.

LUCY'S EMERALD, *Agyrtrina luciae.* 3½   Plate 16
    (Listed under genus *Amazilia* by others.)
RANGE: Honduras.

CANIVET EMERALD, *Chlorostilbon canivetii.*   3¼   Plate 16
(Considered a race of *C. mellisugus* by some.)
FIELD MARKS: Bill as long as head, straight, red with a dusky tip
(female has only the base of the lower bill pink). Tail blue black
and plainly forked in male but only slightly (though definitely) so
in female. Female has tail largely green basally, but the outer
feathers are mostly black with pale gray tips; has white stripe back
of eye that is bordered below by a black facial patch; underparts
are light gray or pale brownish gray; sides are glossed with bronze
green.
RANGE: Mexico (uncommon in west from Sinaloa and Durango to
Guerrero; more common and widespread in east from s. Tamaulipas
and e. San Luis Potosí to Chiapas and Yucatán; sea level up to
about 6000 ft.) to n.w. Costa Rica.

ALLIED EMERALD, *Chlorostilbon assimilis.*   3   Plate 16
(Listed as race of *C. canivetii* by some and *C. mellisugus* by others.)
FIELD MARKS: Similar to last species but is darker and has black bill.
RANGE: S.w. Costa Rica and Panama.

GREEN THORNTAIL, *Popelairia conversii.*   4   Plate 16
FIELD MARKS: Bill straight and shorter than head; tail long and forked
in male. Female has short tail, which makes it an inch shorter; has
dull black throat outlined at side with white; breast and belly black
in center (black bordered by white line).
RANGE: Caribbean slope of Costa Rica to w. Ecuador; favors humid
subtropics above 2500 ft.

SLENDER SHEARTAIL, *Doricha enicura.*   4¼   Plate 15
FIELD MARKS: Bill one and a half times as long as head and plainly,
though not decidedly, decurved (bill and tail make up half the
total length of this small-bodied bird). Female has a less deeply
forked and shorter tail (still, it extends a full quarter-inch below end
of wing when bird is perched), the two outer feathers of which
are rufous with a black subterminal band and white tip.
RANGE: Mexico (highlands of Chiapas), Guatemala, El Salvador, and
Honduras.

MEXICAN SHEARTAIL, *Doricha eliza.*   3½   Plate 15
FIELD MARKS: Bill about twice as long as head and decidedly decurved. Similar to last species but has shorter tail (only slightly
longer than wing) that is forked for two-thirds its length. Female
has a shorter tail that is somewhat double-rounded; it extends a
quarter-inch beyond end of wing when bird is perched; underparts
cream-colored.
RANGE: Mexico (semi-arid areas in c. Veracruz where rare; arid regions
in Yucatán).

COSTA RICAN WOODSTAR, *Philodice bryantae.* 3½   Plate 15
FIELD MARKS: Bill about as long as head, straight and black. Male has tail forked and largely black. Female has tail double-rounded and largely rufous; underparts largely rufous with center of breast and belly dull white.
RANGE: Highlands of Costa Rica and w. Panama.

COLOMBIAN WOODNYMPH, *Thalurania colombica.* 4   Plate 14
(Considered a race of *T. furcata* by some.)
FIELD MARKS: Bill about as long as head, straight or very slightly decurved, and black; tail blue black and forked. Forehead of male bluish violet. Female is brownish gray below (throat paler); under tail-coverts and femoral tufts white.
RANGE: Humid tropical and subtropical woods of s. Nicaragua and Costa Rica to Venezuela and n.e. Colombia.

HONDURAS WOODNYMPH, *Thalurania townsendi.* 4.   Plate 14
(Considered a race of *T. colombica* by some.)
FIELD MARKS: Similar to previous species but male has breast and belly green instead of violet blue.
RANGE: E. Guatemala and Honduras.

GREEN-CROWNED WOODNYMPH, *Thalurania fannyi.* 4
Plate 14
(Considered a race of *T. colombica* by some.)
FIELD MARKS: Similar to Colombian Woodnymph, but male has shining green crown, usually edged with blue at back.
RANGE: E. Panama to w. Colombia and Ecuador.

DUPONT HUMMINGBIRD, *Tilmatura dupontii.* 3½   Plate 15
FIELD MARKS: Bill shorter than head or barely equal to it, straight and black; a white or buffy white spot on each side of rump; male has long, deeply forked tail. Female has slightly forked tail that is so short it does not extend beyond the wing tips of the perched bird; underparts are rufous (lighter on throat).
RANGE: Mexico (from Jalisco in west and c. Veracruz in east, southward to Chiapas; mostly above 3000 ft.) to Nicaragua.

LUCIFER HUMMINGBIRD, *Calothorax lucifer.* 3½
RANGE: S.w. United States and south to Chiapas, Mexico; from sea level to about 8000 ft., but more common above 3000 ft.

BEAUTIFUL HUMMINGBIRD, *Calothorax pulcher.* 3½   Plate 15
FIELD MARKS: Bill longer than head, very slightly decurved, and black. Very similar to last species, but male has a straighter, somewhat shorter bill and a slightly longer forked tail, the outer feathers of which are rounded at the tip instead of being gradually tapered

to a sharp point (difficult to see because tail is seldom spread). The female has the throat and median underparts creamy or buffy gray instead of dull, as in Lucifer Hummingbird, and only sides and flanks are cinnamon-buff (this slight difference is not too dependable as there is overlapping, but the difference is best observed at the side of the throat just below the ear region). The tail-length ratios of the males and females of the two species is just the reverse: when perched the wing tips of the female Beautiful extend to the end of the tail or a tiny bit beyond, whereas the tips of the wings of the female Lucifer lack a full quarter-inch of reaching the end of the tail (in both females the tails are double-rounded instead of forked).

RANGE: Mexico (Distrito Federal and Morelos south through Guerrero and Pueblo to Chiapas; mostly in arid regions and high basins).

BOUCARD'S HUMMINGBIRD, *Lepidopyga boucardi.*   4   Plate 17
(Listed as *Amazilia boucardi* by some.)
FIELD MARKS: Bill longer than head and faintly decurved, the lower mandible pink at base; tail forked. Female has the throat white, more or less speckled with green.
RANGE: Mangrove swamps along Pacific coast of Costa Rica.

IRAZU HUMMINGBIRD, *Panterpe insignis.*   4½   Plate 17
FIELD MARKS: Bill slightly longer than head, straight and black, with a bit of pink at base of mandible.
RANGE: Mts. (near tops) of Costa Rica and w. Panama.

CUVIER'S HUMMINGBIRD, *Phaeochroa cuvierii.*   4½   Plate 14
FIELD MARKS: Bill slightly longer than head, straight and dark, the lower mandible pink at base.
RANGE: Guatemala and British Honduras south to n. Colombia.

BERYLLINE HUMMINGBIRD, *Saucerottia beryllina.*   3½   Plate 17
(Listed as *Amazilia beryllina* by some.)
FIELD MARKS: Bill longer than head, essentially straight, the mandible pink at base.
RANGE: Mexico (Sonora and Chihuahua south to Chiapas; Veracruz to Chiapas; from sea level up to 9000 ft; more common in west), Guatemala, El Salvador, and Honduras.

BLUE-TAILED HUMMINGBIRD, *Saucerottia cyanura.*   3½
(Listed as *Amazilia cyanura* by some.)   Plate 17
RANGE: Mexico (Pacific slope in Chiapas) to Costa Rica.

SOPHIA'S HUMMINGBIRD, *Saucerottia sophiae.*   3½   Plate 17
(Listed as *Amazilia saucerottei hoffmanni* by some.)
RANGE: Nicaragua and Costa Rica.

EDWARD'S HUMMINGBIRD, *Saucerottia edward.* 3½   Plate 17
(Listed as *Amazilia edward* by others.)
RANGE: S. Panama; n.w. Ecuador.

SNOWY-BREASTED HUMMINGBIRD, *Saucerottia niveoventer.*
(Listed as *Amazilia edward niveoventer* by some.)   3½   Plate 17
RANGE: S.w. Costa Rica and w. Panama.

VIOLET-CROWNED HUMMINGBIRD, *Cyanomyia verticalis.*   4
(Listed as *Amazilia verticalis* by some.)
FIELD MARKS: Bill longer than head, essentially straight and red
basally. Female and immatures have the crown duller and greenish
blue or green instead of violet blue.
RANGE: Mexico (Sonora and Chihuahua through Hidalgo and Guerrero
to Chiapas); from sea level to 7000 ft. or more; accidental in
Arizona.

AZURE-CROWNED HUMMINGBIRD, *Cyanomyia cyanocephala.*   4
(Listed as *Amazilia cyanocephala* by some.)   Plate 17
RANGE: Highlands of e. Mexico (cloud forests and oak-pine forests of
. w. Tamaulipas and e. San Luis Potosí to Chiapas) to Nicaragua.

BUFF-BELLIED HUMMINGBIRD, *Amazilia yucatanensis.* 3½
FIELD MARKS: Bill longer than head, faintly decurved and dusky with
a red base. Birds of this genus have cinnamon-rufous tails.
RANGE: S. Texas, Mexico (Tamaulipas to Chiapas and Yucatán; from
sea level up to about 3000 ft.) to Guatemala and British Honduras.

RIEFFER'S HUMMINGBIRD, *Amazilia tzacatl.* 3½   Plate 17
RANGE: Mexico (Tamaulipas south through e. Oaxaca to Chiapas and
Quintana Roo) to w. Venezuela and Ecuador; sea level to 6000 ft.

CINNAMON HUMMINGBIRD, *Amazilia rutila.* 4   Plate 17
RANGE: Mexico (Sinaloa to Chiapas; Yucatán and Quintana Roo) to
c. Costa Rica.

RIVOLI HUMMINGBIRD, *Eugenes fulgens.* 5
RANGE: S.w. United States, Mexico (Sonora to w. Tamaulipas and
south to Chiapas; from 6000 to 10000 ft., but lower in winter) and
south to n. Nicaragua.

ADMIRABLE HUMMINGBIRD, *Eugenes spectabilis.* 5½ Plate 17
(Considered a race of *E. fulgens* by others.)
FIELD MARKS: Female has crown sooty green; a small white spot back
of eye; tail tipped with light brownish gray.

RANGE: Mts. of Costa Rica and w. Panama; above 5000 ft.

BLUE-THROATED HUMMINGBIRD, *Cyanolaemus clemenciae.* 5
(Listed as *Lampornis clemenciae* by others.)
RANGE: Mts. of s.w. United States; Mexico (Sonora and Durango
south to Oaxaca and sometimes Chiapas; Nuevo León to Hidalgo
and Veracruz).

AMETHYST-THROATED HUMMINGBIRD
Lampornis amethystinus. 4½   Plate 15
FIELD MARKS: Bill slightly longer than head, faintly decurved and
black. The female has the throat dull cinnamon or brown, some-
times with a pink glint on the feathers.
RANGE: Mexico (Nayarit and south; s. Tamaulipas and e. San Luis
Potosí to Chiapas; cloud forests and oak-pine woods; 3000 to 8000
ft.) to Honduras.

GARNET-THROATED HUMMINGBIRD, *Lamprolaima rhami.* 4½
Plate 17
FIELD MARKS: Bill about as long as head, straight and black. The
female is dark brownish gray below, the throat sometimes showing
metallic purplish red feathers; femoral tufts white.
RANGE: Mexico (Guerrero, Oaxaca, Mexico, Veracruz, and Chiapas;
from 3000 to 10000 ft., but mostly from 5000 to 8000 ft.) to
Honduras.

DUCHASSAIN'S HUMMINGBIRD, *Lepidopyga coeruleogularis.* 3½
Plate 16
FIELD MARKS: Bill longer than head, faintly decurved, base of lower
mandible pink; tail forked. Female is white below; outside tail
feathers are black with white tip.
RANGE: S.w. Costa Rica and Panama.

PANAMA HUMMINGBIRD, *Damophila panamensis.* 3½   Plate 16
(Considered a race of *D. julie* by others.)
FIELD MARKS: Bill about as long as head, straight, the lower mandible
pink. Female has the underparts pale gray (breast is whiter) and
sometimes a few green spots at side of throat. Julie's Hummingbird,
erroneously reported in e. Panama, might yet be found there.
RANGE: Panama.

GUIMET'S HUMMINGBIRD, *Klais guimeti.* 3   Plate 14
FIELD MARKS: Bill shorter than head and straight. Female has the underparts pale gray and the outer tail feathers tipped grayish white.
RANGE: Honduras to Panama; w. Venezuela to Bolivia; tropical and
subtropical regions; favors semi-open areas.

ABEILLE'S HUMMINGBIRD, *Abeillia abeillei.* 3 Plate 14
FIELD MARKS: Bill shorter than head, straight and black. Female is
gray below (lighter on throat); sides washed with bronze green.
RANGE: Mexico (humid subtropical forests of s. Veracruz, e. Oaxaca,
and c. Chiapas) to n. Nicaragua; highlands.

STRIPED-TAILED HUMMINGBIRD, *Eupherusa eximia.* 3½
Plate 17
FIELD MARKS: Bill as long as head, straight (or faintly decurved) and
black. Female has the underparts buffy gray; femoral tufts white.
RANGE: Mexico (s. Veracruz, e. Oaxaca, and Chiapas; 400 to 4000 ft.)
to w. Panama; uncommon forest bird.

BLACK-BELLIED HUMMINGBIRD, *Eupherusa nigriventris.* 3
Plate 17
FIELD MARKS: Female lacks black on head; below pale brownish gray;
outer tail feathers white.
RANGE: Caribbean highlands of Costa Rica and w. Panama; rare.

WHITE-TAILED HUMMINGBIRD, *Eupherusa poliocerca.* 3
Plate 17
(Considered a race of *E. eximia* by some.)
FIELD MARKS: Similar to the Striped-tailed Hummingbird, but with
the inner web of four, instead of just two, of the outer tail feathers
on each side white, and with the outer web of these feathers gray
instead of black.
RANGE: Mexico (confined to the Sierra Madre del Sur of s. Guerrero
and nearby Oaxaca); rare.

BLACK-FRONTED HUMMINGBIRD, *Eupherusa cyanophrys.* 3
Plate 17
(Considered a race of *E. eximia* by some.)
FIELD MARKS: Similar to last species, but the forecrown is blue instead
of green.
RANGE: Mexico (cloud-forest area on Pacific slope of c. Oaxaca).

XANTUS HUMMINGBIRD, *Hylocharis xantusii.* 3½ Plate 16
FIELD MARKS: Bill slightly longer than head, faintly decurved, and red
with a dark tip. Female has the forehead brown and the underparts
wholly cinnamon-buff, except for white femoral tufts.
RANGE: Mexico (s. Baja California).

WHITE-EARED HUMMINGBIRD, *Hylocharis leucotis.* 4
FIELD MARKS: The female is distinguished by the red base to the bill,
the conspicuous white line back of the eye, white tips to tail

feathers, and green speckling on the throat, all of which resembles Rivoli female.

RANGE: S. Arizona and Mexico (Sonora and Chihuahua in mt. oak-pine woods, south to Chiapas; Tamaulipas south to Quintana Roo) to Nicaragua.

ELICIA'S HUMMINGBIRD, *Hylocharis eliciae.*   3½   Plate 16
FIELD MARKS: Female has blue feathers of throat margined with white and is paler below than male.
RANGE: Mexico (s. Veracruz and e. Oaxaca to Chiapas; rare) to w. Panama; favors shady forest areas.

GRAY'S HUMMINGBIRD, *Hylocharis grayi.*   4   Plate 16
FIELD MARKS: Female has blue black tail with outer feathers tipped grayish white; throat speckled with green.
RANGE: E. Panama to n.w. Colombia.

GOLDMAN'S HUMMINGBIRD, *Goldmania violiceps.*   3½   Plate 16
FIELD MARKS: Bill somewhat longer than head, the lower mandible pink. Female has chestnut markings on outer tail feathers; under-parts are grayish white, except for white plumes on under tail-coverts.
RANGE: E. Panama (collected on Cerro Azul at 3000 ft.).

GOETHAL'S HUMMINGBIRD, *Goethalsia bella.*   3½   Plate 16
FIELD MARKS: Female has forehead green like rest of crown; under-parts shade from almost white on throat to light cinnamon-buff on belly; under tail-coverts are white plumes.
RANGE: E. Panama (Darien; 200 to 5000 ft.; rare); adjacent Colombia.

LOVELY HUMMINGBIRD, *Polyerata amabilis.*   3¼   Plate 16
   (Listed under genus *Amazilia* by some.)
FIELD MARKS: Bill longer than head, straight; lower mandible pink at base. Male has upper throat dull black (in most lights) and lower throat metallic violet blue. Female crown is not brighter green than back; underparts brownish white with some green speckles.
RANGE: Humid Caribbean lowland of Nicaragua to c. Panama; also Colombia and n.w. Ecuador.

CHARMING HUMMINGBIRD, *Polyerata decora.*   3½   Plate 16
   (Listed in genus *Amazilia* by some and as race of *amabilis* by others.)
FIELD MARKS: Similar to previous species, but male has whole crown and nape glittering metallic green, and central tail feathers are

blacker; female has crown brighter (a more shining bluish-green) than back.

RANGE: Pacific slope lowlands of s.w. Costa Rica and Panama.

BROAD-BILLED HUMMINGBIRD, *Cynanthus latirostris.* 3¼

RANGE: S.w. United States and Mexico (Sonora and Chihuahua to n. Guerrero; Nuevo León and Tamaulipas to Hidalgo and Veracruz; from sea level up to 7000 ft.)

DOUBLEDAY HUMMINGBIRD, *Cynanthus doubledayi.* 3¼

Plate 16

(Considered a race of the previous species by others.)

FIELD MARKS: Similar to previous species but tail plainly forked instead of just notched when spread; the forehead and crown are brilliant metallic bluish green instead of bronze green; the throat shows much more blue.

RANGE: S.w. Mexico (Pacific slope of s. Guerrero to Puebla and Oaxaca).

DUSKY HUMMINGBIRD, *Cynanthus sordidus.* 4   Plate 16

FIELD MARKS: Bill longer than head, faintly decurved, red at base with a dusky tip; tail double-rounded. Female tail is greenish bronze, the four outer feathers on either side crossed by a broad, dull black subterminal band and tipped with pale grayish brown; the crown and forehead are brown.

RANGE: Mexico (Jalisco to Morelos and Guerrero, Hidalgo, Pueblo, and Oaxaca).

ANNA HUMMINGBIRD, *Calypte anna.* 3½

RANGE: California, Arizona, and n.w. Mexico (Baja California; in winter to Sonora).

COSTA HUMMINGBIRD, *Calypte costae.* 3.

FIELD MARKS: Female has the outermost tail feather narrower than any of the others, and it tapers more gradually to a point (this can be seen only when the tail is widely spread, but it is a feature not found in other members of the genus).

RANGE: California and n. Baja California; winters to Sonora.

HELOISE HUMMINGBIRD, *Atthis heloisa.* 2¾   Plate 15

FIELD MARKS: Bill scarcely as long as head, straight and black. Female is similar to the female Calliope Hummingbird, but the bill is a bit shorter and the tail is shorter; both these give the bird a plumper look.

RANGE: Mexico (Sinaloa, Chihuahua, Nuevo León, and Tamaulipas south to Oaxaca and Veracruz; mostly in mts. at 5000 to 8000 ft.).

ELLIOT HUMMINGBIRD, *Atthis ellioti.*   2½   Plate 15
FIELD MARKS: Similar to previous species but smaller and with a darker
head; jaw is grayish brown instead of white; purple of throat is
more tinted with red.
RANGE: S. Mexico (mts. of Chiapas) to Honduras.

HELIODOR HUMMINGBIRD, *Acestrura heliodor.*   2¾   Plate 16
FIELD MARKS: Gorget of male is metallic purple and extends out at
side of neck; breast gray; tail black. Female has white line back of
eye; tail is black with a rufous tip, but upper tail-coverts are rufous;
below largely buff.
RANGE: E. Panama to Venezuela and Ecuador.

CALLIOPE HUMMINGBIRD, *Stellula calliope.*   2¾
RANGE: British Columbia, w. United States, and Mexico (mts. of n.
Baja California, Sonora, and Durango, south to Distrito Federal and
Guerrero).

BLACK-CHINNED HUMMINGBIRD, *Archilochus alexandri.*   3.
RANGE: British Columbia, w. United States, and n. Mexico (Baja
California across to Tamaulipas; in winter south as far as Guerrero
and Veracruz).

RUBY-THROATED HUMMINGBIRD, *Archilochus colubris.*   3.
RANGE: E. North America; winters through Mexico to Panama.

BROAD-TAILED HUMMINGBIRD, *Selasphorus platycercus.*   3½
RANGE: W. United States, Mexico (Sonora and Chihuahua south to
Oaxaca; Coahuila, Nuevo León, and Tamaulipas south to Veracruz;
4000 to 12000 ft.), and Guatemala.

LESSER BROAD-TAILED HUMMINGBIRD, *Selasphorus flammula.*
                                                       3   Plate 15
FIELD MARKS: Similar to Broad-tailed Hummingbird but with more
rufous on tail feathers; throat of males duller and more nearly
purple (rose purple).
RANGE: High mts. of Costa Rica.

VOLCANO HUMMINGBIRD, *Selasphorus torridus.*   3   Plate 15
(Considered either a race or a color phase of the last species by
others.)
FIELD MARKS: Similar to last species, but males have the gorget dull
metallic grayish green glossed with purple.
RANGE: High mts. of w. Panama.

SIMON'S HUMMINGBIRD, *Selasphorus simoni.*   2½   Plate 15
FIELD MARKS: Similar to Lesser Broad-tailed Hummingbird, but the

male has the middle tail feathers black (instead of green) and narrowly edged with rufous only on the outer web; the gorget is metallic reddish purple.

RANGE: Highlands of Costa Rica (apparently confined to Poas and Barba volcanoes).

GLOW-THROATED HUMMINGBIRD, *Selasphorus ardens.* 2¾

Plate 15

FIELD MARKS: Similar to last species, but male has a broad rufous edging on the middle tail feathers, and the outer ones have rufous on both edges; also the throat is redder (purplish red).

RANGE: Higher mts. of w. Panama.

RUFOUS HUMMINGBIRD, *Selasphorus rufus.* 3¼

RANGE: W. North America; winters to Mexico (Guerrero to Veracruz).

ALLEN HUMMINGBIRD, *Selasphorus sasin.* 3¼

RANGE: California; winters to c. Mexico (Guanajuato and D. F.)

SCINTILLANT HUMMINGBIRD, *Selasphorus scintilla.* 2½

Plate 15

FIELD MARKS: Similar to Allen Hummingbird but smaller; the male has a black line extending up tail feathers from the tip; the female has the outside tail feathers tipped cinnamon instead of white.

RANGE: Costa Rica and w. Panama; favors middle altitudes above 4000 ft.

TROGONS: Trogonidae

GUATEMALAN QUETZAL, *Pharomachrus mocinno.* 14½ Plate 18

VOICE: The song is made up of a series of similar calls. A single motif may be represented as *cuauk cuoo*, or possibly *cuak ca;* the pitch is about F^2D^2 sharp E^2. The complete motif with the pause between the figures requires nearly two sec.; it is repeated after a rest of about one sec. The series may continue for several minutes. Although it is heavier, the quality is similar to that of the Jalapa Trogon.

RANGE: Mexico (virgin cloud forest in s. Oaxaca and s.w. Chiapas; rare and likely to be exterminated shortly, as the birds are still being killed for skins and the habitat is being destroyed) to mts. of w. Panama.

GOLDEN-HEADED QUETZAL, *Pharomachrus auriceps.* 14

Plate 18

(Considered a race of *P. pavoninus* by some.)

RANGE: Mts. of e. Panama to n. Bolivia.

EARED TROGON, *Euptilotis neoxenus.* 13½   Plate 18
RANGE: Mexico (pine forests in w. Chihuahua and e. Sinaloa south to Michoacán and Zacatecas).

MASSENA TROGON, *Curucujus massena.* 13½   Plate 18
(Listed in the genus *Trogon* by others.)
FIELD MARKS: All members of this genus have vermiculations on the secondaries and wing-coverts; none have white tips to the outer tail feathers (those which show on the under side of tail). This species has no white on the under parts.
VOICE: The usual "song" is a series of *ook* figures given at a rate of three per sec.; the pitch is about C¹. A pair of birds will sometimes "duet"; the pitch of the female is about a half tone higher.
RANGE: Mexico (c. Veracruz and e. Oaxaca to Chiapas and Campeche; in humid lowland forest) to n.w. Ecuador.

LATTICE-TAILED TROGON, *Curucujus clathratus.* 12   Plate 18
(Listed in the genus *Trogon* by others.)
RANGE: Humid woods on Caribbean slope of Costa Rica and w. Panama.

LARGE-TAILED TROGAN, *Curucujus macrourus.* 13   Plate 18
(Listed as *Trogon melanurus* by others.)
RANGE: E. Panama and n. Colombia.

GENUS *TROGON*: Birds of this group tend to go about in small flocks, at least during the "courtship" season (flocks of 6 to 10 common, but sometimes up to 20 or so); they have a characteristic song phrase in common that might be called a rattle of the "bouncing ball" type; middle tail feathers (in male) are metallic greenish blue (or green) and tipped black; the lateral tail feathers are broadly tipped white and otherwise largely or entirely white.

BAIRD'S TROGON, *Trogon bairdii.* 11½   Plate 18
(Considered a race of *T. viridis* by some.)
FIELD MARKS: Belly orange red; central tail feathers metallic greenish blue with black tip in male and slate black in female; outer tail feathers white in male and tipped and narrowly barred with white in female.
VOICE: Similar to other members of genus.
RANGE: S.w. Costa Rica and adjacent n.w. Panama.

WHITE-TAILED TROGON, *Trogon chionurus.* 10½   Plate 18
(Considered a race of *T. viridis* by others.)
FIELD MARKS: Belly yellow; central tail feathers in male green with black tip; outer tail feathers of male are white; outer tail feathers

of female are tipped white as in Baird's Trogon, but the other parts show much less regular barring.

RANGE: E. Panama (from c. Bocas del Toro along Caribbean slope to San Blas and on both slopes of the Darien region) and n. Colombia.

BLACK-HEADED TROGON, *Trogon melanocephalus.*   11 Plate 18
(Considered a race of *T. citreolus* by some.)

FIELD MARKS: Bare eyelids azure blue, forming a ring around eye.

VOICE: The typical "song" phrase is the "bouncing ball" type of rattle. It consists of some fifteen to twenty-five *cuk* figures and requires from two to three sec. to deliver. It begins somewhat slowly, quickly accelerates, and sometimes slows down a bit at the end (this gives the bouncing ball effect). The quality is Cuckoo-like; the pitch is about G^2. (The overall effect might be compared to a laugh or giggle or to the song phrase of the Barred Antshrike.) Other vocalizations include a single *cop,* or a slow series of them, which resembles efforts of the Massena Trogon as well as those of other species of the present genus.

RANGE: E. Mexico (s. Tamaulipas and e. San Luis Potosí through Veracruz, e. Puebla, and e. Oaxaca to Chiapas and Yucatán) to n.w. Costa Rica; favors savannas or open woods.

CITREOLINE TROGON, *Trogon citreolus.* 10½   Plate 18
FIELD MARKS: Similar to the Black-headed Trogon but noticeably paler below, with a much wider white band on the breast and a different tail pattern (a narrow, dark slate blue eye ring mentioned in museum descriptions is not visible in the field).

VOICE: Similar to other members of the genus.

RANGE: Pacific slope of Mexico from Sinaloa to n.w. Chiapas.

GENUS, *TROGONURUS:* Birds of this group have the tails distinctly longer than the wing; adult males have the chest metallic bronze, green, or blue, and the secondaries and wing-coverts are vermiculated; adult females have the chest and upper parts brown or slate (according to Ridgway, the young have spotted plumage); the song phrases are made up of distinctly separated figures of Cuckoo-like quality.

MEXICAN TROGON, *Trogonurus mexicanus.*   12   Plate 18
(Listed in the genus *Trogon* by some.)

VOICE: The "song" is composed of eight to twenty figures (*cuc*) delivered one each half sec.; pitch about C^2. There is also a softer ("whisper") phrase, which is more hurried (*cu cu cu,* etc.) and of lower pitch (7 figures in 2½ sec.). The alarm call is a low, sharp *cut.*

RANGE: Mts. of Mexico (w. Chihuahua and s. Tamaulipas to Chiapas;

favors cloud forest and mixed pine-oak woods at 3000 to 8000 ft.)
to Guatemala and Honduras.

ELEGANT TROGON, *Trogonurus elegans.* 11½   Plate 18
(Listed in the genus *Trogon* by others.)

FIELD MARKS: Similar to Coppery-tailed Trogon, but the adult male
has the under side of the tail regularly, though narrowly, barred
with black and the secondaries and wing-coverts more coarsely
vermiculated; the adult female has narrower black tip to the middle
tail feathers, and the under side of tail is regularly and more broadly
barred with black.

VOICE: The song of the male is a series of hoarse calls, *coaa*, delivered
about 3 per sec. The pitch at the start of a figure is about C^2,
but is slurred down to B^2. In the female the pitch is higher and the
voice not hoarse; hence, its song sounds more nearly like that of the
Mexican Trogon.

RANGE: Pacific slope from Guatemala to n.w. Costa Rica; favors rather
dry woods.

COPPERY-TAILED TROGON, *Trogonurus ambiguus.* 11 Plate 18
(Listed as a race of *T. elegans* by others.)

FIELD MARKS: Similar to the previous species, but has a shorter tail,
which in the male is finely vermiculated with dusky lines or flecks
on the under side instead of showing distinct bars.

RANGE: S.w. United States and Mexico (Sonora and Chihuahua to
Guerrero and Oaxaca; Nuevo León and Tamaulipas to Veracruz);
favors rather dry woods from sea level up to the pines.

JALAPA TROGON, *Trogonurus puella.* 10   Plate 18
(Listed as a race of *Trogon collaris* by some.)

FIELD MARKS: Belly red, salmon pink, or reddish orange. The orange-
bellied forms are considered a distinct species by some (*aurantiiventris*), but since the various color forms are found in the same
habitat in Costa Rica, have the same habits and the same vocalizations, they cannot be separated in the field.

VOICE: The "song" phrase is composed usually of two figures (sometimes three but rarely more). These may be represented by *keeuk*
or *keeah* (some say it sounds like *cow*); pitch is about A^3. A three-
figure phrase requires about 2 sec.; after a rest of 4 or 5 sec., the
phrase is repeated.

RANGE: Mexico (e. San Luis Potosí, e. Puebla, Veracruz, e. Oaxaca,
Tabasco, Chiapas, and in the Sierra Madre del Sur of Guerrero;
also in Campeche, Yucatán, and Quintana Roo) to w. Panama; in
humid, subtropical regions and cloud forests in the mts., but,
strangely, down to sea level in the Yucatán Peninsula.

COLLARED TROGON, *Trogonurus collaris.* 9 Plate 18
(Listed in genus *Trogon* by others.)
FIELD MARKS: Similar to Jalapa Trogon but with a different pattern on under side of tail (white bars much wider).
RANGE: Mts. of e. Panama to Guiana and Bolivia.

GRACEFUL TROGON, *Trogonurus tenellus.* 9 Plate 18
(Listed as a race of *Trogon rufus* by some.)
FIELD MARKS: Has noticeably longer tail than the Gartered Trogon.
VOICE: Similar to Jalapa Trogon.
RANGE: S.e. Honduras to extreme w. Colombia; favors virgin forest from sea level up to 3000 ft. or more.

GENUS, *CHRYSOTROGON:* Birds of this group have relatively short tails (equal in length to the wing); according to Ridgway the nestlings are colored more or less like the adults (no spotting).

GARTERED TROGON, *Chrysotrogon caligatus.* 8 Plate 18
(Listed as a race of *Trogon violaceus* by others.)
FIELD MARKS: Eye ring of male is yellow, that of female white.
VOICE: "Song" is a series of "whistled" figures (about 3 per sec.; pitched about F³). It is somewhat similar to the song of the Ferruginous Pygmy-Owl, but of higher pitch. There is a similar "whisper song" that is much softer and faster. There is also a still softer rattle of about one-sec. duration.
RANGE: E. Mexico (s. Tamaulipas and e. San Luis Potosí to Chiapas and Yucatán) to w. Ecuador; favors forest edge or open woods from sea level up to about 5000 ft.

KINGFISHERS: Alcedinidae

RINGED KINGFISHER, *Ceryle torquata.* 15 Plate 3
RANGE: S. Texas to Tierra del Fuego.

BELTED KINGFISHER, *Ceryle alcyon.* 11
RANGE: North America, winters through Mexico to Venezuela and Colombia.

AMAZON GREEN-KINGFISHER, *Chloroceryle amazona.* 10
Plate 3
FIELD MARKS: This bird is the "Big Green-Kingfisher" and is the only one of its genus that shows much of a crest, which is even less conspicuous than the crests of members of the other genus in the family.
RANGE: Mexico (s. Sinaloa to Chiapas; s. Tamaulipas and e. San Luis Potosí to Quintana Roo) to Tierra del Fuego.

SPOTTED GREEN-KINGFISHER, *Chloroceryle inda.*   8   Plate 3
FIELD MARKS: The female has a black belt across the breast that is
   conspicuously spotted with white or buffy white.
RANGE: Nicaragua to Brazil and Peru; rare in Central America.

LITTLE GREEN-KINGFISHER, *Chloroceryle americana.*   7
FIELD MARKS: Collar across hindneck, throat, belly, under wing-
   coverts, and base of under side of tail white. The white base of the
   outer tail feathers may show well in flight. The female has no
   rufous on the breast.
RANGE: S.w. United States, Mexico (Sonora to Tamaulipas and southward; from sea level up to about 6000 ft.) to Argentina and Bolivia.

LEAST GREEN-KINGFISHER, *Chloroceryle aenea.*   5   Plate 3
FIELD MARKS: Throat, breast, sides, and flanks rufous; female has black
   band across breast.
RANGE: S. Mexico (Oaxaca and e. San Luis Potosí to Chiapas and
   Quintana Roo) to Brazil and Bolivia; tropical lowlands.

MOTMOTS: Momotidae

Forest birds of medium size; their colors are green, blue, and rufous;
their two long middle tail feathers are stripped of their webs for a short
distance, forming a racquet-shaped tip (except for two species). Sexes
are similar. Most often seen sitting upright, occasionally swinging the
tail like a pendulum. Among the first to call in the morning; readily
respond to imitation. Nest in holes in banks.

TODY MOTMOT, *Hylomanes momotula.*   6½   Plate 19
FIELD MARKS: Lacks racquet at end of relatively short tail.
VOICE: "Song" is a series of figures at varying tempo; pitch about C^2.
   A single figure is similar to one of a Ferruginous Pygmy-Owl, but the
   phrase is quite different. The first figure may have a slight burr,
   werb, but this is followed by clear sounds (*cu* or *cuc* figures) at a
   rate of 2 to 3 per sec.. These may continue for 15 to 20 sec., with a
   gradual drop in pitch and a "slow-down" near the end. Just before
   dawn the song usually begins with a slow, measured beat for 3 or 4
   figures and is then accelerated (perhaps 21 figures in next 11 sec.,
   including the terminal slow-down). At times the song suggests a
   slow laugh.
RANGE: Mexico (c. Veracruz and south) to n.w. Colombia.

BLUE-THROATED MOTMOT, *Aspatha gularis.*   11   Plate 19
FIELD MARKS: So closely related to the preceding species that one
   might think they should be placed in the same genus. The only large

Motmot within our range without a racquet-tipped tail and the only one with an extensive blue throat patch.

VOICE: Rather similar to that of the Tody Motmot.

RANGE: Highlands of Chiapas and south to Honduras; favors cliffs and cañons in forests at 6000 to 9000 ft.

KEEL-BILLED MOTMOT, *Electron carinatum.*   12   Plate 19

VOICE: "Song" is a series of low-pitched figures, *daw* (each one drawn out about a half sec.), repeated at two-sec. intervals. Call is a hoarse, vibratory *aw*, something like the *caw* of a crow (as though C^1 and F^1 were sounded simultaneously), or, at times, *ca-daw*.

RANGE: Mexico (humid lowland forests of s. Veracruz, Tabasco, and e. Chiapas) to n. Costa Rica.

BROAD-BILLED MOTMOT, *Electron platyrhynchum.*   11½
Plate 19

FIELD MARKS: Whole head rufous.

VOICE: Similar to last species.

RANGE: Costa Rica to Brazil and Peru; humid tropical and subtropical woods (mostly on Caribbean slope in Central America).

TURQUOISE-BROWED MOTMOT, *Eumomota superciliosa.*   14
Plate 19

FIELD MARKS: Conspicuous turquoise and black trim.

VOICE: Somewhat like that of Keel-billed Motmot, but not so loud and pitched about an octave higher. The *caw*, or *daw*, is held for about a half sec. and is usually repeated after a rest, so that about four will be sounded in ten sec. There are also some faster calls, some of them given in flight. A *keuk-keuk* is pitched about G^1 and takes one sec. for delivery; a rapid *cu-a* is given at the rate of two per sec.; the last is sometimes lengthened to *cuwa* or *uh-cawa*.

RANGE: Mexico (on the Pacific slope of Oaxaca and Chiapas; and from s. Veracruz to Chiapas, Campeche, Yucatán, and Quintana Roo) to n.w., Costa Rica; favors semi-arid woods.

RUFOUS MOTMOT, *Urospatha martii.*   17   Plate 19
   (Considered a race of *Baryphthengus ruficapillus* by some.)

VOICE: The "song" is a bubbling *hu-hu-hu-hu;* this motif is delivered in about one sec. There are also stronger single calls or hoots.

RANGE: E. Nicaragua to the Pacific slope of Colombia and w. Ecuador; favors humid lowlands, but found at times up to 4000 ft.

MEXICAN MOTMOT, *Momotus mexicanus.*   12   Plate 19

VOICE: A quite soft, low *hough* or *huhh,* as though someone were exhaling quickly with the mouth open; the pitch is about F^2; the quality is burry, as though it were an extremely fast roll; the mate will frequently call at almost the same time, but the individual will usually wait five or ten sec. before repeating.

RANGE: Mexico (from s. Sonora and Durango to Chiapas; has been collected as far east as Orizaba, Veracruz); mostly in semi-arid regions.

CHESTNUT-HEADED MOTMOT, *Momotus castaneiceps.* 14
Plate 19

(Considered a race of *M. mexicanus* by some.)

FIELD MARKS: Similar to last species, but crown bright chestnut and black area beneath eye bordered below by greenish white (not blue).

RANGE: Arid region of c. Guatemala.

BLUE-CROWNED MOTMOT, *Momotus coeruliceps.* 16 Plate 19

(Considered a race of *M. momota* by some.)

VOICE: A soft, low, owl- or dove-like *oot-goot*, repeated at four-sec. intervals; pitch F¹. Also a softer, rapid, bubbling *oot-oot-oot-oot-oot*.

RANGE: N.e. Mexico (Tamaulipas, Nuevo León, e. San Luis Potosí to c. Veracruz); in humid woods below 4000 ft.

LESSON MOTMOT, *Momotus lessonii.* 15½ Plate 19

(Considered a race of *M. coeruliceps* by some and of *M. momota* by others.)

RANGE: S. Mexico (s. Veracruz to Chiapas and Yucatán) to w. Panama.

RUFOUS-BELLIED MOTMOT, *Momotus subrufescens.* 15
Plate 19

(Considered a race of *M. momota* by others.)

RANGE: E. Panama to c. Colombia and Venezuela.

JACAMARS: Galbulidae

The slender bodies, brilliant colors, and long thin bills of these birds, as well as the habit of hawking for insects, serve to give one the impression of a giant Hummingbird. They nest in burrows, as do Motmots and Kingfishers.

SALMON'S JACAMAR, *Brachygalba salmoni.* 7 Plate 32

RANGE: E. Panama to c. Colombia.

RUFOUS-TAILED JACAMAR, *Galbula ruficauda.* 9½ Plate 32

FIELD MARKS: Two central tail feathers golden green; chin white.

RANGE: E. Panama (Darien), e. Colombia, and Venezuela to Brazil.

BLACK-CHINNED JACAMAR, *Galbula melanogenia.* 9 Plate 32
(Considered a race of *G. ruficauda* by some.)
FIELD MARKS: Four central tail feathers metallic golden green; chin black; tail longer than wing and graduated.
VOICE: A number of calls suggest those of the Myiarchus Flycatchers. There is a *weep* and numerous longer motifs, such as *weep-eep-eep-ep-ep-e-e-e-e-e,* which begins with a figure like that of a Crested Flycatcher, after which each succeeding figure becomes shorter and the tempo faster until it finally runs into a rattle. There is also a well-accented (almost barking) *queeo-quip-quip-quip-quip-queeo.* This may be varied to three figures that sound like some given by the Olivaceous Flycatcher.
RANGE: Mexico (lowlands in s. Veracruz, Tabasco, and Chiapas) and south to w. Panama (not found in El Salvador).

GREAT JACAMAR, *Jacamerops aurea.* 11 Plate 32
FIELD MARKS: White patch on throat of male but not of female.
RANGE: Caribbean slope of Costa Rica to Guiana and Peru; favors humid virgin forest.

PUFFBIRDS: Bucconidae

Medium-sized forest birds with pointed bills that are somewhat decurved; their plumage is full and lax; they nest in holes after the fashion of Jacamars and Kingfishers and are likely to perch quietly for long periods before darting out to catch an insect or to disappear into the forest. There are two different sub-groups: one (Puffbirds) with quite heavy bills that are sharply decurved at the tip to form a sharp "tooth"; the other with weaker bills without the tooth.

WHITE-NECKED PUFFBIRD, *Notharchus hyperrhynchus.* 9
Plate 19
(Considered a race of *N. macrorhynchos* by others.)
FIELD MARKS: Broad area on forehead (reaching back beyond the middle of the eye), throat, belly, and collar on hindneck white.
RANGE: Mexico (s. Veracruz, e. Oaxaca, Tabasco, Chiapas, and Campeche) and south to Bolivia; also w. Venezuela and w. and s. Brazil; favors fairly open tropical woods, either humid or dry.

BLACK-BREASTED PUFFBIRD, *Notharchus pectoralis.* 8 Plate 19
RANGE: E. Panama to c. Colombia.

PANAMA PUFFBIRD, *Notharchus subtectus.* 6 Plate 19
(Considered a race of *N. tectus* by others.)
RANGE: E. Costa Rica to w. Colombia and Ecuador.

BARRED PUFFBIRD, *Nystalus radiatus.*   8   Plate 19
RANGE: C. Panama to w. Ecuador.

PANAMA SOFTWING, *Malacoptila panamensis.*   7   Plate 19
FIELD MARKS: Feathers on jaw at each side of chin are white and elon-
   gated and form a limp tuft.
RANGE: S. Mexico (Tabasco) to w. Ecuador.

LANCEOLATED MONKLET, *Micromonacha lanceolata.*   5
                                                                    Plate 19
RANGE: Costa Rica to w. Brazil and Peru.

GRAY-CHEEKED NUNLET, *Nonnula frontalis.*   5½   Plate 19
RANGE: E. Panama to c. Colombia.

COSTA RICAN NUNBIRD, *Monasa grandier.*   11   Plate 19
   (Considered a race of *M. morphoeus* by others.)
FIELD MARKS: Forehead, lores, and chin white in adults (rusty in
   young); jaw adjacent to chin black; hindneck slate gray.
RANGE: S.e. Honduras to n.w. Panama; humid Caribbean lowlands.

GOLDMAN'S NUNBIRD, *Monasa fidelis*   10   Plate 19
   (Considered a race of *M. morphoeus* by others.)
FIELD MARKS: Similar to last species, but the jaw area next to chin
   (in adults) is white; hindneck and chest black. Black extends farther down on breast and sides than in previous species. A few birds
   found with black chins are believed to be hybrids with following
   species.
RANGE: E. Panama (Canal Zone, Cerro Azul, and Chepo region).

PALE-WINGED NUNBIRD, *Monasa pallescens.*   11   Plate 19
   (Considered a race of *M. morphoeus* by others.)
FIELD MARKS: Chin black; wing-coverts pale gray.
RANGE: S.e. Panama and n.w. Colombia.

BARBETS: Capitonidae

Forest birds related to both Woodpeckers and Toucans; the bill is
stout and shorter than the head; the tail is shorter than the wing; they
eat berries and insects and nest in holes in trees.

SPOTTED-CROWNED BARBET, *Capito maculicoronatus.*   6
                                                                    Plate 30
FIELD MARKS: Male has throat and belly white; breast band yellow.
   Female is largely black with a yellow or red flank patch.
RANGE: E. Panama to w. Colombia.

PRONG-BILLED BARBET, *Semnornis frantzii.* 6½   Plate 30
FIELD MARKS: Plumage rather plain; male has black tuft on back of head.
RANGE: Humid highlands of Costa Rica and w. Panama.

RED-HEADED BARBET, *Eubucco bourcierii.* 6   Plate 30
FIELD MARKS: Female has forehead black, ear spot grayish blue, and throat grayish yellow.
RANGE: Highlands of Costa Rica to w. Venezuela and Peru.

TOUCANS: Ramphastidae

Forest birds with highly specialized bills that, though greatly inflated and several times longer than the head, are very light (a hollow shell made quite strong by fiber-like reinforcements within). They are frequently found in small flocks, feeding along the tree tops; the food consists largely of fruit, but eggs and young of other birds are often taken; they nest in abandoned woodpecker holes or in other cavities in trees.

EMERALD TOUCANET, *Aulacorhynchus prasinus.* 14   Plate 12
VOICE: Varies from a low, guttural croak to a high-pitched staccato bark. When given in series, the low croaks may be given at the start at a rate of about eight in five sec.; the tempo and pitch may go up until ten to twelve of the "barks" (*wac*) are given in five sec. and the pitch reaches about B².
RANGE: S.e. Mexico (e. San Luis Potosí, Veracruz to Chiapas) to n. Nicaragua; typically a cloud-forest bird.

WAGLER'S TOUCANET, *Aulacorhynchus wagleri.* 14   Plate 12
(Considered a race of *A. prasinus* by some.)
FIELD MARKS: Similar to the last species but forehead much lighter than crown and has a different bill pattern.
RANGE: S.w. Mexico (mts. in Guerrero and w. Oaxaca).

BLUE-THROATED TOUCANET, *Aulacorhynchus caeruleogularis.*
                                                     12   Plate 12
(Considered a race of *A. prasinus* by some.)
FIELD MARKS: Spot near base of upper bill chestnut or black.
RANGE: Highlands of Costa Rica and Panama.

COLLARED ARACARI, *Pteroglossus torquatus.* 16   Plate 12
VOICE: The thin, shrill call is composed of two hurried figures that are a fourth apart (sometimes probably only a third apart); the pitch is about F⁴ for the first figure and B⁴ for the second. The call requires no more than one-quarter sec.; it is so hurried that it sounds almost

like a squeak or the chirp of an insect; various words or sounds have been used to describe it, such as *we-zit, wee-tit,* or *wich-it,* but the call is best imitated by whistling the figures.

RANGE: S. Mexico (Pacific slope in Oaxaca and Chiapas; Veracruz to Chiapas and Quintana Roo) to Venezuela and Colombia; favors humid lowland woods, but is sometimes found in woods that are only slightly moist and up to 5000 ft.

FRANTZIUS' ARACARI, *Pteroglossus frantzii.*   13   Plate 12
(Considered a race of *P. torquatus* by some.)
FIELD MARKS: Upper bill largely bright orange.
RANGE: S.w. Costa Rica and w. Panama (replaces previous species).

CASSIN ARACARI, *Selenidera spectabilis.*   14   Plate 12
FIELD MARKS: Male has tuft of yellow feathers near ear region.
RANGE: From s.e. Honduras to w. Colombia; favors humid tropics, but at times is found up into the "subtropical" zone.

KEEL-BILLED TOUCAN, *Ramphastos sulfuratus.*   18   Plate 12
VOICE: A long series of calls something like that of the Emerald Tou-
canet but of quite different quality and pitch. At the start of a series the sound may be hoarse and the tempo slow, but it will quickly work up to a steady rate of between one and a half and two figures per sec. at a pitch of about F^3 (sometimes on up to G^3 or even A^3). The hoarse figures may be represented as *crunch* and the others as *creet.* This *creet* might be said to resemble the call of a tree frog or a cricket or some other insect.
RANGE: Tropical Mexico (e. San Luis Potosí, Veracruz, Oaxaca, Ta-
basco, Chiapas to Yucatán) to w. Venezuela and Colombia (not found in El Salvador); humid lowlands up to 3000 ft.

SWAINSON'S TOUCAN, *Ramphastos swainsonii.*   20   Plate 12
(The similar Black-billed Toucan, *R. ambiguus,* once erroneously reported near the Colombian border of Panama, is shown on Plate 12; it might yet be found.)
RANGE: S. Honduras to Venezuela and w. Ecuador.

WOODPECKERS: Picidae

OLIVACEOUS PICULET, *Picumnus olivaceus.*   4   Plate 22
FIELD MARKS: Lacks prop feathers in tail; crown black dotted with white and in male also with orange.
RANGE: E. Guatemala to Venezuela and Ecuador.

RED-SHAFTED FLICKER, *Colaptes cafer.* 11
(Considered a race of *C. auratus* by some.)
RANGE: W. North America to Isthmus of Tehuantepec; mostly in oak-pine regions in the mts., but also in the semi-deserts of the high interior basins; also a winter visitor in the coastal lowlands of n.e. Mexico.

MEXICAN FLICKER, *Colaptes mexicanoides.* 11   Plate 20
(Considered a race of *C. cafer* by some.)
FIELD MARKS: Similar to Red-shafted Flicker, but the cap and the hindneck are cinnamon-rufous instead of grayish brown; adult male has a red mustache line with black marks on it; the female has a cinnamon mustache line.
RANGE: Mexico (highlands below the Isthmus of Tehuantepec), Guatemala, El Salvador, Honduras, and Nicaragua.

YELLOW-SHAFTED FLICKER, *Colaptes auratus.* 11
RANGE: E. North America; Mexico (rare winter visitor in n.e. Tamaulipas).

GILDED FLICKER, *Colaptes chrysoides.* 11
(Considered a race of *C. auratus* by some.)
RANGE: Arid regions in s.w. United States and n.w. Mexico (Baja California, Sonora, and n.w. Sinaloa).

SPOTTED-BREASTED WOODPECKER, *Chrysoptilus punctigula.*
8½   Plate 20
RANGE: E. Panama to w. Brazil and n. Bolivia.

GRAY-CROWNED WOODPECKER, *Piculus auricularis.* 8
Plate 20
RANGE: Highland oak-pine woods of w. Mexico (except Baja California) southward to Guerrero.

LICHTENSTEIN WOODPECKER, *Piculus aeruginosus.* 9 Plate 20
(Considered a race of *P. rubiginosus* by some.)
FIELD MARKS: Largely green with a gray crown bordered behind by a red patch that extends forward as a border to the crown until it reaches the back angle of the eye in males (on the nape only in females).
VOICE: The call is a sharp, Flicker-like *keeo*, or *keeer* (pitch C^4 or a bit higher), which is slightly nasal and which is almost identical with the "Flicker call" of the Ivory-billed Woodhewer. There is also a softer roll or repercussion (might carelessly be called a rattle or even a "trill" by some) that lasts about one and a half sec. The roll holds rather well to one pitch but swells somewhat in volume near the

middle. This roll may be confused with the song of the Thin-billed
Woodhewer, but the latter contains scarcely more than half as many
figures per sec.

RANGE: N.e. Mexico (Tamaulipas, s. Nuevo León, n. Veracruz, e. San
Luis Potosí, e. Puebla, and Oaxaca; from sea level up to 6000 ft.).

GREEN WOODPECKER, *Piculus rubiginosus.*   8   Plate 20
FIELD MARKS: So similar to last species that many will prefer to call
both Green Woodpeckers. In the present form the red border to the
gray crown patch in the male continues on from the eye to the lores
or thereabouts; the yellow bars on the chest are somewhat narrower
and sharper.

RANGE: S. Mexico (c. Veracruz to Chiapas and Yucatán) to Argentina
and Bolivia; favors the subtropical region in the mts.

PANAMA WOODPECKER, *Piculus callopterus.*   7   Plate 20
(Considered a race of *P. leucolaemus* by some.)
FIELD MARKS: Line below eye dull buffy white; throat barred.
RANGE: E. Panama.

BUGABA WOODPECKER, *Piculus simplex.*   7   Plate 20
RANGE: Honduras to w. Panama; uncommon; favors upper tropical
zone but ranges into the subtropical.

BRONZE WOODPECKER, *Piculus chrysochloros.*   8   Plate 20
FIELD MARKS: Chin and throat immaculate orange yellow.
RANGE: E. Panama to Brazil and Bolivia.

CHESTNUT-COLORED WOODPECKER, *Celeus castaneus.*   9
                                                              Plate 20
FIELD MARKS: Yellowish brown crest; red cheeks in male.
VOICE: The call may be represented by *queeo-yayaya.* The *queeo* is
a relatively soft, mellow "whistle" lasting about a half sec.; it begins
at about F^3 and is slurred down to D^3. The first figure is accented;
the *yayaya* is softer and faster and has a suggestion of nasal quality.
Together with the infinitesimal pause after the *queeo*, the *yayaya* requires a half sec.; this makes the complete motif about one sec.
long. The drumming is also moderate in volume; there are about
twelve taps per sec.

RANGE: Mexico (c. Veracruz and e. Oaxaca to Chiapas and Yucatán)
to n.w. Panama.

CINNAMON WOODPECKER, *Celeus loricatus.*   8   Plate 20
RANGE: S.e. Nicaragua to w. Ecuador; favors humid lowland forests.

WHITE-BILLED WOODPECKER, *Dryocopus scapularis.* 12
Plate 21

(Considered a race of *D. lineatus* by some.)

VOICE: The song phrase is something like that of the Pileated Woodpecker of the United States; it consists of a series of about twenty figures given in four sec. A figure may be likened to *quee;* the pitch is about E^3 There is frequently a drop in pitch at the end so that the last figure may be shown as *quah;* there is a slight swell in volume near the middle of the phrase. A call that is a high, sharp *peek* or *pip* is frequently followed by a low rattle, as *cuchurrrrrr.* The drum is loud and distinct—about 20 taps in one and three quarters sec.

RANGE: Mexico (Sonora south to Guerrero and w. Oaxaca; Nuevo León and Tamaulipas to Chiapas and Yucatán) to n. Costa Rica.

LINEATED WOODPECKER, *Dryocopus lineatus.* 12½   Plate 21

RANGE: S. Costa Rica (overlaps range of preceding species over a wide area, and some hybrids are found; however pure forms are found in the same habitat) to n. Argentina and Bolivia.

LEWIS' WOODPECKER, *Asyndesmus lewis.* 10

RANGE: W. North America; winters to n.w. Mexico.

ANT-EATING WOODPECKER, *Melanerpes formicivorus.* 8

RANGE: W. United States to w. Panama; also Colombia; usually found in the pine-oak region of the mts., but at times down to sea level in Mexico.

GENUS *CENTURUS*: Back regularly barred with black and white; rump white; a narrow white band shows on the wing in flight; no black band running back from eye; males have red crowns and females gray crowns; voices rather similar in all species. This genus is lumped with *Melanerpes* by some authors.

GRAY-BREASTED WOODPECKER, *Centurus hypopolius.* 8
Plate 20

FIELD MARKS: Front white (varies to brownish gray in some birds—probably immatures); a quite narrow black area around eye that may not be visible at a distance; a partially hidden red spot on the face below the eye may be visible under very favorable conditions; nape drab (no red or yellow).

RANGE: S.w. Mexico (Morelos, Guerrero, Mexico, Puebla, and Oaxaca).

GILA WOODPECKER, *Centurus uropygialis.* 8½
(Considered a race of *C. hypopolius* by some.)
RANGE: W. United States and n.w. Mexico (Baja California, Sonora,
Chihuahua, and south to Jalisco; mostly in semi-desert regions).

GOLDEN-CHEEKED WOODPECKER, *Centurus chrysogenys.* 8½
                                                                       Plate 20
FIELD MARKS: A black ring around the eye is enlarged considerably
at the top; resembles Golden-fronted Woodpecker in having a yellow nape and relatively wide white bars on the back.
RANGE: W. Mexico (Sinaloa to Oaxaca).

UXMAL WOODPECKER, *Centurus dubius.* 9   Plate 20
(Considered a race of *C. aurifrons* by some.)
FIELD MARKS: Prefrontal region (nasal tufts) red; white bars on back
much narrower than the black interspaces (this gives the back a
dark appearance); central tail feathers black. In areas where the
range of this species overlaps that of any of the next three species,
some hybrids will be found.
RANGE: S.e. Mexico (Veracruz and adjacent e. Oaxaca, Tabasco, n.e.
Chiapas, Campeche, Yucatán, and Quintana Roo; Cozumel Is.), n.
British Honduras, and n.e. Guatemala.

SANTACRUZ WOODPECKER, *Centurus santacruzi.* 9   Plate 20
(Considered a race of *C. aurifrons* by some.)
FIELD MARKS: Similar to the previous species in having the narrow
white bars on the back (hence, the two make up a Narrow-barred
Woodpecker species group and may be so listed by those who prefer to lump them); nasal tufts and belly yellow; central tail feathers
largely black but may show a few white bars. There may be hybrids
in areas of overlap with other species of the genus to the north and
west (these hybrids may show a gray area between the red of the
crown and the orange red of the nape instead of a smooth blend of
colors).
RANGE: S. Mexico (s.e. Chiapas), Guatemala, El Salvador, s. British
Honduras, Honduras, and n. Nicaragua.

GOLDEN-FRONTED WOODPECKER, *Centurus aurifrons.* 9
FIELD MARKS: White bars on back about as wide as the black interspaces; a gray band separates the red crown patch in the male from
the yellow area on the nape; the central tail feathers are black. There
are hybrids of this form and the Uxmal Woodpecker in s. Tamaulipas, e. San Luis Potosí, and n. Veracruz.
RANGE: Texas to Mexico (Durango across to Tamaulipas and south to
Michoacán, San Luis Potosí, and Hidalgo).

OAXACA WOODPECKER, *Centurus polygrammus.* 9   Plate 20
(Listed as a race of *C. aurifrons* by some.)
FIELD MARKS: Similar to last species, except that the central tail feathers are largely white instead of black, and the white bars on the back may be somewhat narrower; belly yellow; the gray area on back of crown may be almost, if not completely, obsolete in a few cases. (*C. aurifrons* and *C. polygrammus* make up the Golden-fronted Woodpecker species group.)
RANGE: S.w. Mexico (Pacific slope in Oaxaca and c. and w. Chiapas).

HOFFMANN WOODPECKER, *Centurus hoffmanni.* 7   Plate 20
(Considered a race of *C. aurifrons* by some.)
FIELD MARKS: Similar to last species, but much smaller; central tail feathers black barred with white; underparts darker; belly yellow.
RANGE: S.w. Honduras to n.w. and c. Costa Rica; dry woods.

YUCATAN WOODPECKER, *Centurus pygmaeus.* 6½   Plate 20
RANGE: Yucatán peninsula and Cozumel Island; Bonacca Island.

WAGLER'S WOODPECKER, *Centurus rubricapillus.* 6½   Plate 20
RANGE: Costa Rica (open areas in humid woods of southwest from sea level up to 4500 ft.), Panama, Venezuela, and Colombia.

PUCHERAN'S WOODPECKER, *Tripsurus pucherani.* 7½   Plate 20
(Listed in genus *Centurus* by some and *Melanerpes* by others.)
FIELD MARKS: Members of this genus have a black line running back from eye down side of neck. In this species the male has the crown and nape red (nape only in female); sides and flanks yellow, more or less barred with black.
RANGE: Mexico (s. Veracruz, Puebla, Oaxaca, Tabasco, and e. Chiapas), e. Guatemala, British Honduras, e. Honduras, Caribbean slope in Nicaragua, and Costa Rica to w. Ecuador.

GOLDEN-NAPED WOODPECKER, *Tripsurus chrysauchen.* 7
Plate 20
(Listed in genus *Centurus* by some and *Melanerpes* by others.)
RANGE: S.w. Costa Rica and w. Panama.

YELLOW-BELLIED SAPSUCKER, *Sphyrapicus varius.* 7½
RANGE: North America; winters through Mexico to Panama.

RED-NAPED SAPSUCKER, *Sphyrapicus nuchalis.* 7½
(Usually listed as a race of *S. varius.*)
RANGE: W. United States; in winter in w. Mexico.

RED-BREASTED SAPSUCKER, *Sphyrapicus ruber.* 7½
(Considered a race of *S. varius* by some.)
RANGE: Pacific coast of North America; winters to Baja California.

WILLIAMSON SAPSUCKER, *Sphyrapicus thyroideus.* 8
RANGE: W. North America; winters to w. Mexico.

BROWN WOODPECKER, *Veniliornis fumigatus.* 6½ Plate 20
FIELD MARKS: Ear region, chin, and throat white or pale grayish brown;
back tawny olive, at times tinged red; female lacks red on head.
RANGE: Mexico (Nayarit and Jalisco; s.w. Tamaulipas, e. San Luis
Potosí, to Chiapas and Yucatán) to Venezuela, n.w. Argentina,
and Bolivia.

RED-RUMPED WOODPECKER, *Veniliornis kirkii.* 6 Plate 20
FIELD MARKS: Underparts pale brown or grayish white, barred with
dark grayish brown. Red rump is usually hidden by wings.
RANGE: S. Costa Rica to Venezuela and Ecuador; favors humid tropical forest.

HAIRY WOODPECKER, *Dendrocopos villosus.* 7
RANGE: North America and mts. of Mexico (Baja California across to
Tamaulipas and south to Chiapas) to w. Panama; mostly from
5000 to 10000 ft. in south.

NUTTALL WOODPECKER, *Dendrocopos nuttallii.* 7
RANGE: Upper Sonoran Life Zone in California and Baja California.

LADDER-BACKED WOODPECKER, *Dendrocopos scalaris.* 6
RANGE: S.w. United States, Mexico, British Honduras, and e. Honduras;
favors semi-arid regions.

ARIZONA WOODPECKER, *Dendrocopos arizonae.* 7
RANGE: Mts. of s.w. United States and w. Mexico (Sonora and Chihuahua to Michoacán).

STRICKLAND WOODPECKER, *Dendrocopos stricklandi.* 6½
Plate 20
FIELD MARKS: Similar to Arizona Woodpecker, but the male has top
of head red as well as nape, and the back is barred.
RANGE: Mts. of c. Mexico (Michoacán, Puebla, and Veracruz).

GENUS, *CAMPEPHILUS:* Birds of this specialized group are set
apart by a peculiar behavior character: they use a loud double rap
in lieu of the usual drumming of other woodpeckers. They are relatively large birds, and most of them have ivory-colored bills.

GUATEMALAN IVORYBILL, *Campephilus guatemalensis.* 13
Plate 21

(Listed in genus *Phloeoceastes* by some.)
FIELD MARKS: Whole head and crest in male is red (in female the forehead and front of crest is black); white lines starting just below
the head run down either side of the neck and continue on down to
the middle of the back where they meet to form a narrow V.
VOICE: There is a loud call that may be represented by *ka ka ka ka-
dacky;* It sounds something like a squirrel barking or may suggest a
chicken cackling. There is another call that resembles somewhat
that of a Nuthatch.
RANGE: Mexico (Sonora to Oaxaca; Tamaulipas and e. San Luis Potosí to Chiapas and Yucatán) to w. Panama.

MALHERBE'S WOODPECKER, *Campephilus malherbii.* 13
Plate 21

(Listed as a race of *Phloeoceastes melanoleucos* by some.)
FIELD MARKS: Similar to last species, but the bill, chin, and throat are
black; there is a spot of white at the base of the bill (in the female a
white line runs along the cheek from the white spot to the white
line on the neck). A spot near ear is black (above) and white.
RANGE: Panama (c. Bocas del Toro and c. Chiriquí eastward) to w.
Venezuela and n. Colombia.

SPLENDID WOODPECKER, *Campephilus splendens.* 12 Plate 21
(Listed as a race of *Phloeoceastes haematogaster* by some.)
FIELD MARKS: Lower foreneck and breast red.
RANGE: Panama, c. and w. Colombia, and n.w. Ecuador.

IMPERIAL IVORYBILL, *Campephilus imperialis.* 22 Plate 21
RANGE: Restricted to virgin pine forests of n.w. Mexico; probably present only in s.w. Durango and n.e. Nayarit if not exterminated.

WOODHEWERS : Dendrocolapidae

Forest birds adapted for climbing tree trunks; the tails are graduated
and stiff pointed so as to make good props. They are various shades
of brown and have cinnamon-rufous or chestnut tails. They are closely
related to the tropical Ovenbirds—the coloration in many species is
similar, and even some of the habits are alike. They resemble Creep-
ers somewhat in coloration and in the manner of tree climbing, although they are not closely related to that family. They resemble
Woodpeckers in voice in some cases and also in some habits (some of
them tap or hammer on tree trunks or decayed wood). They nest in
abandoned Woodpecker holes or natural cavities or occasionally in
burrows in banks that have been abandoned by Motmots. Most of

them have distinctive calls; however, a few calls so closely resemble those of certain Woodpeckers that they may not be safely used for identification by man. In searching for food, some species fly to the base of a tree and rather rapidly work up the trunk and then out the branches (which they work both top and bottom), after which they drop down to the base of another tree; however, they are able to back down a trunk when they desire. Some occasionally feed on the ground.

TAWNY-WINGED WOODHEWER, *Dendrocincla anabatina.* 7

Plate 22

FIELD MARKS: Bill as long as head, rather stout and nearly straight (tip of upper bill slopes down giving a slightly decurved effect); streak back of eye, chin, and throat pale buff; wing dark brown with contrasting tawny secondaries.

RANGE: Mexico (s. Veracruz, Oaxaca, Tabasco, Chiapas, Campeche, Yucatán, and Quintana Roo; mostly at low elevation but sometimes up to 2000 ft.) and south to w. Panama (not found in El Salvador).

RIDGWAY'S WOODHEWER, *Dendrocincla ridgwayi.* 8   Plate 22
(Considered a race of *D. meruloides* by some and of *D. fuliginosa* by others.)

FIELD MARKS: Wing-coverts brown; primaries more rufescent; throat buffy gray.

RANGE: S.e. Honduras to w. Ecuador; in humid tropical forest.

RUDDY WOODHEWER, *Dendrocincla homochroa.* 7   Plate 22

RANGE: Mexico (Oaxaca, Campeche, Yucatán, and Quintana Roo; in cool subtropical regions in mts. except in the Yucatán Peninsula) to w. Venezuela and Colombia.

CHERRIE'S WOODHEWER, *Deconychura typica.* 7½   Plate 22
(Considered a race of *D. longicauda* by some.)

FIELD MARKS: Back, rump, and wing-coverts olive brown; tail, upper tail-coverts, and secondaries chestnut; chest dark olive, spotted buff.

RANGE: S.e. Honduras to n.w. Colombia.

MEXICAN WOODHEWER, *Sittasomus sylvioides.* 6   Plate 22
(Listed as a race of *S. griseicapillus* by others.)

FIELD MARKS: Bill straight, noticeably shorter than head and rather slender; head olive gray; underparts lighter gray.

VOICE: A forced buzz or fast rattle, rising slightly in pitch at the start and then descending rapidly. The song phrase lasts about one sec.

RANGE: Mexico (s.w. Tamaulipas and e. San Luis Potosí to Chiapas and Yucatán; Jalisco to Oaxaca) to n.e. Colombia.

WEDGE-BILLED WOODHEWER, *Glyphorynchus spirurus.* 5½

Plate 22

FIELD MARKS: Bill much shorter than head; crown dark brown; line over eye buffy white; throat buff; chest spotted with pale buff. These birds hammer vigorously on the trunks of thin-barked trees, knocking off bark (pieces an inch or two across) in just a few sec.

RANGE: Mexico (e. Veracruz and south) and south to Brazil and Bolivia (not found in El Salvador).

GUATEMALAN WOODHEWER, *Xiphocolaptes emigrans.* 12

Plate 21

(Considered a race of *X. promeropirhynchus* by some.)

FIELD MARKS: Bill longer than head, stout, slightly decurved, and light horn color with a dusky base.

VOICE: The song phrase is a series of motifs given at a rate of about ten in five and a half sec. The main figure of the motif, which is strongly accented, may be called *wowk,* or *wack;* the first three or four motifs in the phrase may have a short, soft, preliminary figure, *oo,* in effect something like a person saying *ah* before speaking a word; at the end of the *wack* there is a short figure, *ee,* like a person quickly drawing in breath. After the first three or four motifs the preliminary *oo* is excluded and the final figure, *ee,* is lengthened to *eety* so that the motif becomes *wackety.* The terminal motif in the phrase is a simpler, but strongly accented, *wack.* The pitch of the *oo* is about C⁴; the *wack* is the next tone up; the *ee* is the next tone, E⁴; the *eety* is D⁴ sharp E⁴. A full song phrase might be represented as *ooWackee-ooWackee-ooWackee-ooWackee-Wackity-Wackity-Wackity-Wackity-Wack.* (Main motif could be *Riperty.*)

RANGE: Mexico (cloud forests and pine woods of Guerrero; e. San Luis Potosí, Veracruz, Oaxaca and Chiapas) to c. Costa Rica.

BARRED WOODHEWER, *Dendrocolaptes sanctithomae.* 10

Plate 22

(Listed as a race of *D. certhia* by others.)

VOICE: The "song" phrase is made up of a series of softly and slowly "whistled" figures, each with a rising inflection (something like that used to call a dog). An individual figure requires about a half sec. at the slowest tempo, and there may be as much as one sec. rest before it is repeated; it could be called a whistled *wert.* The pitch is about F³ at start, but the rising inflection makes it end a tone or tone and a half higher; the tempo varies somewhat, and there may be seven or eight figures in a phrase of five sec.

RANGE: Mexico (humid forests of c. Veracruz and Oaxaca to Campeche and Quintana Roo; also Pacific lowlands of Chiapas) to w. Panama.

BLACK-BANDED WOODHEWER, *Dendrocolaptes picumnus* 10
Plate 22
RANGE: S. Mexico (s. Chiapas) to Argentina and Bolivia; wet forest
in mts. (above range of previous species).

LIGHT-THROATED WOODHEWER, *Dendroplex picirostris.* 8
Plate 22
(Listed as *Xiphorhynchus picus* by others.)
RANGE: Semi-arid regions of c. Panama (Pacific slope), n. Venezuela,
and Colombia.

BUFF-THROATED WOODHEWER, *Xiphorhynchus guttatus.* 9
Plate 22
FIELD MARKS: Bill slightly longer than head, the lower bill straight;
wing-coverts same color as back and unstreaked.
VOICE: The song phrase is similar to that of the Ivory-billed Woodhewer in form, tempo, and length (though sometimes tending to be
much longer), but the individual figures have a rising inflection more
nearly like that of the Barred Woodhewer.
RANGE: Guatemala, Honduras, Nicaragua, Costa Rica, and Panama and
south to Brazil and Bolivia; favors humid lowland forests.

IVORY-BILLED WOODHEWER, *Xiphorhynchus flavigaster.* 9¼
Plate 22
FIELD MARKS: Similar to last species but with black-edged buff streaks
on the wing-coverts. The upper bill is variable in color.
VOICE: The song phrase is a series of loud, clear, liquid figures delivered rapidly but varying in pitch, volume, and tempo. The pitch
varies from about G^3 up to E^4, the volume varies at least fifty percent, and at the slowest tempo the figures are about twice the duration as at the opposite extreme. Length of phrase varies from five to
ten sec. There may be twenty figures in a five-sec. song phrase and
as many as sixty in a ten-sec. phrase. A short phrase reaches its peak
pitch, fastest tempo, and greatest volume in the first sec., and after
holding steady for a short time will gradually fade and slow down as
the pitch drops at the end (it might be represented as *ee-ee-ee-ee-
er-er-err-err-errrr*). A longer phrase might swell in volume again
after a "slowdown." There are also some short calls. One is a sharp,
Flicker-like figure almost identical to the call of the Green Woodpecker. Also, there is a loud, sharp *kleeo*, or *cheeo*, or *keeyo;* this begins at about E^4 and slides down to D^4 and lasts about one half sec.
RANGE: Mexico (s.e. Sonora through Guerrero to Oaxaca; e. Tamaulipas and San Luis Potosí south to Chiapas and Yucatán; from sea
level up to about 4000 ft.) to n.w. Costa Rica.

BLACK-STRIPED WOODHEWER, *Xiphorhynchus lachrymosus.*
9¼   Plate 22

RANGE: Nicaragua to n.w. Ecuador; favors humid lowland forests.

SPOTTED WOODHEWER, *Xiphorhynchus erythropygius.*   9
Plate 22

(Considered a race of *X. triangularis* by some.)

FIELD MARKS: Crown and back marked plainly with small buff streaks; throat buff, the feathers tipped with olive causing a barred effect; breast and belly spotted with buff.

VOICE: The "song" phrase is a series of soft, almost plaintive, "whistled" figures; usually three or four, each one weaker in volume than the preceding so that the fourth fades away entirely. The quality is between that of the Crested Flycatcher (*weep*) and the Olivaceous Flycatcher; there is a rest of about a sec. between figures. The louder first figure is also used as a call.

RANGE: Mexico (humid mt. forests or cloud forests in Guerrero; e. San Luis Potosí to Chiapas), Guatemala, and Honduras.

SPOTTED-THROATED WOODHEWER
Xiphorhynchus punctigulua.   8½   Plate 22

(Considered a race of *X. erythropygius* by some.)

FIELD MARKS: Similar to Spotted Woodhewer, but crown and back not plainly streaked with buff and the throat spotted rather than barred with dusky olive.

RANGE: Humid, subtropical woods of s. Nicaragua to n.w. Colombia.

WHITE-STRIPED WOODHEWER, *Lepidocolaptes leucogaster.*   9
Plate 22

FIELD MARKS: Bill longer than head and noticeably decurved.

VOICE: A short, thin, high-pitched rattle.

RANGE: W. and c. Mexico (Sonora and Durango to Oaxaca; San Luis Potosí to c. Veracruz; mostly from 5000 to 8000 ft. in oak, pine, and fir woods).

THIN-BILLED WOODHEWER, *Leptidocolaptes compressus.*   7½
Plate 22

(Considered a race of *L. souleyetii* by some.)

FIELD MARKS: Feathers of crown and nape marked with a center streak of buff and edged with black; breast tricolored.

VOICE: The "song" phrase is a rattle of about twenty-six figures that lasts about two sec. (it may be a bit faster and up to 31 figures in length so that it is a buzz). The pitch of the introductory figure (which is held longer than the others) is near C^5; the remainder are lower in pitch (A^4 flat); the last figure seems to fall a bit. The phrase might be represented as *quee-hee-hee-hee-hee-hee-hee-heh*. The tempo is so fast that one will not notice the slight differences in pitch unless one listens carefully.

RANGE: Mexico (Guerrero to Oaxaca; c. Veracruz to Chiapas; in humid woods from sea level up to 3000 ft.) to w. Panama.

STRIPED-CROWNED WOODHEWER, *Lepidocolaptes lineaticeps.*
8   Plate 22

(Listed as *L. souleyetii* by some.)

FIELD MARKS: Crown and nape dark brown, streaked with pale fulvous.

RANGE: E. Panama to Brazil and Peru.

ALLIED WOODHEWER, *Lepidocolaptes affinis.*   8   Plate 22

FIELD MARKS: Crown dark brown, feathers edged with black and marked with a center spot of dull buff (in dark woods may appear plain brown); back and wing-coverts brown; throat buff; breast tri-colored.

VIOCE: There is a low call, *yseeyup,* and a louder *huip* (the latter something like the call of a Hairy Woodpecker). The "song" phrase is a rattle of about nineteen figures delivered in one and three-fourths sec.; there is a drop in pitch during each of the last four or five figures, and the tempo is retarded.

RANGE: Mexico (Guerrero to Oaxaca and Chiapas; s.w. Tamaulipas and San Luis Potosí to Veracruz and Chiapas; from 3000 to 8000 ft. in humid oak-pine woods or cloud forest) to w. Panama.

VENEZUELAN WOODHEWER, *Campylorhamphus venezuelensis.*
9   Plate 21

(Considered a race of *C. trochilirostris* by some.)

FIELD MARKS: Bill much longer than head, strongly arched (cycle-shaped), and reddish brown; primaries and tail feathers chestnut.

RANGE: E. Panama, n. Colombia, and Venezuela.

COSTA RICAN WOODHEWER, *Campylorhamphus borealis.*   9
Plate 21

(Considered a race of *C. pusillus* by some.)

RANGE: Costa Rica and w. Panama; favors humid woods, mostly in mts.

OVENBIRDS: Furnariidae

This family is composed of a number of subgroups of rather different appearance and habits; all are more closely related to the Woodhewers than to any other family, and some of them look and act like Wood-hewers while others look and act more nearly like Antbirds. None are related to the North American Ovenbird, which is a Warbler.

SPINETAIL SUBFAMILY

SYNALLAXIS. Short-billed (two-thirds as long as head), long-tailed (one and one-third times as long as wing) birds that always have some cinnamon-rufous color (except in the young). The tail is graduated, and the long central feathers are usually tapered to a point. They are usually found working their way through low, dense shrubbery and are seldom seen more than three feet above the ground.

PALE-BREASTED SYNALLAXIS, *Synallaxis albescens.* 5 Plate 23
RANGE: Costa Rica to Brazil and Bolivia; favors savanna regions.

SOOTY SYNALLAXIS, *Synallaxis brachyura.* 5¼ Plate 23
RANGE: Honduras to Brazil and Ecuador; avoids forest.

RUFOUS-BREASTED SYNALLAXIS, *Synallaxis erythrothorax.* 5½
Plate 23
VOICE: The usual song phrase requires about one sec. for delivery and may be represented as *ka-ka-key-keh*. It is repeated after a pause of about one sec. The pitch is about C^4 for the first two figures, the third figure is a bit higher (D^4 sharp) and accented, and the last figure drops down to A^3. A seldom heard "dawn song" is somewhat similar but has some extra figures in the phrase.
RANGE: S. Mexico (c. Veracruz to Chiapas and Yucatán) and British Honduras to Honduras.

RED-FACED SPINETAIL, *Cranioleuca erythrops.* 5½ Plate 23
FIELD MARKS: Behavior is the most noticeable difference between this bird and a *Synallaxis*. The Spinetail is most likely to be found no lower that six feet above the ground. (The Rusty-backed Spinetail, *C. vulpina,* which is shown on Plate 23, is found on Coiba Island off the Pacific coast of Panama and might possibly appear on the mainland sometimes.)
RANGE: Costa Rica to w. Ecuador; favors "edge" in cloud forest.

DOUBLE-BANDED SOFTTAIL, *Xenerpestes minilosi.* 4½ Plate 23
FIELD MARKS: The tail is rounded in this genus.
RANGE: E. Panama and Colombia.

TREERUNNER SUBFAMILY

BEAUTIFUL TREERUNNER, *Margarornis bellulus.* 5 Plate 23
FIELD MARKS: Birds of this group act like and resemble Woodhewers.
RANGE: E. Panama; mts.

PLATE 1

PLATE 2

PLATE 3

PLATE 4

PLATE 5

PLATE 6

PLATE 7

PLATE 8

PLATE 9

PLATE 10

PLATE 11

PLATE 12

PLATE 13

PLATE 14

PLATE 15

PLATE 16

PLATE 17

PLATE 18

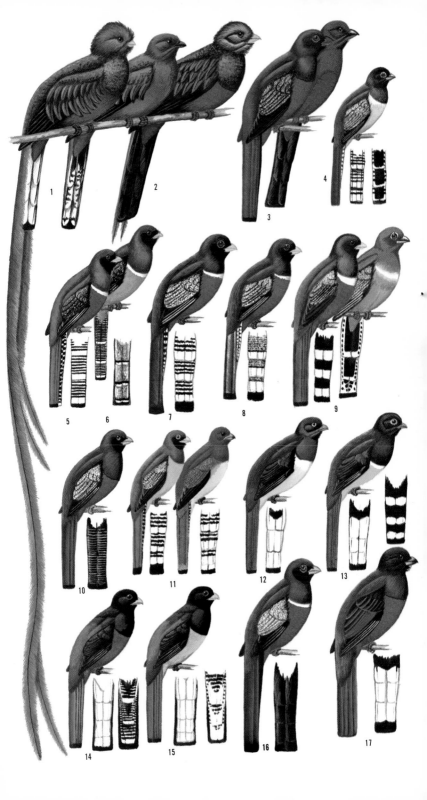

PLATE 19

PLATE 20

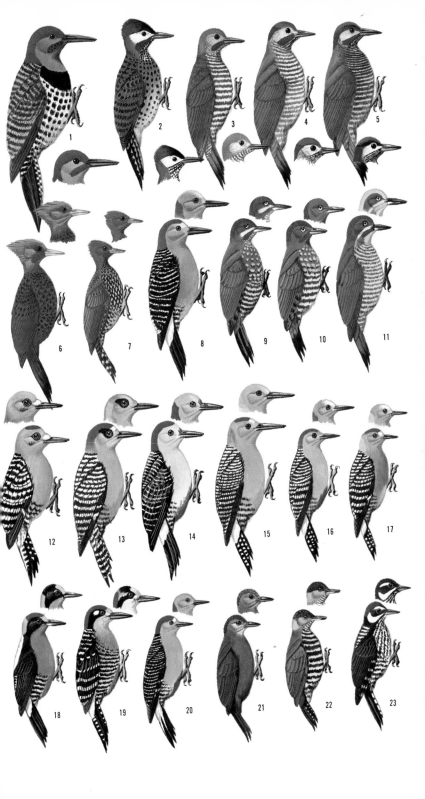

PLATE 21

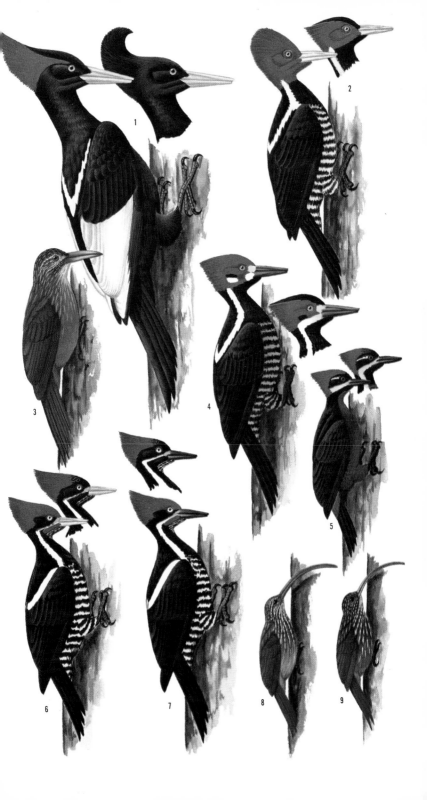

PLATE 22

PLATE 23

PLATE 24

PLATE 25

PLATE 26

PLATE 27

PLATE 28

PLATE 29

PLATE 30

PLATE 31

PLATE 32

PLATE 33

PLATE 34

PLATE 35

PLATE 36

PLATE 37

PLATE 38

PLATE 39

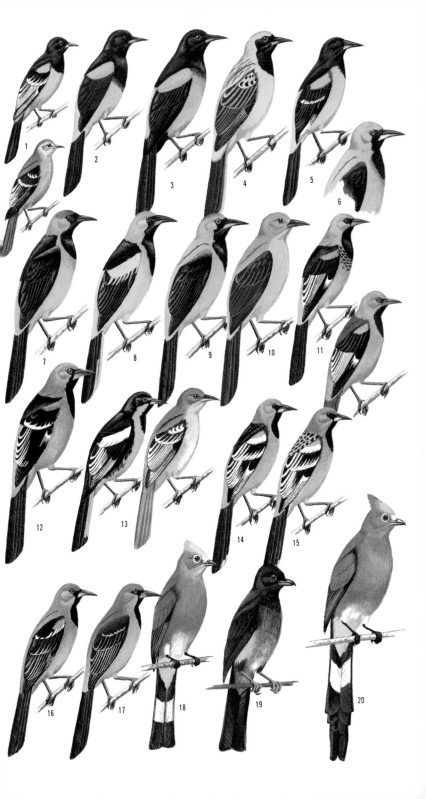

PLATE 40

PLATE 41

PLATE 42

PLATE 43

PLATE 45

PLATE 46

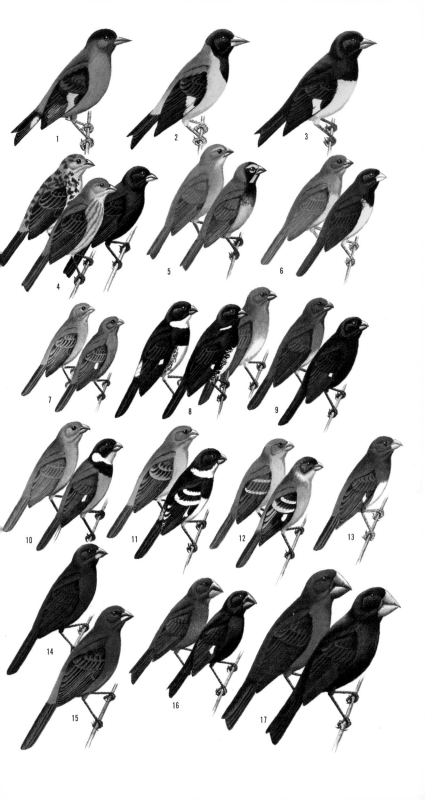

PLATE 47

PLATE 48

RUDDY TREERUNNER, *Margarornis rubiginosus.* 5½   Plate 23
RANGE: Mts. (up to timber line) of Costa Rica and n.w. Panama.

SPOTTED TREERUNNER, *Premnoplex brunnescens.* 5   Plate 23
RANGE: Mts. of Costa Rica to Venezuela and Bolivia; favors humid
   subtropical areas.

LAWRENCE'S PSEUDOCOLAPTES, *Pseudocolaptes lawrencii.* 7½
                                                        Plate 23
   (Considered a race of *P. boissonneautii* by some.)
FIELD MARKS: Tail cinnamon-rufous as in a Woodhewer; looks like and
   acts like a Woodhewer.
RANGE: Open woods on higher mts. of Costa Rica to w. Ecuador.

FOLIAGEGLEANER SUBFAMILY

STRIPED FOLIAGEGLEANER, *Hyloctistes virgatus.* 7   Plate 23
   (Considered a race of *H. subulatus* by some.)
RANGE: Nicaragua, Costa Rica, and Panama in humid tropical forests.

LINEATED FOLIAGEGLEANER, *Syndactyla subalaris.* 7
                                                        Plate 23
RANGE: Costa Rica to Venezuela and Peru; humid subtropical woods.

SCALY FOLIAGEGLEANER, *Anabacerthia variegaticeps.* 6
                                                        Plate 23
   (Considered a race of *A. striaticollis* by some.)
RANGE: S. Mexico (Guerrero to Oaxaca; c. Veracruz to Chiapas), Guatemala, Honduras, Costa Rica, and w. Panama; in underbrush of
   humid mt. forests.

OCHRACEOUS FOLIAGEGLEANER, *Philydor panerythrus.* 7½
                                                        Plate 23
   (Considered a race of *P. rufus* by some.)
RANGE: Subtropical forests in Costa Rica and w. Panama.

DUSKY-WINGED FOLIAGEGLEANER, *Philydor fuscipennis.* 6
                                                        Plate 23
   (Listed as *P. erythrocercus* by some.)
RANGE: E. Panama to w. Ecuador.

RUDDY AUTOMOLUS, *Automolus rubiginosus.* 8   Plate 23
RANGE: Mexico (Guerrero to Oaxaca; e. San Luis Potosí and Veracruz
   to Chiapas; dense underbrush in cloud forests) to w. Panama.

BLACK-TAILED AUTOMOLUS, *Automolus nigricauda.* 8 Plate 23
(Considered a race of *A. rubiginosus* by some.)
RANGE: E. Panama to w. Ecuador.

BUFF-THROATED AUTOMOLUS, *Automolus cervinigularis.* 7
Plate 23
(Considered a race of *A. ochrolaemus* by some.)
FIELD MARKS: Line back of eye dark brown; throat deep buff.
RANGE: Mexico (c. and s. Veracruz and e. Oaxaca to Chiapas; humid woods up to 3000 ft.) to the Caribbean slope of Costa Rica.

PALE-THROATED AUTOMOLUS, *Automolus pallidigularis.* 7
Plate 23
(Considered a race of *A. ochrolaemus* by some.)
FIELD MARKS: Similar to preceding species, but line back of eye usually missing; throat light creamy buff to white; chest feathers without dark margins.
RANGE: Humid areas in s.w. Costa Rica to w. Ecuador.

STREAKED AUTOMOLUS, *Thripadectes rufobrunneus.* 8 Plate 23
RANGE: Subtropical regions in Costa Rica and w. Panama.

STREAKED XENOPS, *Xenops rutilans.* 5½   Plate 23
FIELD MARKS: Bill (in this genus) short, stout, and wedge-shaped; lower bill strongly recurved at the end. Nape brown and distinctly streaked buff.
RANGE: Costa Rica to n. Argentina and Bolivia; favors tall, humid woods in subtropical regions.

LITTLE XENOPS, *Xenops minutus.* 5   Plate 23
RANGE: Mexico (c. Veracruz to Chiapas and Quintana Roo) to n. Argentina and Bolivia. (Not found in El Salvador.)

LEAFSCRAPER SUBFAMILY

GRAY-THROATED LEAFSCRAPER, *Sclerurus canigularis.* 6
Plate 23
(Considered a race of *S. albigularis* by some.)
FIELD MARKS: Bill about as long as head, almost straight and slender. (All birds of this group feed mostly on the ground, knocking aside leaves and sticks with the bill and probing into mud, rotted logs, or into moss-covered muck on rocks or logs.)
RANGE: Costa Rica and w. Panama; subtropical regions.

MEXICAN LEAFSCRAPER, *Sclerurus mexicanus.* 8 Plate 23
RANGE: Mexico (c. Veracruz to Chiapas; humid cloud forest) to Brazil and Bolivia. (Not found in British Honduras or El Salvador.)

GUATEMALAN LEAFSCRAPER, *Sclerurus guatemalensis.* 6½
Plate 23
RANGE: Mexico (s. Veracruz to Chiapas) to w. Ecuador; favors humid tropical forest. (Not found in El Salvador.)

COLOMBIAN LEAFSCRAPER, *Lochmias sororia.* 6 Plate 23
(Considered a race of *L. nematura* by some.)
FIELD MARKS: No white line over eye; underparts spotted white.
RANGE: Highlands of e. Panama to Venezuela and Ecuador; favors streamside habitats.

ANTBIRDS : Formicariidae

Forest or brush birds of many forms (subgroups) and sizes; all groups have lax, fluffy plumage on the rump, and all have a bill with a sharp hook (sometimes very small) at the end, something like that of a Shrike; none is brightly colored and most are partly or wholly tawny, rufous brown, or black and white.

LINEATED ANTSHRIKE, *Cymbilaimus lineatus.* 6 Plate 24
RANGE: S.e. Honduras to Brazil and Bolivia.

GREAT ANTSHRIKE, *Taraba major.* 8 Plate 24
VOICE: The "song" phrase is a series of *cu* figures; it begins slowly but accelerates gradually. A phrase of twenty figures requires about four sec. for delivery; the pitch is about B^1. This may be confused with the song of the Black-headed Trogon, but it is slower and softer.
RANGE: Mexico (from c. Veracruz and e. Oaxaca to Chiapas) to Argentina and Bolivia.

BARRED ANTSHRIKE, *Thamnophilus doliatus.* 6 Plate 24
FIELD MARKS: Crest feathers white at base; throat streaked.
VOICE: When disturbed, a low, somewhat hoarse call, *curr*, may be given. The "song" phrase might be said to resemble a giggle with a hiccup at the end. It begins rather deliberately and then picks up speed until it becomes a rattle; the last figure in the phrase is longer than the others and has a nasal quality and an upward inflection. The effective pitch is about A^3, and the end of the last figure is about C^4. A phrase of twenty-six or twenty-seven figures will require about 5 sec. for delivery, but only about ten of the figures will be sounded in the first 2½ sec.

RANGE: Mexico (Pacific slope of Chiapas; s. Tamaulipas and e. San Luis Potosí to Chiapas and Yucatán) to Guiana and Colombia; favors semi-arid brushland or open woods.

BLACK-CROWNED ANTSHRIKE, *Thamnophilus nigricristatus.* 6
Plate 24
(Considered a race of *T. doliatus* by some.)
FIELD MARKS: Crown black (crest feathers not white at base) in male.
RANGE: E. Panama and Colombia.

BRIDGES' ANTSHRIKE, *Thamnophilus bridgesi.* 6   Plate 24
FIELD MARKS: No crest; male largely black with a few white spots on wing-coverts; female black to slaty brown, streaked with white.
RANGE: Pacific slope of Costa Rica and w. Panama.

BLACK ANTSHRIKE, *Thamnophilus nigriceps.* 5½   Plate 24
FIELD MARKS: Male black except for under wing-coverts.
RANGE: E. Panama and Colombia.

SLATY ANTSHRIKE, *Thamnophilus punctatus.* 5½   Plate 24
FIELD MARKS: Tail feathers (except middle pair) white-tipped; wing spots white.
RANGE: Caribbean lowlands up to about 3000 ft. from Guatemala and British Honduras to Panama and on to Brazil and Bolivia.

SPECKLE-BREASTED ANTSHRIKE, *Xenornis setifrons.* 5
Plate 24
RANGE: E. Panama and n.w. Colombia.

TAWNY ANTSHRIKE, *Thamnistes anabatinus.* 5½   Plate 24
RANGE: Mexico (humid lowland forests of Tabasco and South) to w. Venezuela and Bolivia. (Not found in El Salvador.)

OLIVACEOUS ANTVIREO, *Dysithamnus mentalis.* 4¼   Plate 24
RANGE: Mexico (s. Campeche) to Argentina and Bolivia.

STREAKED-CROWNED ANTVIREO, *Dysithamnus striaticeps.* 4
Plate 24
RANGE: Caribbean slope from s.e. Honduras to n.w. Panama.

SPOTTED-CROWNED ANTVIREO, *Dysithamnus puncticeps.* 4¼
Plate 24
RANGE: Caribbean slope in Costa Rica and Panama to n. Colombia.

LEAST ANTWREN, *Myrmotherula ignota.* 2¾   Plate 24
(Considered a race of *M. brachyura* by some.)
FIELD MARKS: Bill slender and somewhat shorter than head; tail less than half as long as wing; throat white (buff in female).
RANGE: E. Panama and n.w. Colombia; tropical zone.

SURINAM ANTWREN, *Myrmotherula surinamensis.* 4   Plate 24
FIELD MARKS: Female underparts buff; chest tawny.
RANGE: Panama to Brazil and Bolivia.

FULVOUS-BELLIED ANTWREN, *Myrmotherula fulviventris.* 4¼
                Plate 24
FIELD MARKS: Throat, black and white (male) or buff (female).
RANGE: S. Honduras to Pacific slope in Colombia and Ecuador; Caribbean tropical zone only in Honduras and Costa Rica.

WHITE-FLANKED ANTWREN, *Myrmopagis axillaris.* 3½
                Plate 24
(Listed in the genus *Myrmotherula* by some.)
FIELD MARKS: In this genus the bill is much shorter than head and is relatively stouter than in the previous genus; also, the tail is relatively longer (two-thirds as long as wing). The female has the crown and nape slate gray in this species.
RANGE: Caribbean slope of s. Honduras to Panama; on to Brazil and Bolivia.

SLATY ANTWREN, *Myrmopagis schisticolor.* 4   Plate 24
(Listed in the genus *Myrmotherula* by some.)
FIELD MARKS: Female crown is brown.
RANGE: Mexico (s. Chiapas to Venezuela and n. Peru.) (Not in British Honduras or El Salvador.)

RUFOUS-WINGED ANTWREN, *Herpsilochmus rufimarginatus.* 5
                Plate 24
RANGE: E. Panama to Brazil and Bolivia.

BOUCARD ANTWREN, *Microphopias boucardi.* 4½   Plate 24
(Listed as a race of *M. quixensis* by some.)
FIELD MARKS: Bill shorter than head; tail about as long as wing. Male largely black but with white markings on wings and tail (white tips to outside tail feathers less than a half inch long) and a concealed white spot on the middle of the back that may be shown in display. Female rufous below (no black on throat).
RANGE: Mexico (humid lowlands of s. Veracruz and e. Oaxaca south) to w. Ecuador.

SAN MIGUEL ANTWREN, *Formicivora alticincta.*   4½   Plate 24
(Listed as a race of *F. grisea* by others.)
FIELD MARKS: Female dark brown above; below pale buff.
RANGE: Bay of Panama, Swan Island.

RUFOUS-RUMPED ANTWREN, *Terenura callinota.*   4   Plate 24
FIELD MARKS: Birds of this genus show at least four bright or contrast-
ing colors; the bill is slender and a bit longer than that in the genus
Microphopias, and the tail is also relatively longer. The male in this
species has a black cap; female does not.
RANGE: W. Panama to Peru.

LONG-BILLED ANTWREN, *Ramphocaenus rufiventris.*   4½
                                                          Plate 24
(This species and the following one are placed in the Gnatcatcher
family by many authors. Listed as a race of *R. melanura* by some.)
FIELD MARKS: Bill longer than head, straight and slender; tail slightly
shorter than wing. Throat white; breast and belly buff.
VOICE: The call is a very soft *chip* or *chip-chip.* The usual vocalization
is a rattle of short figures (13 to 23 in a series lasting from one and a
half to three sec.). There is usually a pause of about four sec. before
the phrase is repeated. One type is preceded by a soft *chuc* that is so
close to the first figure that it is scarcely heard. This may be represented by *chuc-e-e-e-e-e.* The pitch is about A^4. Another type of
phrase may be shown as *re-re-re-re-re.* In this about twenty-three
figures will be voiced in three sec. The pitch is about G^4 at the start
of the phrase and drops down to F^4 before the end. (The song
phrase of the Tyrannine Antwren may be confused with this unless
one is familiar with details of form and quality.)
RANGE: Mexico (s. Veracruz and e. Oaxaca to Chiapas and Yucatán;
lowlands up to 2000 ft.) to w. Ecuador; favors dense thickets of tangled vines.

HALF-COLLARED ANTWREN, *Microbates semitorquatus.*   4
(Considered a race of *M. cineriventris* by some.)   Plate 24
FIELD MARKS: Bill almost as long as head; tail half as long as wing.
Throat white, bordered on each side by a line of black; no black line
back of eye.
RANGE: Nicaragua to c. Panama.

TYRANNINE ANTWREN, *Cercomacra tyrannina.*   5   Plate 24
FIELD MARKS: The bill in this genus is moderately thick and shorter
than the head; the tail is almost as long as the wing and graduated.
In this species the male is dark slate above (female olive to brown)
and lighter below (female tawny); the outer tail feathers have little,
if any, white at the tip.
VOICE: There is a soft call, *chee-r-r-r*; if the last part is rolled a bit, the

word *cheaper* could be used to represent it. It is given in about one-third sec. and sounds rather like the call of the Beardless Flycatcher. The usual vocal composition consists of a series of figures that may be represented by *chu* (may sound more like *quee* to some). There are from eight to fourteen figures in the phrase, which requires from one to one and a half sec. for delivery; the tempo is increased after the first four or five figures; the pitch is about G^4. The phrase of the Long-billed Antwren is about twice as long and does not speed up as it progresses. In form the phrase is similar to that of the Black-headed Trogon, but the tempo is about doubled.
RANGE: Mexico (s. Veracruz to Chiapas) to Brazil and Ecuador.

GLOSSY ANTWREN, *Cercomacra nigricans.* 5½   Plate 24
FIELD MARKS: Male glossy black (female dark gray); outer tail feathers broadly tipped white.
RANGE: C. Panama to Venezuela and w. Ecuador.

BARE-CROWNED ANTBIRD, *Gymnocichla nudiceps.* 6   Plate 25
FIELD MARKS: Bill about as long as head; tail somewhat shorter than wing. Bare skin of head blue.
RANGE: S.w. Costa Rica to n. Colombia; favors dense thickets.

BARE-FRONTED ANTBIRD, *Gymnocichla chiroleuca.* 6   Plate 25
(Considered a race of *G. nudiceps* by others.)
FIELD MARKS: Bill not black; bend of wing white.
RANGE: Guatemala to e. Costa Rica (Caribbean slope).

WHITE-BELLIED ANTBIRD, *Myrmeciza longipes.* 5½   Plate 25
FIELD MARKS: Bill shorter than head; tail three-fourths as long as wing. Crown gray or brown; wings and back cinnamon-rufous.
RANGE: E. Panama to Guiana and Colombia.

SCLATER'S ANTBIRD, *Myrmeciza exsul.* 5   Plate 25
FIELD MARKS: Small area at bend of wing and line extending along edge of wing white.
RANGE: E. Nicaragua, Costa Rica, and w. Panama.

SPOTTED-WINGED ANTBIRD, *Myrmeciza maculifer.* 5   Plate 25
(Considered a race of *M. exsul* by some.)
FIELD MARKS: Head slate black; wing-coverts spotted white.
RANGE: E. Panama to w. Ecuador.

SALVIN'S ANTBIRD, *Myrmeciza laemosticta.* 5½   Plate 25
FIELD MARKS: Throat black (in female spotted white).
RANGE: Costa Rica to n.w. Colombia.

ZELEDON'S ANTBIRD, *Myrmeciza zeledoni.* 7   Plate 25
(Considered a race of *M. immaculata* by others.)
FIELD MARKS: Female brown and black.
RANGE: Costa Rica to w. Panama.

BICOLORED ANTBIRD, *Gymnopithys bicolor.* 5½   Plate 25
(Listed as a race of *G. leucaspis* by some.)
FIELD MARKS: Bill shorter than head; tail half as long as wing.
RANGE: E. Panama and extreme n.w. Colombia.

OLIVE-SIDED ANTBIRD, *Gymnopithys olivascens.* 5½   Plate 25
(Considered a race of *G. leucaspis* by some and of *G. bicolor* by others.)
FIELD MARKS: No gray on crown.
RANGE: Honduras to w. Panama; humid mature forest up to 4000 ft.

OCELLATED ANTBIRD, *Phaenostictus mcleannani.* 7½   Plate 25
RANGE: S. Honduras to w. Ecuador; favors humid forest underbrush
and follows army ants.

MEXICAN ANTTHRUSH, *Formicarius moniliger.* 7   Plate 25
(Considered a race of *F. analis* by some.)
FIELD MARKS: Bill shorter than head; a distinct rufous collar below
black throat.
VOICE: The "song" phrase varies in length from about 1.5 to 3.0 sec.
and consists of a series of mellow, "whistled" figures that slur downward slightly; the first figure is a bit over 0.1 sec. long and is followed by a rest of slightly over 0.2 sec. The other figures are about
half as long as the first, and the rest between them is the same length
as a figure. Thus, a short phrase may contain a total of nine figures
in a space of 1.3 sec. The pitch averages about C^4; however, the
long first figure may start about D^4. The phrase may be represented
as *keee-cu-cu-cu-cu* (there is greater slurring toward the end).
RANGE: Mexico (humid forests of c. Veracruz to Yucatán and Chiapas;
from sea level up to 5000 ft.) to n.e. Honduras.

HOFFMANN ANTTHRUSH, *Formicarius hoffmanni.* 6½   Plate 25
(Considered a race of *F. analis* by some.)
VOICE: The song phrase is made up of three figures in most cases, but
frequently four figures and rarely more (up to eight or ten); however, the timing (arrangement of the figures in time) is the same
(that is, the figures are all of about 0.2-sec. duration, the rest after
the first figure is about 0.6 sec., and the space between the others is
about 0.3 sec.). The average pitch is about C^4, but each figure is
slurred downward very slightly, but evenly, so that the total drop is
about a semi-tone; the introductory figure begins about a semi-tone

higher than the others. The phrase may be represented as per—pur-pur. The quality is that of a clear whistle.

RANGE: S.e. Honduras to w. Venezuela and n. Colombia.

BLACK-HEADED ANTTHRUSH, *Formicarius nigricapillus.* 6½
Plate 25

RANGE: Costa Rica to w. Ecuador (rare in N. Am.).

RUFOUS-BREASTED ANTTHRUSH, *Formicarius rufipectus.* 6½
Plate 25

RANGE: Costa Rica to Peru (rare).

SPOTTED ANTCATCHER, *Hylophylax naevioides.* 4   Plate 25
FIELD MARKS: Female has throat buffy white instead of black; breast spotted with olive-gray instead of black.

RANGE: Honduras to w. Ecuador; Caribbean slope in Central America.

RICHARDSON'S ANTCATCHER, *Myrmornis strictoptera.* 5½
Plate 25

(Listed as a race of *M. torquata* by some.)

FIELD MARKS: Bill about as long as head; tail very short (less than half as long as wing); wing bars bright buff; tail brown.

RANGE: E. Nicaragua, e. Panama, and n.w. Colombia.

BLACK-CROWNED ANTPITTA, *Pittasoma michleri.* 7   Plate 25
RANGE: Costa Rica to n.w. Colombia; wet forest. (Rare.)

COSTA RICAN ANTPITTA, *Grallaricula costaricensis.* 3¾
Plate 25

(Listed as a race of *G. flavirostris* by some.)

FIELD MARKS: Bill shorter than head and relatively stout; tail not quite one-third so long as wing; throat ochraceous; belly white or buffy white; belly and sides usually marked with dusky flecks.

RANGE: Humid subtropical woods in Costa Rica and Panama.

GUATEMALAN ANTPITTA, *Grallaria guatimalensis.* 6½   Plate 25
FIELD MARKS: Feathers of crown and back margined with black, producing a squamate effect.

RANGE: Mexico (subtropical forests in Chiapas) to w. Panama.

DIVES ANTPITTA, *Grallaria dives.* 5   Plate 25
(Listed as a race of *G. fulviventris* by some.)

FIELD MARKS: Upper wing-coverts not spotted with buff; crown, hind neck, and upper back slate gray; chest tawny, narrowly streaked with black.

RANGE: Humid tropics, Caribbean slope in Nicaragua and Costa Rica.

PACIFIC ANTPITTA, *Grallaria barbacoae.*   6   Plate 25
   (Listed as a race of *G. fulviventris* by some.)
FIELD MARKS: Back olive, contrasting with slate black crown and nape.
RANGE: E. Panama to Pacific slope of Colombia.

SPECTACLED ANTPITTA, *Grallaria perspicillata.*   5   Plate 25
FIELD MARKS: Wing-coverts spotted with buff; eye ring buffy white;
   back olive, streaked with buff; breast and sides streaked black.
RANGE: Nicaragua to w. Ecuador; humid woods.

TAPACULOS: Rhinocryptidae

Small, dark birds of Wren-like appearance except for shorter, stouter
bills and larger feet.

SILVER-FRONTED TAPACULO, *Scytalopus argentifrons.*   4
                                                       Plate 25
FIELD MARKS: Bill much shorter than head; tail much shorter than wing;
   forehead and area over eye silver gray.
RANGE: Mts. of Costa Rica and w. Panama.

PANAMA TAPACULO, *Scytalopus panamensis.*   5   Plate 25
RANGE: E. Panama to Ecuador.

MANAKINS: Pipridae

Small, fruit-eating birds with short, broad-based bills. In most cases
the body is plump and the tail quite short, which gives the bird an egg-
shaped appearance and makes it seem much larger than it is. The males
are usually highly colored, and the females are mostly olive-green
above and yellow below. They frequent dense thickets in tropical
woods.

GRAY-HEADED MANAKIN, *Piprites griseiceps.*   4   Plate 26
FIELD MARKS: Female has head tinged with olive-green.
RANGE: Wet woods, Caribbean slope; Nicaragua and Costa Rica.

VELVET MANAKIN, *Pipra velutina.*   3½   Plate 26
   (Listed as a race of *P. coronata* by some.)
FIELD MARKS: Male black; female green.
RANGE: S.w. Costa Rica to n.w. Ecuador.

YELLOW-THIGHED MANAKIN, *Pipra mentalis.*   4   Plate 26
FIELD MARKS: Female olive-green, lighter below.

VOICE: There is a very thin, high-pitched *pzzzzz-Zit*. The *zit* is very strongly accented. Persons who no longer hear the upper frequencies well are quite likely to miss this call entirely; however, they can hear the wing snapping, which is sharp.

RANGE: S. Mexico (s. Veracruz and south in humid lowland woods) to w. Ecuador.

ORANGE-HEADED MANAKIN, *Pipra erythrocephala*. 3½ Plate 26

FIELD MARKS: Female is olive-green.

RANGE: E. Panama to Guiana and Peru.

WHITE-CROWNED MANAKIN, *Pipra pipra*. 3½   Plate 26

FIELD MARKS: Rump black in male and grayish green in female.

RANGE: Costa Rica to Brazil and Peru; wet woods at 3000 to 4000 ft.

GREEN MANAKIN, *Chloropipo holochlora*. 5   Plate 26

RANGE: E. Panama to Peru.

LONG-TAILED MANAKIN, *Chiroxiphia linearis*. 9; 5¼   Plate 26

FIELD MARKS: Male—body, 3 in.; tail, 6 in.; female—body, 3 in.; tail, 2¼ in.

VOICE: A loud, clear, "whistled" call may be shown as *errlo*. It is pitched at the start at about C^4, and the *lo* drops down to A^3 flat. It requires just under one sec., and almost all the time is taken up by the *err*. Another clear phrase may be shown as *toe-le-doe*. This is the phrase that the males sing in duet. It is sometimes followed by a short rattle. There is also a hoarse, frog-like call that may be represented as *ery-aaa*.

RANGE: Mexico (Pacific slope of Oaxaca and Chiapas; favors coastal lowlands, but up to 3000 ft.) to n. Costa Rica; favors dry brushy woods.

LANCE-TAILED MANAKIN, *Chiroxiphia lanceolata*. 5   Plate 26

VOICE: Some calls very similar to those of preceding species, but others are more distinctive.

RANGE: S.w. Costa Rica to Venezuela and n. Colombia.

COSTA RICAN MANAKIN, *Corapipo altera*. 3½   Plate 26

(Considered a race of *C. leucorrhoa* by some.)

FIELD MARKS: Outermost primary neither conspicuously narrowed nor pointed.

RANGE: S.e. Honduras to n.w. Colombia; favors underbrush in subtropical woods.

SALVIN'S MANAKIN, *Manacus aurantiacus.*   4   Plate 26
   (Considered a race of *M. vitellinus* by some.)
FIELD MARKS: Orange collar of male extends down onto the back; female has distinct yellow wash below.
RANGE: S.w. Costa Rica and w. Panama.

ALMIRANTE MANAKIN, *Manacus cerritus.*   4   Plate 26
   (Considered a race of *M. vitellinus* by some.)
FIELD MARKS: Similar to last species, but collar is yellow.
RANGE: N.w. Panama (Almirante).

GOULD'S MANAKIN, *Manacus vitellinus.*   4   Plate 26
FIELD MARKS: Yellow collar of male does not extend down upon upper back as in the Almirante Manakin.
RANGE: S. and e. Panama and adjacent parts of Colombia.

CANDE'S MANAKIN, *Manacus candei.*   4¼   Plate 26
FIELD MARKS: Female has olive-green breast; belly is yellow.
VOICE: Various calls of Flycatcher quality, as is suggested by *cheert, cheewit, zeer-uip,* or *bizurit* (the *rit* is accented in the last). (This species snaps wings rather like the Yellow-thighed Manakin, but the noise is louder and not quite as sharp.)
RANGE: Mexico (s. Veracruz and e. Oaxaca to Chiapas and Quintana Roo; favors tangled vines and thickets in humid lowlands) and along Caribbean slope to Costa Rica.

COTINGAS: Cotingidae

This family is made up of a heterogeneous group of genera, some of which have no natural affinity with the others; they are more or less intermediate between the Manakins and the Flycatchers and some resemble Flycatchers in appearance and habits.

LOVELY COTINGA, *Cotinga amabilis.*   7¼   Plate 27
   (Considered a race of *C. maynana* by some.)
FIELD MARKS: Purple patch on breast of male separated from purple throat by a band of blue; no black bars on throat.
RANGE: Mexico (humid forests of c. Veracruz and Oaxaca s.) and south along Caribbean slope to Costa Rica.

RIDGWAY'S COTINGA, *Cotinga ridgwayi.*   7   Plate 27
   (Considered a race of *C. maynana* by some.)
FIELD MARKS: There is a black border to the front of the forehead and a narrow black ring around the eye.
RANGE: Pacific slope of s.w. Costa Rica and adjacent Panama.

NATTERER'S COTINGA, *Cotinga nattererii.* 7¼   Plate 27
  (Considered a race of *C. maynana* by some.)
FIELD MARKS: Male has throat narrowly barred with black.
RANGE: E. Panama to c. Colombia and n.w. Ecuador.

SNOWY COTINGA, *Carpodectes nitidus.* 8   Plate 27
RANGE: Caribbean slope of Honduras to w. Panama.

ANTONIA'S COTINGA, *Carpodectes antoniae.* 8   Plate 27
  (Considered a race of *C. nitidus* by some.)
FIELD MARKS: Similar to last species, but bill is yellow.
RANGE: Pacific slope of s. Costa Rica and w. Panama.

HOPKE'S COTINGA, *Carpodectes hopkei.* 9½   Plate 27
FIELD MARKS: Bill, tips to primaries and to central tail feathers black.
RANGE: E. Panama to Ecuador.

POLYMORPHIC ATTILA, *Attila spadiceus.* 8   Plate 27
FIELD MARKS: Rather like a Myiarchus Flycatcher, but has yellow or
  tawny rump.
VOICE: There are a number of rather loud calls, such as may be represented by *weeba, webeeba,* or *wuweebawebeewebee.* The *wee* is
  pitched about F⁴, and the *ba* drops down a bit to E⁴ flat. The last
  motif, being longer, is more nearly musical; it requires about two
  sec. to deliver. Frequently in the early morning or sometimes in the
  evening a dawn song is heard. Its phrases are made up of an indefi-
  nite number of motifs that become louder and more emphatic as the
  phrase develops. It may be represented as *weba-aweba-aweeba-
  weebee-weebee-ahweeeoo.*
RANGE: Mexico (Sinaloa and Durango to Oaxaca; e. San Luis Potosí
  and Veracruz to Chiapas and Yucatán; from sea level up to 6000 ft.;
  favors dense foliage at top of tall trees) to Brazil and Bolivia.

BROAD-BILLED MOURNER, *Sapayoa aenigma.* 6   Plate 27
  (Placed in the Manakin family by some.)
FIELD MARKS: Male has a more or less hidden yellow crown patch.
RANGE: E. Panama to n.w. Ecuador.

BROWN MOURNER, *Schiffornis turdinus.* 6¼   Plate 27
  (Placed in Manakin family by some.)
FIELD MARKS: Olive-brown, somewhat paler below; tail slightly more
  than two-thirds as long as wing.
VOICE: A plaintive "whistle," *chee-a-wewe.* It might be said to resemble a phrase of the E. Pewee, but it is drawn out more and is somewhat more mellow.
RANGE: Mexico (s. Veracruz and south in lowland rain forest) to Brazil and Bolivia; favors humid forest up to 4500 ft.

SPECKLED MOURNER, *Laniocera rufescens*.   8   Plate 27
  (Placed in Manakin family by some.)
FIELD MARKS: A yellow patch of slightly elongated feathers is located
  on each side below the wing (sometimes entirely hidden when wing
  is folded, but sometimes shows conspicuously); distinct dark brown
  and rufous-mottled wing bars. Basal part of bill may be pink.
VOICE: Similar in volume, quality, and phrasing to that of the Brown
  Mourner but more varied. A phrase may be represented as *chee-a-
  wewe-we-we-we*. It is almost exactly the same as one given by the
  Brown Mourner except for the three added *we* figures that ascend
  as *do, re, mi* at the end. There is a low chatterlike *tit-te-rr*.
RANGE: Mexico (s. Veracruz to Chiapas in lowland rain forest) to n.w.
  Ecuador; humid lowlands to subtropical areas.

RUFOUS MOURNER, *Rhytipterna holerythra*.   8   Plate 27
FIELD MARKS: Mandible sometimes largely flesh-colored; tail about
  three-fourths as long as wing.
VOICE: A drawn-out somewhat mournful "whistle" might be said to
  fit the words *Right heere;* a longer phrase may be shown as *wheeo-
  wheeo-wheeo-wheeo-weeo-weeo-weeo-wheee*. This last is similar to
  the "song" phrase of the Mexican Royal-Flycatcher but is more decidedly accented, and the succeeding figures do not seem to be
  spaced so far apart. In using the first-mentioned call, the Mourner
  sometimes repeats the *right* before voicing the *here*. The *right* is
  pitched about F^4, and the *here* begins about a half tone higher but
  slurs down to E^4. The two-figure motif requires slightly over two
  sec.
RANGE: Mexico (s. Veracruz and adjacent Oaxaca to Chiapas; lowland humid forest) to n.w. Ecuador. Not in British Honduras or El
  Salvador.

RUFOUS PIHA, *Lipaugus unirufus*.   9   Plate 27
FIELD MARKS: Except for size (which is not useful unless the birds are
  together) this species appears almost identical to the Rufous
  Mourner. It does not have pink on the bill, and the voice is different.
VOICE: Loud, strongly accented, "whistled" calls. One may be represented as *aweeoo*. Since *wee* is strongly accented and pitched about
  E^4, this call requires about a half sec. Another is similar to the so-
  called wolf whistle and may be shown as *Right here*. The *right* is
  about D^4, the *here* goes up about a half tone and then slurs down to
  about G^3, and the whole call requires about one sec. or a bit less
  (the reverberation is considerable among the big trees). This call is
  frequently given in answer to loud noises. Compared to the first figure in the *right here* of the Rufous Mourner, that of the Piha is
  quick and sharp without the plaintive quality.
RANGE: Mexico (s. Veracruz to Chiapas in lowland rain forest) to w.
  Ecuador. Not found in El Salvador.

BARRED BECARD, *Pachyramphus versicolor.* 4½   Plate 27
FIELD MARKS: Underparts barred (sometimes indistinctly).
RANGE: Costa Rica to w. Venezuela and Bolivia; favors subtropics.

WHITE-FRONTED BECARD, *Pachyramphus rufus.* 5½   Plate 27
FIELD MARKS: Female has rufous, instead of white, forehead.
RANGE: E. Panama to Brazil and Peru.

CINNAMON BECARD, *Pachyramphus cinnamomeus.* 5½   Plate 27
RANGE: Mexico (s. Veracruz and e. Oaxaca to Chiapas; lowland, humid woods; uncommon) along Caribbean slope to w. Venezuela and Ecuador.

BLACK-BACKED BECARD, *Pachyramphus polychopterus.* 5½
Plate 27
FIELD MARKS: Nape of male black; below slate to black.
RANGE: Guatemala to w. Panama; Guiana to Colombia and Argentina.

BOGOTA BECARD, *Pachyramphus dorsalis.* 5½   Plate 27
(Considered a race of *P. polychopterus* by some.)
RANGE: E. Panama to c. Colombia.

BLACK-AND-WHITE BECARD, *Pachyramphus albogriseus.* 5
Plate 27
RANGE: W. Nicaragua to Venezuela and Peru.

MEXICAN BECARD, *Pachyramphus major.* 6   Plate 27
FIELD MARKS: Crown black in both sexes.
VOICE: The "song" phrase is a series of Titmouse-like motifs, as *er-chip er-chip er-chip er-chip.* A phrase of five such calls requires five sec. The *er* is held a bit longer than the *chip*; it is pitched about D^4 while the *chip* is a bit higher at F^4.
RANGE: Mexico (Sinaloa to Guerrero; Nuevo León and Tamaulipas to Chiapas, Yucatán, and Quintana Roo; mostly at 3000 to 4000 ft. in oak woods except in Yucatán peninsula) to e. Nicaragua.

ONE-COLORED BECARD, *Platypsaris homochrous.* 6   Plate 27
FIELD MARKS: Female has crown, nape, back, and rump rufous.
RANGE: C. Panama to n.w. Venezuela and n.w. Peru.

ROSE-THROATED BECARD, *Platypsaris aglaiae.* 6½   Plate 27
FIELD MARKS: Climatic conditions vary greatly over the range of this species. In general the drier the climate, the lighter the color of the birds. This is especially true of the underparts of the males, which are almost white in dry regions and almost black in extremely humid ones. However, there seems to be a color-phase difference, too, for an individual male that is completely gray below is sometimes found in

Texas where one expects it to be almost white below. In Central America the male tends to be slate gray below with only a small purplish red throat spot showing on old birds.

VOICE: The call is a thin "whistle," *seeoo*, which begins about B⁴ and slurs rapidly down to about F⁴. The time required is about one sec. There is sometimes some preliminary chatter, which is also rather weak. When used it adds another half sec. or a bit more to the whole call.

RANGE: S.w. United States, Mexico (Sonora and s.w. Chihuahua to Oaxaca; Nuevo León and Tamaulipas to Chiapas and Yucatán; favors habitats that are open enough to provide flight room below nest); south to Costa Rica.

MASKED TITYRA, *Tityra semifasciata*.   8   Plate 27

VOICE: Low-pitched, soft calls are given by both sexes. Since both "talk" at the same time, it is difficult to determine the form of the phrase used by either. One may give a low, buzzy *dewy*, while the other utters a soft, but less buzzy, *da-da*. This may go on for some time as though it were a whispered conversation; however, the effect may be said to suggest pigs grunting softly in the distance.

RANGE: Mexico (Sonora to Chiapas; Tamaulipas to Chiapas and Yucatán; in humid or semi-arid woods where more common in lowlands) to Brazil and Bolivia; up to 5000 ft.

WHITE-COLLARED TITYRA, *Erator albitorques*.   7½   Plate 27
(Listed as a race of *Tityra inquisitor* by some.)

FIELD MARKS: Cap black; ear region white (brown in female); tail with basal half pale gray or grayish white, a black subterminal band and a white tip.

RANGE: Mexico (e. San Luis Potosí and Veracruz to Chiapas and Yucaán; tropical lowlands) to Peru. Not in El Salvador.

PURPLE-THROATED FRUITCROW, *Querula purpurata*.   10
Plate 38

FIELD MARKS: Bill much shorter than head; tail about one-third shorter than wing.

RANGE: Costa Rica to n. Brazil and Bolivia; tropical lowlands.

BARE-NECKED UMBRELLABIRD, *Cephalopterus glabricollis*.   15
(Considered a race of *C. ornatus* by some.)   Plate 38

RANGE: Costa Rica and w. Panama; breeds in highlands and descends into Caribbean lowlands at other seasons.

THREE-WATTLED BELLBIRD, *Procnias tricarunculata*.   10
Plate 38

RANGE: Highlands of Nicaragua to w. Panama; descends into lowlands after breeding season.

FLYCATCHERS: Tyrannidae

SUBFAMILY: FULVICOLINAE

EASTERN PHOEBE, *Sayornis phoebe.* 6
RANGE: E. North America; winters through e. Mexico.

BLACK PHOEBE, *Sayornis nigricans.* 6
RANGE: W. North America, Mexico (mostly above 1000 ft.; partially
migratory), and south to w. Panama; favors boulder-strewn mountain streams.

WHITE-WINGED PHOEBE, *Sayornis latirostris.* 6   Plate 28
(Considered a race of *S. nigricans* by some.)
RANGE: Highlands of e. Panama (Darien) to Argentina and Bolivia.

SAY'S PHOEBE, *Sayornis saya.* 6¼
RANGE: W. North America and Mexico (breeds in highlands south as
far as Oaxaca; winters east to Tamaulipas and Veracruz).

WHITE-BACKED FLYCATCHER, *Colonia leuconotus.* 8   Plate 28
(Considered a race of *C. colonus* by some.)
FIELD MARKS: Crown, sooty gray; grayish white streak down center
of back; body 3 in.; slender tail 5 in.
RANGE: S. Honduras to w. Ecuador; favors semi-open areas in humid
Caribbean lowlands in Central America.

PIED FLYCATCHER, *Fluvicola pica.* 5   Plate 28
RANGE: E. Panama to Argentina and Bolivia; favors streamside or
marsh habitats.

VERMILION FLYCATCHER, *Pyrocephalus mexicanus.* 5
(Listed as a race of *P. rubinus* by others.)
RANGE: S.w. United States to Honduras; migratory in north.

SUBFAMILY: TYRANNINAE

SWALLOW-TAILED FLYCATCHER, *Muscivora tyrannus.* 14
(Listed as *Tyrannus savana* by some.)   Plate 28
FIELD MARKS: Tail feathers rather flexible (bend in the wind).
RANGE: Mexico (savannas of Atlantic slope from c. Veracruz south;
migratory and occasionally straggles north to Rio Grande Delta) to
Argentina.

EASTERN KINGBIRD, *Tyrannus tyrannus.* 7
RANGE: North America; in winter to South America.

SCISSOR-TAILED KINGBIRD, *Tyrannus forficata.*   13
(Listed as *Muscivora forficata* by some.)
RANGE: S.c. United States and Mexico (n.e. Tamaulipas); winters to
Panama.

ARKANSAS KINGBIRD, *Tyrannus verticalis.*   8
RANGE: W. North America to Mexico (n. Baja California, Sonora, and
Chihuahua); south on migration as far as Nicaragua.

CASSIN KINGBIRD, *Tyrannus vociferans.*   8
RANGE: W. North America and Mexico (n. Baja California, Sonora,
and Chihuahua, and south to Chiapas; mostly in high interior basins,
but also in relatively dry, open pine forests).

TROPICAL KINGBIRD SPECIES GROUP: There is much confusion
concerning the relationship among various populations of this group
at present, and careful field observations by students visiting different
regions may aid materially in clarifying the situation. It appears that
a number of mutations involving the structure and patterns of the
voice have taken place in Mexican populations (the following three
species) that are usually lumped into a single species. (Voice studies
on the whole genus suggest that all species found in North America
may have developed from a primitive song type such as the Tropical
Kingbird.)

TROPICAL KINGBIRD, *Tyrannus melancholicus.*   8   Plate 28
FIELD MARKS: Tail almost black ("dusky grayish brown") and slightly
notched; throat grayish white.
VOICE: The vocalizations are of the primitive type: simple cries that
build up quickly to a maximum pitch and then immediately drop
back to the starting pitch with the decay rate about the same as the
build-up. Most of the figures used are of the type that will be
referred to as *wit* (0.03 to 0.04 sec. duration), but there are some
referred to as *pit* that are shorter and some called *chip* that are
longer (about 0.1 sec.). The overall pitch varies from about A^4 to
E^5. The dawn song is a series of rhythmic phrases made up of figures of different length and pitch. The phrase is introduced by one
or more *wit* figures and is terminated by three rather closely joined
motifs that have a combined duration of slightly over one sec. in
northern birds and slightly under one sec. in southern birds. A song
phrase of a Yucatán bird may be shown as *wit wit-wit-wit-wit*
pit-pit-wit-chip-wit   wit-wit-wit-chip-pit. The fast tempo, the irregular timing and the variable peak pitch, together with the very
high overall pitch, gives a tinkling effect. These songs are of such
fast tempo that the field student will not be able to properly

evaluate them unless he records them and plays them back at one-fourth speed.

RANGE: C. Mexico (Veracruz and Oaxaca and south) to Argentina; in savanna and edge situations from sea level up to 3000 ft.

WESTERN KINGBIRD, *Tyrannus occidentalis.* 8   Plate 28

(Considered a race of *T. melancholicus* by others.)

VOICE: The *wit*s of this species are of about the same pitch as those of the northern Tropical Kingbirds. The fast tempo, the tinkling effect, and the crowded arrangement of the figures in the motifs of the song phrase are likely to cause the observer to think the songs are the same also. But if the phrase is studied, it will be found that many mutations have taken place and that the songs are really quite different. The dawn song heard in Sonora is made up of a long series of phrases that are individually about fifty percent longer than those of a Tropical Kingbird. There are a few introductory figures followed by four well-developed motifs. As in other species of the genus, the terminal motif is the most stable and the most distinctive or typical of the species. The introductory figures are entirely different from the *wit* used by the Tropical Kingbird and are all alike, being slightly downward-slurred vibrato figures (the modulating frequency is about 120 Hz and hence can be appreciated by the student only when a recording is played back at one-fourth speed). Along with some of the introductory vibrato figures, the entire song phrase may be represented as *tr tr tr tr tr wit-wit-wit-wit wit-wit-wit-wit wit-wit-wit-wit illwit-e-a-ill-awi-wi-wi-wi-wi.* The duration is about two sec.

RANGE: S.w. Arizona and Mexico (Sonora to Guerrero along the Pacific slope). (It is said that hybrids are found in areas where this form comes in contact with the Tropical Kingbird, but no voice studies have been made on any of the supposed hybrids.)

COUCH'S KINGBIRD, *Tyrannus couchii.* 8½

(Considered a race of *T. melancholicus* by some.)

FIELD MARKS: Similar to the last species, but larger and with a lighter grayish brown tail that is relatively shorter in comparison with the wing.

VOICE: A *wit* is used as a call in this species, but such a figure is apparently never used in the song phrase. The peak pitch of these *wit* figures is about E^4, which is much lower than in the Tropical Kingbird. The typical daytime call is a vibrato figure of about a half sec. duration (this is much longer and differently inflected as well as lower in pitch than the vibrato figures used by the Western Kingbird. In this the average pitch bows up and then down in the form of a simple cry). Frequently this figure is preceded by a *wit*, so that we have a two-figure call, which may be shown as *wit pleerrr* (some think the ending drops down so low that it would be better shown as *pleeooo*). The dawn song is made up of a series of long, slowly delivered phrases, for instance, *pleerrr pleerrr pleerrr plity plity plity-plitecheu*. The main variations are the leaving off of the first vibrato figure or the exclusion of one of the figures shown as *plity*. The little variation that occurs in the terminal motif is mostly confined to the second figure, which may be lengthened or shortened a bit (this motif, shown as *plity-plitecheu* is really made up of four or five figures, the last three or four being crowded together). This song is seldom heard in southern Veracruz but is fairly common in the Yucatán peninsula where it and the high-pitched song of the Tropical Kingbird may be heard and recorded simultaneously.

RANGE: S. Texas and Mexico (Tamaulipas and Nuevo León to Campeche, Yucatán, and Quintana Roo); partly migratory.

THICK-BILLED KINGBIRD, *Tyrannus crassirostris.*   9
FIELD MARKS: Crown grayish brown; belly pale yellow.
VOICE: There is a loud vibrato call that corresponds to the longer *pleerrr* of Couch's Kingbird. It may be represented as *weeerr*. There is also a sharply accented *chweeeet* that is about the same length but is inflected upward throughout the last segment. The song that may be heard at dawn at the beginning of the nesting season is made up of a long series of phrases, each of which may be represented as *wit wu-wu-wu-wuwuah wit-wuah wu-weeea-yah*. The *weeea* in the last motif is another of the vibrato figures, but the modulating frequency is so high that it may not be noticed by the observer. A phrase as shown requires about two sec.
RANGE: S. Arizona, Mexico along the Pacific slope, and w. Guatemala; mostly in semi-arid regions from sea level up to 5000 ft.

GRAY KINGBIRD, *Tyrannus dominicensis.*   8
FIELD MARKS: Belly pale yellow (almost white); a dark line through the eye. (The Giant Kingbird, *T. cubensis*, which was found once on an island off coast of Quintana Roo, lacks the dark face stripe.)
RANGE: Extreme s.e. United States, West Indies, and Cozumel Island; in winter to Central America and South America.

PANAMA SIRYSTES, *Sirystes albogriseus.*   7   Plate 29
(Considered a race of *S. sibilator* by some.)
FIELD MARKS: Bill plainly shorter than head; tail black, narrowly tipped white; wing bars grayish white.
RANGE: C. Panama to n.w. Colombia.

STRIPED FLYCATCHER, *Legatus leucophaius.*   6   Plate 28
FIELD MARKS: Bill about half as long as head.
VOICE: A weak "whistle," *sweeee*, which lasts about a half sec. or a

fraction more. It is pitched about A⁴ and drops a bit at the end. There is also a soft, high-pitched *dee-da-de-du* that lasts less than a sec.; it is almost like a slow trill.

RANGE: Mexico (e. San Luis Potosí and Veracruz south to Chiapas in humid lowlands) to Argentina. Not found in El Salvador.

SULPHUR-BELLIED FLYCATCHER, *Myiodynastes luteiventris.* 7½
Plate 28

FIELD MARKS: Bill about as long as head; line over eye white, plainly lighter than the pale yellow line along jaw.

VOICE: The quick call sounds rather like *squeegee.* The song phrase (heard at dawn in breeding season) is quite short and sounds something like *kee-zwick.* The *kee* is pitched about A⁴, and the whole phrase lasts about a half sec. The phrase is repeated at such a rate that five will be sounded in ten sec. At times this phrase may sound like *kee-zwicky.* (A variant is *chee weutut.*)

RANGE: S.w. United States, Mexico (Sinaloa to Chiapas; Nuevo León and Tamaulipas to Chiapas and Yucatán; from sea level up to about 4000 ft.; favors semi-arid regions, but is usually found along streams where the trees are larger; migratory) and south to Costa Rica; migrates south as far as Peru.

STREAKED FLYCATCHER, *Myiodynastes maculatus.* 7½   Plate 28

FIELD MARKS: Similar to Sulphur-bellied Flycatcher, but belly is much paler (almost white in most cases) and line over eye is pale yellow, although not as light as the belly (the Sulphur-bellied has just the opposite effect).

VOICE: The song phrase is composed of six or seven steeply inflected figures crowded into a space of about 0.7 sec. (about the same as for Sulphur-bellied). The effect is similar to that of Sulphur-bellied Flycatcher, but the form of the figures is different; it may be likened to *weet where-are-yo weet.* One call may be suggested by *ah wee-erer*; it requires 0.25 sec. (pitch and length same as for Sulphur-bellied Flycatcher call).

RANGE: Mexico (in tropical woods from s. Tamaulipas to Chiapas and Yucatán; uncommon and migratory), Central America (except El Salvador), and on to Brazil and Peru.

GOLDEN-CROWNED FLYCATCHER
Myiodynastes chrysocephalus. 7½   Plate 28

FIELD MARKS: Yellow crown patch is hidden; line through eye dull black and bordered below by yellowish white; line over eye white; line along jaw dull black; streaks on breast dull black.

RANGE: E. Panama to Venezuela and Bolivia.

GOLDEN-BELLIED FLYCATCHER, *Myiodynastes hemichrysus.*
7½   Plate 28
(Considered a race of *M. chrysocephalus* by some.)
FIELD MARKS: Similar to previous species, but bright golden yellow below instead of pale yellow and without the black streaks on breast.
RANGE: Highlands of Costa Rica and w. Panama.

GIRAUD'S FLYCATCHER, *Myiozetetes texensis.*   6½   Plate 28
(Considered a race of *M. similis* by others.)
FIELD MARKS: Similar to the preceding species, but there is no black edging at the top of the white line over the eye; also the rusty patch on the wing is missing; red crown patch seldom, if ever, seen.
VOICE: There are a number of rather shrill calls that are lacking in the nasal quality used by various Flycatchers with the same color pattern. Most of these are of a hurried or insistent nature, such as *chip-cheer,* or, in series, *chipcheer-chipcheer-chipcheer,* or *cheer-cheer-cheer chipcheer chipcheer-acheer.*
RANGE: Mexico (s. Sonora to Chiapas; s. Tamaulipas and e. San Luis Potosí to Chiapas and Yucatán; sea level up to 5000 ft.) to n. and w. Colombia and Venezuela.

GRAY-CAPPED FLYCATCHER, *Myiozetetes granadensis.*   6½
Plate 28
FIELD MARKS: Similar to preceding species, but lacks the white line over the eye.
RANGE: S.e. Honduras to n. Brazil and Bolivia.

CAYENNE FLYCATCHER, *Myiozetetes cayanensis.*   6½   Plate 28
FIELD MARKS: Bill half as long as head; orange crown patch shows usually in part; white line over eye edged above and below with black; rusty patch on lower part of wing.
RANGE: Panama to Brazil and Ecuador.

BOAT-BILLED FLYCATCHER, *Megarynchus pitangua.*   9
Plate 28
FIELD MARKS: Bill about as long as head and heavy. Very similar to Derby Flycatcher but more olive-brown above and lacks the rufous edging to the wing and tail feathers that shows on the Derby when the feathers are spread slightly.
VOICE: The call most often heard is a relatively short, nasal, complaining *kerrr* that lasts about a half sec. A louder call, rather frequently heard, may be represented as *cheweey.* Another call sometimes given in the daytime is something like *cherrt;* this figure is more frequently heard at dawn when repeated monotonously as a "song."
RANGE: Mexico (Sinaloa to Chiapas; s. Tamaulipas and e. San Luis

Potosí to Chiapas and Yucatán; from sea level up to 5000 ft.) and south to Argentina and Bolivia.

WHITE-RINGED FLYCATCHER, *Coryphotriccus albovittatus*. 6
Plate 28

(Considered a race of *Conopias parva* by some.)
FIELD MARKS: Bill shorter than head; throat white.
RANGE: E. Costa Rica to w. Ecuador (e. lowlands in Central America).

DERBY FLYCATCHER, *Pitangus sulphuratus*. 9 Plate 28
FIELD MARKS: Bill about as long as head; rufous tint shows when wings and tail are spread.
VOICE: All calls are quite nasal in quality, and most are loud. The commonest is a simple one that may be likened to *e-yeh,* which is held about a half sec. There is a somewhat louder *der-Bey* and a still more emphatic, though less often heard, *Get-ta-heck* (sometimes *Get-ta-here*). Although seldom heard, there is a soft "roll" or repercussion that lasts a sec. or more. The dawn song is made up of motifs that are apparently never used as calls. They are rhythmically combined into long phrases, one of which may be shown as *dewey tittit-adewy tittit-adewy tittit-adoo.* Such a phrase will require three sec.
RANGE: S. Texas, Mexico (s. Sonora to Chiapas; Nuevo León and Tamaulipas to Chiapas and Yucatán; also in interior basin states of Guanajuato and Zacatecas; sea level up to 5000 ft.; in semi-arid regions favors pondside habitats), and south to Argentina and Bolivia.

LICTOR FLYCATCHER, *Pitangus lictor*. 7½ Plate 28
FIELD MARKS: Similar to last species but much smaller; bill more slender.
RANGE: E. Panama to Brazil and Peru.

SUBFAMILY: MYIARCHINAE

MYIARCHUS FLYCATCHERS: The following seven forms are all crested Flycatchers with yellow bellies and, except in one case, with more or less rufous on the wing and tail feathers. They are best identified by voice.

CRESTED FLYCATCHER, *Myiarchus crinitus*. 7½
FIELD MARKS: Bill slightly shorter than head and brown; light gray throat and chest joins abruptly with yellow breast.
VOICE: The *weeep* call is usually the only one heard in our range.
RANGE: E. North America; south on migration as far as South America; a few winter as far north as Tamaulipas.

ASH-THROATED FLYCATCHER, *Myiarchus cinerascens.*   7½

FIELD MARKS: Throat almost white; breast pale gray; belly pale yellow.

VOICE: Clear calls shown as *ke-werr* and *pwit-Ke-wherr* set this species off from the others of the genus. The various calls are softer than those of the Mexican Flycatcher but are about the same pitch and volume as those of the Nutting Flycatcher. The dawn song is composed of a series of three-figure motifs, but there is another motif that may be called a soft roll, *r-r-r*, that is inserted occasionally. The first motif may be represented as *tea fo you.* The *tea* is sharply accented, and the whole motif is hurried, lasting only a half sec. The other motif, when used, lasts probably no more than a tenth of a sec. These two motifs are very similar to #1 and #4 of the Mexican Flycatcher's Song.

RANGE: W. United States and n. Mexico (Baja California, Sonora, Sinaloa, e. to Tamaulipas, and s. to Hidalgo; in east restricted to semi-arid regions at 3000 to 5000 ft.); in winter to Guatemala and El Salvador.

NUTTING FLYCATCHER, *Myiarchus nuttingi.*   7   Plate 28

FIELD MARKS: Very similar to Mexican Flycatcher. It has been claimed that hybrids of this species and of the Ash-throated Flycatcher are sometimes found in southern Sonora. Such hybrids would cause considerable confusion should a field student encounter one; however, the vocalizations of such a bird should not be typical of either parent type.

VOICE: The *wit* call of this species is similar to that of the Mexican Flycatcher but is less emphatic; a *weep* rather like that of the Crested Flycatcher is sometimes used. Other calls are softer and less harsh than those of the Mexican Flycatcher. The dawn song is made up of a long series of two-figure motifs. The figures used by different individuals are not always identical but are always short and always delivered in the same manner. Such a motif may be represented by *wert weeo.* Each motif has a duration of about a half sec., and there is a rest of nearly one sec. between motifs.

RANGE: Mexico (s. Sonora and Chihuahua to Chiapas, including the interior basin as far east as Zacatecas, Guanajuato, and Puebla; from sea level up to 5000 ft.) to n.w. Costa Rica. Not in British Honduras.

MEXICAN FLYCATCHER, *Myiarchus tyrannulus.*   8

FIELD MARKS: Throat and chest pale gray, which gradually shades into the yellow of the breast; the bill is black.

VOICE: The commonest call is an emphatic *wit*, but this seems to be the same in form as the one used by various other members of the genus. However, this together with several other calls may be used to identify the species in most cases after one has become familiar with the style or manner of calling. The dawn song is a long period (may last an hour) of two-motif phrases. This song is firmly fixed in the species and does not differ from Texas to Venezuela. The first motif may be represented as *wit-will-do* and the second as *Three-for you*. The *will-do* and *for-you* are identical in form, but it is helpful to most people to use different words to represent the figures in the two motifs. The *Three* is more strongly accented and goes higher in pitch than any other figure in the phrase. Since motif #2 drops down from a higher pitch, it has more finality than #1; consequently, it is easy to see that it terminates the phrase. There is a somewhat longer rest between the phrases than between the two motifs of a given phrase. A variant of motif #1, which is observed in all parts of the range of the species, may be represented as *will-can-do*. Only the first figure is changed, but we will call it motif #3. There is also, at times another short motif (#4) which is inserted between the phrases so that it appears as an introductory motif to the next phrase. This is a very soft *churr*.

RANGE: S.w. United States, Mexico (Sonora across to Tamaulipas and south to Chiapas and Yucatán), and south to n.w. Costa Rica; also the Lesser Antilles, the Guianas, Venezuela, and n. Colombia to Argentina; favors coastal land savannas or open areas usually below 3000 ft.

YUCATAN FLYCATCHER, *Myiarchus yucatanensis*.   7   Plate 28

FIELD MARKS: Bill largely black; throat and chest light gray (this color occupies approximately half the distance from the chin to the under tail-coverts).

VOICE: The phrases of this species bring to mind those of the Olivaceous Flycatcher but are even more plaintive, softer, and more drawn out. The dawn song is a succession of phrases that vary in content only by the exclusion of motifs in a somewhat random way; it may begin as early as 2:00 A.M. A song phrase is typically made up of from one to four or more motifs but there seem to be only three different motifs available. Motif #1 is made up of three identical, very soft, short figures, *de*; it requires about two-tenths sec. Motif #2 is a drawn-out *aheeet* and requires one sec. or a bit more. Motif #3 may be shown as *aheehoo* and requires just under one sec. The most pleasing phrase is 1-2-1-3, but more often it is likely to be simply 1-3. The song period frequently ends with what may be called a terminal motif. In it there is an introductory figure that shows a slight vibrato and is inflected upward slowly for about a half sec., whereupon it runs into a slow rattle that lasts about a sec. more. Total pitch range is from G^3 to E^4, and the introductory figure of the terminal motif spans this whole range, as does the *aheehoo*.

RANGE: The Yucatán peninsula of Mexico.

OLIVACEOUS FLYCATCHER, *Myiarchus lawrenceii.*   7

(Considered a race of *M. tuberculifer* by others.)

FIELD MARKS: Bill at base is wider than it is high; crown chocolate brown; underparts as in Crested Flycatcher.

VOICE: The commonest call is a plaintive and somewhat subdued *weeur*. It is held about one sec. and slurs down slightly more at the end than it does up at the start; the high point is about B³. Other calls may range upward a bit higher, but all are softer than the various calls of the Mexican Flycatcher and even when emphasized lack the harsh quality of the latter species. There is a more emphatic *peweer* and a more burry *threebeers* as well as a call that runs into a roll, *berrrrrrr*. The last is more frequently given at the end of a series, such as *weeur threebeers berrrrrrr*. The song is made up of musical phrases that resemble those of the Yucatan Flycatcher except that they are pitched a bit higher and everything is speeded up about three to one. Motif #1 is a simple *wip* (like a *wit,* but cut off sharply at its highest peak); motif #2 is a single figure, *weeo*; motif #3 is composed of two figures usually fused together as *weehoo*. There is frequently a terminal motif introduced by a figure resembling motif #2. This introductory figure runs into a roll of some twenty or thirty short figures having an overall duration of about one sec. The usual song phrase is 1–2–3; less common is 1–2–1–3 and rarely 1–1–2–2–3. However, some individuals use motif #1 seldom or not at all. The last motif, #3, may be inflected just before the terminal motif up to a higher pitch than usual and the figures separated distinctly as *wee hoo*. Various parts of the song are used as daytime calls.

RANGE: S.w. United States, Mexico (Sonora and Chihuahua to Chiapas; Nuevo León and Tamaulipas to Chiapas and Yucatán; up to 4000 feet or more) to Panama and adjacent Colombia.

FIERCE FLYCATCHER, *Myiarchus ferox.*   7   Plate 28

FIELD MARKS: No rufous shades in wings or tail.

VOICE: The song is a long series of identical two-figure motifs and may end with a terminal phrase of two figures followed by a rattle that brings to mind the rattle used by the Yucatan Flycatcher. The two-figure motif may be likened to a quick *digit doo*.

RANGE: Pacific coast of Costa Rica south to Argentina and Bolivia.

FLAMULATED FLYCATCHER, *Deltarhynchus flammulatus.*   6

Plate 28

FIELD MARKS: Looks like a small *Myiarchus* but has a grayish white throat and a pale gray breast that is indistinctly streaked with yellowish white.

VOICE: Somewhat plaintive, the quality being rather like that of the Olivaceous Flycatcher, although the pitch is higher. The phrasing is perhaps intermediate between that of a Buff-breasted Flycatcher and an Olivaceous. There is usually a drawn-out, loud motif followed closely by a hurried, weaker one that may sound like mumbling. This may be represented as *churrreeee urweba.* The first requires one sec., and the last a half sec. Sometimes the first may be shortened somewhat, and sometimes the second may be lengthened and made more distinct so that it might be represented by *a-free-beer.* There is also a bubbling rattle, *we-we-we-we-we.*

RANGE: W. Mexico (from Sinaloa to Guerrero and Oaxaca to Chiapas; mostly from 1000 to 4000 ft.)

OLIVE-SIDED FLYCATCHER, *Nuttallornis borealis.* 7

FIELD MARKS: A dividing white line down center of breast.

RANGE: North America to mts. of Baja California; in winter south to n. South America.

COUES' FLYCATCHER, *Contopus pertinax.* 7

(Considered a race of *C. fumigatus* by some.)

FIELD MARKS: Slight but noticeable crest; lacks distinct wing bars (the appearance and voice of this species suggest that it is placed in the wrong genus; hence, field students do not call it a Pewee); looks more like an Olive-sided Flycatcher than a Pewee, but lacks the white line down center of the breast.

VOICE: A low *pip* or *beep,* frequently given as a double call, *beep-beep.* The song may be indicated as *Ave-a ma-re-ah,* or a shorter *Av-a me-ah.*

RANGE: Highlands of Arizona south to n. Nicaragua; pine-oak woods.

EASTERN PEWEE, *Contopus virens.* 6

FIELD MARKS: Relatively long wings (when perched, the wing tips extend beyond the middle of the tail).

RANGE: E. North America; on migration as far as South America (a late spring migrant; some still present in Mexico latter part of May).

WESTERN PEWEE, *Contopus sordidulus.* 6

(Considered a race of *C. virens* by some.)

FIELD MARKS: Lower bill usually partly brown; breast olive-gray; when perched the wing tips usually extend slightly past middle of tail but not always.

VOICE: The call is nasal and burry and may be indicated by *dearre dearra,* or a more emphatic *dear-ie.* Sometimes it is more burry and sounds like *zerrre.* There are less-often used calls that lack the vibratory character, such as *pa-paah-we.* The dawn song heard during the breeding season is a series of two-motif phrases. One motif corresponds to the *pee-a-wee* of the Eastern Pewee, but the tempo is much faster, so that only a half sec. is required for delivery instead of one sec. This motif may be shown as *dearr-reeea.* Motif #2 is quite different and apparently is never used as a call. There is no vibrato in any of its four figures. It may be shown as *aaaa wit wit-'l-we,* the first two figures being distinctly separated and the last two being slurred together by the effect indicated by the '*l*. The last figure is slurred up to the end and hence lacks "finality." Consequently, the musical phrase is really 2–1. Either motif may be modified by having one or more very short "introductory" figures (possibly this is stuttering) added. These may be shown as *a*. Motif #2 is approximately the same length as #1.

RANGE: W. North America to Mexico (Baja California to Nuevo León and south to Chiapas; also Veracruz, at least in winter) and Guatemala (possibly breeding further south in Central America); mostly in mts. in the west; in winter south to Venezuela and Bolivia.

SHORT-LEGGED PEWEE, *Contopus brachytarsus.* 5½   Plate 29
(Considered a race of *C. cinereus* by some.)
FIELD MARKS: Throat, median portion of breast, belly, and under tail-coverts yellowish white; wings relatively short (when perched, the wing tips extend barely or not quite to the middle of the tail); back and sides olive-gray.
RANGE: Mexico (c. Veracruz and e. Oaxaca to Chiapas and the Yucatán peninsula; from sea level up to 2000 ft.) to w. Panama.

GUANACASTE PEWEE, *Contopus rhizophorus.* 5   Plate 29
(Considered a race of the previous species by others.)
FIELD MARKS: Similar to previous species but bill shorter, and olive-gray color replaced by light gray.
RANGE: Pacific coast mangrove area of n.w. Costa Rica.

DARK PEWEE, *Contopus lugubris.* 6   Plate 29
(Considered a race of *C. fumigatus* by some.)
FIELD MARKS: Olive-slate, slightly paler below, and passing to dull yellowish white at center of belly.
RANGE: Subtropical highlands up to 7000 ft. or more in Costa Rica and w. Panama.

OCHRACEOUS PEWEE, *Contopus ochraceus.* 6   Plate 29
FIELD MARKS: Chest and sides ochraceous-olive; throat and center of breast yellow; belly slightly paler yellow.
RANGE: Higher mts. of Costa Rica and w. Panama; rare.

EMPIDONAX FLYCATCHERS: Most museum taxonomists at present list a confusing number of species in this genus. Their field characters overlap to such an extent that it is impossible to identify most of them in the field except by voice. Since migrants and winter residents do not sing and since most of the birds in our range come under the category of migrants, it seems best to divide the genus into what might be called "natural" groups, thus giving the field student something possible to work with. Except for two species (which he does not list in the genus), the complexes used herein closely follow the natural groups of the genus as suggested by Pierce Brodkorb.

YELLOW-BELLIED FLYCATCHERS. 5   Plate 29
(The taxonomic forms *flavescens, imperturbans, dwighti, difficilis, cineritus, culicani, hellmayri, immodulatus, salvini,* and *flaviventris* are included in this complex.)

FIELD MARKS: Bill wide and relatively short (not much longer than the width at the base); upper parts olive-green; tail usually notched or double-rounded but sometimes almost straight across; eye ring yellowish white or yellow; wing bars yellowish white, pale yellow, or light buff; throat pale yellowish gray to light grayish yellow, somewhat lighter than breast but not in notable contrast; breast olive, with a slight yellow wash or a buffy or tawny tint; belly yellow to pale yellow. The eggs of these birds are spotted. Those who wish to do so may split this complex during the breeding season on the basis of range and habitat. If definitely of this complex, in most of Mexico (Chiapas excepted) birds found in the pines (and also in cloud forest in San Luis Potosí and Tamaulipas) may be called Western Flycatchers (*E. difficilis*) since all belong to the same subgroup of races; birds found in the cloud forests of s. Veracruz (Sierra de Tuxtla) may be called Yellowish Flycatchers since they belong to the *flavescens* subgroup; and south of Honduras all will be Yellowish Flycatchers. (Both Yellowish and Western Flycatchers may breed in Chiapas; the Yellowish Flycatcher is much brighter yellow below.)

RANGE: North America (in Mexico—Baja California, Sonora, and Chihuahua, south through Michoacán and San Luis Potosí to Veracruz and Chiapas; mostly in pine-oak regions in mts. of the north, but in both pine woods and cloud forests in south) and south to Panama.

LIGHT-THROATED FLYCATCHERS. 5   Plate 29
(Within this Complex are included the taxonomic subgroups known as *albigularis, timidus, subtilis, axillaris, virescens, trailii, brewsteri, lawrencei,* and *euleri*; however, some do not occur within our range and others are not present during breeding season.)

FIELD MARKS: Bill short and wide (frequently only slightly longer than width at the base); tail almost straight across the end or slightly rounded (not plainly notched); eye ring yellowish white, buffy white, or pale yellowish green; wing bars yellowish white, grayish white, or very pale gray; breast olive-gray, noticeably darker than the throat; belly light to pale yellow or buffy yellow. The eggs of these birds are white or almost so, with irregular brown spots. Except in the northern part of Baja California and possibly near the

Arizona border of Mexico, the only birds of this complex found in our range during the breeding season are of the subgroup of races usually called the White-throated Flycatcher, *E. albigularis*. Those who wish to do so may therefore identify this subgroup in midsummer by range. After migrants from the north have arrived, such splitting is no longer possible. The migrant subgroups, *trailii* and *brewsteri*, have some variation in bill and tail characters so that they do not always fit too well in the general pattern, but the contrast of the light throat with the breast should properly place them in this complex.

RANGE: North America (in Mexico—n. Baja California, Sinaloa, Chihuahua, Durango, Mexico, s.w. Tamaulipas, e. San Luis Potosí, Puebla, Veracruz, and Chiapas; elsewhere on migration; in the east mostly from 3000 to 4000 ft. elevation in oak woods and cloud forests but more widespread on migration), Central America (except El Salvador and British Honduras during the breeding season), and South America.

NARROW-BILLED FLYCATCHERS. 5   Plate 29
(The taxonomic units included in this Complex are *affinis*, *pulverius*, *trepidus*, *virgensis*, *minimus*, *hammondii*, *wrightii*, and *oberholseri*.)

FIELD MARKS: Bill narrow and usually more than twice as long as the width at the base; upper parts gray to grayish olive; tail usually notched; eye ring white; wing bars white or grayish white; throat pale gray; breast slightly darker than throat, but what little difference there is shades in so gradually that there is no noticeable contrast (when there is a light yellow or olive wash below, it does not show on the throat); belly yellowish white or pale yellow. Some members of this complex (notably *minimus*) have bills that are too broad to fit the pattern well, but their tails are so plainly notched that there should be no great difficulty in identifying them if they can be carefully studied. The eggs of these birds are white or almost so. Since only one of the subgroups of this complex nests in Mexico, those who wish to split them may call breeding birds there Pine Flycatchers, *E. affinis*. Migrants not present in June.

RANGE: North America (in Mexico—Chihuahua across to Coahuila and south to Guerrero and Veracruz; in pine and oak regions in the mts.; more widespread on migration); south in winter as far as Panama.

PILEATED FLYCATCHER, *Empidonax mexicanus*. 5½   Plate 29
(Listed under genus *Aechmolophus* by others.)

FIELD MARKS: Similar to other grayish brown members of the genus (especially Light-throated Flycatchers) but with a longer crest that is somewhat pointed. The crest is seldom completely raised and frequently is decumbent so that it is not noticed at all. There is no yellow on the underparts unless it be a very faint wash on the belly. The nest is like that of the Acadian Flycatcher.

VOICE: There are some soft, short calls and a more emphatic alarm call. The song starts like a "chatter" but quickly runs into a rattle that becomes louder and faster and finally bursts into a sharply accented *ReeChoo*. The *Ree* is pitched about A⁴. The whole phrase may be represented as *ra re ee-e-e-e-ReeChoo*; it requires about one and a quarter sec.

RANGE: C.w. Mexico in Michoacán, Mexico, Morelos, Guerrero, w. Puebla, and Oaxaca; mostly in deciduous woods at 4000 to 5000 ft.

BELTED FLYCATCHER, *Empidonax callizonus*.   5   Plate 29
(Listed in the genus *Xenotriccus* by others.)

FIELD MARKS: Crest rather long and pointed; breast band rufous.

VOICE: The call is a rather weak *pip*. The song phrase is a hurried *pip-pip Reerrr*. The *Ree* is strongly accented as it goes into a *buzz*. The number of introductory *pip* figures varies somewhat and may be three or only one, but is usually two. With the introductory figures the phrase requires a half sec. or a fraction more. The *pip* is pitched about A⁴, and the *Reerrr* drops down slightly.

RANGE: Central Chiapas and adjacent parts of Guatemala; from 4000 to 7000 ft.

BUFF-BREASTED FLYCATCHER, *Empidonax fulvifrons*.   4½
Plate 29

FIELD MARKS: Throat pale buffy gray; breast tawny buff.

VOICE: The song phrase brings to mind that of the Pileated Flycatcher but is weaker and less distinct.

RANGE: S.w. United States, Mexico (Sonora and Chihuahua to Chiapas; in pine-oak regions mostly from 5000 to 9000 ft.), Guatemala, El Salvador, and Honduras.

BLACK-CAPPED FLYCATCHER, *Empidonax atriceps*.   4½
Plate 29

FIELD MARKS: Crown and hindneck black; breast grayish brown.

RANGE: Higher mts. up to timber line in Costa Rica and w. Panama.

TUFTED FLYCATCHER, *Mitrephanes phaeocercus*.   5   Plate 29

FIELD MARKS: Underparts tawny buff to tawny cinnamon.

VOICE: A thin, high-pitched rattle, *chewe-che-che-che-che* or *che-che-che-tse-tse-tse*.

RANGE: Mexico (Sonora and Chihuahua to Oaxaca; s.w. Tamaulipas, San Luis Potosí, and Hidalgo to Veracruz and Chiapas; mostly in oak-pine forests, but at times—at least in winter—to sea level) to Nicaragua. Not in British Honduras.

YELLOW-VENTED FLYCATCHER, *Mitrephanes aurantiiventris.*
(Considered a race of *M. phaeocercus* by others.)   4½   Plate 29
RANGE: Costa Rica and w. Panama; 2000 to 7000 ft.

OLIVE-BREASTED FLYCATCHER, *Mitrephanes berlepschi.*   4¼
                                                           Plate 29
(Considered a race of *M. phaeocercus* by some.)
FIELD MARKS: Breast buffy olive; center of belly yellow.
RANGE: E. Panama and Pacific lowlands of Colombia to n.w. Ecuador.

RUDDY-TAILED FLYCATCHER, *Terenotriccus erythrurus.*   3½
                                                           Plate 29
RANGE: S. Mexico (Chiapas) to Brazil and Bolivia; humid tropical
woods.

SALVIN'S FLYCATCHER, *Aphanotriccus capitalis.*   4½   Plate 29
FIELD MARKS: Wings black with cinnamon bars.
RANGE: E. Nicaragua and e. Costa Rica; foothills up to 3000 ft.

NELSON'S FLYCATCHER, *Aphanotriccus audax.*   5   Plate 29
FIELD MARKS: Back and tail uniform greenish olive; wing bars and
throat white; belly yellow.
RANGE: E. Panama and n.w. Colombia; tropical woods.

BRAN-COLORED FLYCATCHER, *Myiophobus fasciatus.*   4½
                                                       Plate 29
FIELD MARKS: Bill much shorter than head; hidden crown patch
yellow; underparts buffy yellow, the breast streaked with grayish
brown.
RANGE: S.w. Costa Rica to Argentina and Bolivia; favors shrubby
pastures in lower subtropical or upper tropical zone.

SULPHUR-RUMPED MYIOBIUS, *Myiobius sulphureipygius.*   4½
                                                           Plate 29
(Considered a race of *M. barbatus* by some.)
FIELD MARKS: Rump and hidden crown patch yellow.
RANGE: S.e. Mexico (s. Veracruz to Chiapas; humid woods up to
about 3000 ft.) to Pacific Colombia and Ecuador. Not in El Salvador.

TAWNY-BREASTED MYIOBIUS, *Myiobius villosus.*   5¼   Plate 29
(Considered a race of *M. barbatus* by some.)
FIELD MARKS: Similar to other members of the genus but larger and
with relatively longer tail (longer than wing instead of shorter),
and the usual orange area on breast is larger and more tawny.
RANGE: E. Panama (subtropics) to Venezuela and Bolivia.

BLACK-TAILED MYIOBIUS, *Myiobius atricaudus.* 4½   Plate 29
  (Considered a race of *M. phaeocercus* by others.)
FIELD MARKS: Similar to other members of genus, but tail equal to wing and more rounded at end; rump and belly brighter yellow, and breast somewhat brownish olive.
RANGE: Pacific Costa Rica and south to Brazil and Peru.

MEXICAN ROYAL-FLYCATCHER, *Onychorhynchus mexicanus.* 6½
                                                Plate 29
  (Considered a race of *O. coronatus* by some.)
FIELD MARKS: Bill about as long as head and depressed; when the crest is not visible, this bird might be thought to resemble a *Myiarchus* Flycatcher of the understory of the rain forest.
VOICE: The call is somewhat complaining in quality and a bit like a weak Flicker call; it may be represented as *cleeip.* The song is a slow series of mellow "whistles," such as *Right-here here here here.* This is very similar to the song of the Rufous Mourner, but the second figure in the first motif is less strongly accented, and the subsequent figures are given after rests of about one sec.
RANGE: Mexico (c. Veracruz to Chiapas and Yucatán; mostly in lowland forest; favors understory habitat) to w. Venezuela and n. Colombia.

SUBFAMILY: PLATYRINCHINAE

MEXICAN SPADEBILL, *Platyrinchus cancrominus.* 4   Plate 29
  (Considered a race of *P. mystaceus* by some.)
FIELD MARKS: Bill about half as long as head, very broad and flat; male has a small, concealed yellow crown patch; ring around eye dull white. (All Spadebills have short, stubby tails.)
VOICE: The call is a Thrush-like *titter-up.*
RANGE: Mexico (s. Veracruz to Chiapas and Quintana Roo; tropical forest; favors understory thickets) to n.w. Costa Rica; favors moist to dry lowland woods but rises to wet forest, at times to 4000 ft.

WHITE-THROATED SPADEBILL, *Platyrinchus mystaceus.* 4
                                               Plate 29
FIELD MARKS: Similar to last species but darker, and male has a large patch of yellow on the crown; eye ring buffy white.
RANGE: Wet subtropical woods of Costa Rica to Argentina and Bolivia.

GOLDEN-CROWNED SPADEBILL, *Platyrinchus coronatus.* 3
                                               Plate 29
FIELD MARKS: A narrow black line along side of crown.
RANGE: Honduras to Brazil and Bolivia; humid tropical woods.

BROWN FLATBILL, *Cnipodectes subbrunneus.*   7   Plate 29
RANGE: E. Panama to Brazil and Peru.

GRAY-HEADED FLATBILL, *Tolmomyias cinereiceps.*   4½   Plate 29
(Considered a race of *T. sulphurescens* by some.)
FIELD MARKS: Bill short and flat; iris white; head gray; throat and chest light gray.
RANGE: S. Mexico (Oaxaca to Chiapas; s. Veracruz to Chiapas and Yucatán; mostly in lowlands) to Costa Rica (possibly in w. Panama).

YELLOW-OLIVE FLATBILL, *Tolmomyias sulphurescens.*   5
Plate 29
FIELD MARKS: Similar to last species, but the eye is not white; the gray of throat, which is strongly tinged with olive-yellow, does not extend onto the chest.
RANGE: E. Panama to Argentina and Bolivia.

YELLOW-MARGINED FLATBILL, *Tolmomyias flavotectus.*   4½
Plate 29
(Considered a race of *T. assimilis* by some.)
FIELD MARKS: Greater wing-coverts broadly margined with yellow; gray of throat extends down onto chest.
RANGE: Caribbean Costa Rica to n.w. Ecuador; humid forest.

OLIVACEOUS FLATBILL, *Rhynchocyclus olivaceus.*   5   Plate 29
FIELD MARKS: Chest light grayish olive.
RANGE: E. Panama to Brazil and Ecuador.

SHORT-BILLED FLATBILL, *Rhynchocyclus brevirostris.*   6
Plate 29
FIELD MARKS: Chest olive-green and obscurely streaked gray.
RANGE: Mexico (c. Veracruz to Chiapas and Yucatán; from sea level up to about 6000 ft; uncommon) to n.w. Ecuador.

SUBFAMILY: EUSCARTHMINAE

BLACK-HEADED TODY-FLYCATCHER, *Todirostrum nigriceps.*   3
Plate 26
FIELD MARKS: Tody-Flycatchers are shaped something like Gnatcatchers; they have narrow flat bills that are about as long as the head. The tail in this species is relatively short, the feathers black with yellowish olive edges; the throat is white.
RANGE: Costa Rica to w. Venezuela and w. Ecuador.

WHITE-TIPPED TODY-FLYCATCHER, *Todirostrum cinereum.* 4
Plate 26

FIELD MARKS: Underparts yellow; tail feathers black with narrow yellowish olive edges and narrowly tipped white; iris straw colored.

RANGE: Mexico (s. Veracruz to Chiapas and Yucatán; favors edge and is seldom more than ten ft. above ground) to Brazil and Colombia.

SLATE-HEADED TODY-FLYCATCHER
Todirostrum schistaceiceps. 3½   Plate 26

(Considered a race of *T. sylvia* by others.)

FIELD MARKS: Throat light gray; iris brown.

RANGE: Mexico (s. Veracruz, e. Oaxaca, and south; favors dense thickets) to Venezuela and Colombia. Not found in El Salvador.

GRAY-THROATED BENTBILL, *Oncostoma cinereigulare.* 4
Plate 26

FIELD MARKS: Upper bill arched or decurved; lower bill straight. This species is colored above and below very much like the Gray-headed Flatbill, and it also has a white iris. The different bill and the relatively much shorter tail of the Bentbill (it is porportionately one-fourth shorter) will easily separate the species. The Bentbill hides in dense thickets near the ground.

VOICE: Short, soft rattles lasting from one half to slightly over one sec. Some sound guttural or froglike, and some hold well to one pitch while others climb in pitch. The range is from F^3 to C^4. The rattles are indicated by *burrrr, beerrrr, brerrr,* and *pterrrrt.*

RANGE: Mexico (s. Oaxaca and Chiapas; c. Veracruz to Chiapas and Yucatán; up to 4000 ft. but favors lowlands) to w. Panama.

OLIVACEOUS BENTBILL, *Oncostoma olivaceum.* 3½   Plate 26
(Considered a race of *C. cinereigularie* by some).

FIELD MARKS: Similar to last species, but head and throat not gray; above olive-green; below light olive-yellow.

RANGE: E. Panama and w. Colombia.

SCALED HELMETED-FLYCATCHER, *Lophotriccus pileatus.* 3½
Plate 26

FIELD MARKS: Feathers of crest margined with rufous.

RANGE: Highlands of Costa Rica to Peru.

WHITE-EYED PYGMY-FLYCATCHER, *Atalotriccus pilaris.* 3½
Plate 26

FIELD MARKS: Tail about as long as wing; above olive-green; below grayish white tinged with pale yellow.

RANGE: Panama to Venezuela and Colombia.

BLACK-CAPPED PYGMY-FLYCATCHER

Perissotriccus atricapillus. 2½   Plate 26

(Considered a race of *Myiornis ecaudatus* by some.)

FIELD MARKS: Bill nearly as long as head; tail very short.

RANGE: Costa Rica to n.w. Colombia. (Caribbean slope in Central America.)

BROWN PYGMY-FLYCATCHER, *Pseudotriccus berlepschi.* 4½

Plate 26

(Considered a race of *P. pelzelni* by others.)

FIELD MARKS: Upper parts, breast, and sides dark reddish brown; wings brown, showing rufous margins on feathers; throat dull white.

RANGE: E. Panama to n.w. Colombia.

YELLOW-GREEN PYGMY-FLYCATCHER

Phylloscartes flavovirens. 4   Plate 26

(Considered a race of *P. ventralis* by some and placed in the genus *Leptopogon* by others.)

RANGE: E. Panama.

RUFOUS-BROWED PYGMY-FLYCATCHER

Phylloscartes superciliaris. 4   Plate 26

(Listed as *Mecocerculus superciliaris* by some.)

FIELD MARKS: Crown slate gray.

RANGE: Mts. of Costa Rica to Guiana and Colombia.

YELLOW PYGMY-FLYCATCHER, *Capsiempis flaveola.* 4

Plate 26

FIELD MARKS: Bill slightly shorter than head; wing bars yellow.

RANGE: Nicaragua to Argentina and Bolivia; humid tropics.

SUBFAMILY: SERPOPHAGINAE

TORRENT FLYCATCHER, *Serpophaga cinerea.* 4   Plate 30

RANGE: Costa Rica to w. Venezuela and Bolivia; favors mt. streams in humid subtropics at 3000 to 5000 ft.

SUBFAMILY: ELAENIINAE

YELLOW-BELLIED ELAENIA, *Elaenia flavogaster.* 6   Plate 30

FIELD MARKS: Bill narrow and about half as long as head; white crown patch concealed by long olive feathers that can be erected into a long crest; eye ring white.

VOICE: The call is a hoarse scream or burry "whistle" suggestive of a very hoarse rendition by an Olivaceous Flycatcher. It might be represented as *wheerr;* the duration will be from a half to one sec., depending upon emphasis; the highest pitch reached is about F⁴. There are other longer, hurried, and excited calls and a dawn song.

RANGE: Mexico (c. Veracruz and e. Oaxaca to Chiapas and Yucatán; favors edge and lowland savannas) to Argentina and Bolivia.

LESSER ANTILLEAN ELAENIA, *Elaenia martinica.* 6 Plate 30
RANGE: Islands off coast of Quintana Roo and British Honduras.

LESSER ELAENIA, *Elaenia chiriquensis.* 5 Plate 30
FIELD MARKS: The throat is olive instead of gray, and this color blends in with the yellow breast instead of contrasting with it.
RANGE: Costa Rica to Brazil and Bolivia; open brushland up to 4000 ft.

MOUNTAIN ELAENIA, *Elaenia frantzii.* 6 Plate 30
(Considered a race of *E. obscura* by some.)
RANGE: Guatemala to w. Venezuela and Colombia; favors cloud forest openings from timber line down to about 5000 ft.

MACILVAINE'S FLYCATCHER, *Myiopagis macilvainii.* 5
Plate 30
(Considered a race of *M. gaimardii* by some.)
FIELD MARKS: Hidden crown patch canary yellow; indistinct line over eye brownish white.
RANGE: E. Panama and adjacent Colombia; humid forest.

PARAMBA FLYCATCHER, *Myiopagis parambae.* 5 Plate 30
(Considered a race of *M. caniceps* by others.)
FIELD MARKS: Sexes alike; upper parts, throat, and breast gray; belly white; wings and tail dark, the wing feathers showing some white edging.
RANGE: E. Panama and south along Pacific slope to Bolivia.

PLACID FLYCATCHER, *Myiopagis viridicata.* 5¼ Plate 30
(Listed in genus *Elaenia* by some.)
FIELD MARKS: Bill half as long as head, narrow; no wing bars.
VOICE: Call is high pitched and thin, such as *seeip,* or sometimes *seeip see see* (something like call of Beardless Flycatcher).
RANGE: Mexico (Nayarit to Guerrero and w. Puebla; Pacific slope of Chiapas; s. Tamaulipas and e. San Luis Potosí to Chiapas and Yucatán; lowlands up to 4000 ft.) to Argentina and Bolivia.

PUNTA ARENAS FLYCATCHER, *Sublegatus arenarum.* 5
(Considered a race of *S. modestus* by some.) Plate 30
FIELD MARKS: Crown, wings, and tail, blackish olive; throat grayish white.
RANGE: N.w. Costa Rica (mangroves along shores of Gulf of Nicoya).

SMOOTH FLYCATCHER, *Sublegatus glaber.* 5   Plate 30
(Considered a race of S. *arenarum* by some and S. *modestus* by others.)
FIELD MARKS: Crown grayish brown; throat gray, blending smoothly into the yellow of belly.
RANGE: Panama, Venezuela, and Colombia; favors semi-arid areas.

MOUSE-COLORED FLYCATCHER, *Phaeomyias murina.* 5
Plate 30
FIELD MARKS: Light buffy white wing bars.
RANGE: C. Panama to Argentina and Bolivia; semi-open areas.

BEARDLESS FLYCATCHER, *Camptostoma imberbe.* 4   Plate 30
FIELD MARKS: Wing bars indistinct; breast pale gray; belly yellowish white.
VOICE: One call is a thin *squee-ut.* What might be called a daytime song could be shown as *dee-dee-dee-dee;* it requires about two sec. The dawn song is slightly variable, but the phrase may be represented as *chip ee-chee-FreeBeeeo* or *Chee-chee Free-Beebee.* It is quite thin and high pitched; the introductory figures are weak, but the accented *Free-Beebee* stands out rather well. The phrase is repeated quickly again and again.
RANGE: S.w. United States, Mexico (Sonora and Chihuahua to Chiapas; Nuevo León and Tamaulipas to Chiapas and Yucatán; favors dry lowlands but ranges up to 4000 ft.) to n.w. Costa Rica.

PANAMA FLYCATCHER, *Camptostoma flaviventre.* 4   Plate 30
(Considered a race of C. *obsoletum* by some.)
FIELD MARKS: Back greenish olive; wing bars distinct; underparts yellow.
RANGE: Pacific slope of Costa Rica and Panama; favors more moist conditions than Beardless Flycatcher, but their ranges overlap some.

GRAY-HEADED FLYCATCHER, *Phyllomyias griseiceps.* 4½
Plate 30
FIELD MARKS: Crown olive-gray; no wing bars.
RANGE: Far e. Panama and Pacific coast of Colombia.

PALTRY TYRANNULET, *Tyranniscus vilissimus.* 4   Plate 30
FIELD MARKS: All Tyrannulets have short, thick bills (less than half as long as head) and tails that are shorter than the wing. In this species the crown is dark slate; underparts have no olive-yellow except on sides and flanks.
RANGE: S. Mexico (Chiapas) to Venezuela and Colombia; favors edge in humid woods (tropical and subtropical). Not in British Honduras.

YELLOW-CROWNED TYRANNULET, *Tyrannulus elatus.* 4
Plate 30
FIELD MARKS: Crown dusky slate with hidden yellow patch; wing bars
yellowish white.
RANGE: Panama to Brazil and Bolivia; favors edge habitats.

ZELEDON'S TYRANNULET, *Acrochordopus zeledoni.* 4¼
Plate 30
FIELD MARKS: Lower bill pink; underparts largely yellow.
RANGE: Costa Rica to Peru.

YELLOW-BELLIED TYRANNULET, *Ornithion semiflavum.* 3
Plate 30
(Placed in the genus *Microtriccus* by some.)
FIELD MARKS: Crown slate; line over eye white.
RANGE: Mexico (s. Veracruz and e. Oaxaca, south in tropical woods),
Guatemala, Honduras, Nicaragua, and s.w. Costa Rica.

BROWN-CAPPED TYRANNULET, *Ornithion brunneicapillum.* 3
Plate 30
(Considered a race of *O. semiflavum* by some; placed in genus
Microtriccus by some.)
FIELD MARKS: Crown dark brown; line over eye does not extend back
of ear region.
RANGE: Costa Rica (Caribbean slope) to Ecuador.

GRAY-CAPPED LEPTOPOGON, *Leptopogon superciliaris.* 5
Plate 30
FIELD MARKS: Bill about as long as head; tail somewhat shorter than
wing, dark grayish brown; feathers edged with olive-green.
RANGE: Costa Rica to Brazil and Bolivia; favors subtropical woods.

BROWN-CAPPED LEPTOPOGON, *Leptopogon amaurocephalus.*
4½ Plate 30
FIELD MARKS: Tail brown with olive-brown edging.
RANGE: Mexico (s. Veracruz and e. Oaxaca to Chiapas; humid lowlands), Guatemala, Honduras, and south to Argentina and Bolivia.

OLEAGINOUS PIPROMORPHA, *Pipromorpha oleaginea.* 5
Plate 30
FIELD MARKS: Bill about half as long as head and slender; throat olive-
gray; belly ochraceous-yellow.
RANGE: Mexico (e. San Luis Potosí and Veracruz and south; more
common in lowlands, but up to 5000 ft.) to Brazil and Bolivia.

OLIVACEOUS MIONECTES, *Mionectes olivaceus.* 5 Plate 30
RANGE: Costa Rica to Venezuela and Peru; humid subtropics.

SHARPBILLS: Oxyruncidae

Fruit-eating, forest birds, which superficially resemble Flycatchers.

CRESTED SHARPBILL, *Oxyruncus cristatus.* 6½   Plate 27
FIELD MARKS: Partly concealed crest feathers orange red.
RANGE: Humid mt. forests in Costa Rica to Brazil and Paraguay.

LARKS: Alaudidae

HORNED LARK, *Eremophila alpestris.* 6
RANGE: North America and Mexico (Baja California to Tamaulipas
and south to Oaxaca and Veracruz; mostly in open plains); Colombia; Eurasia.

SWALLOWS: Hirundinidae

PURPLE MARTIN, *Progne subis.* 7   Plate 31
RANGE: North America to c. Mexico (Baja California to Coahuila and
south to Michoacán); winters from e. Mexico to Brazil.

SINALOA MARTIN, *Progne sinaloae.* 6½   Plate 31
(Considered a race of *S. subis* by some and *S. dominicensis* by
others.)
FIELD MARKS: Male is similar to Purple Martin but has median breast
and belly white; female shows a more decided contrast of the somewhat darker chest and sides with the white belly than the Purple
Martin does.
RANGE: Mexico (5000 to 9000 ft. in mts.; s.e. Sonora and s.w. Chihuahua to Nayarit and Jalisco; migratory, uncommon, and local).

GRAY-BREASTED MARTIN, *Progne chalybea.* 6½   Plate 31
FIELD MARKS: Similar to female Purple Martin but more smoothly
colored; lacks pale gray mottling on forehead; the male is purple
above.
RANGE: Mexico (Nayarit to Oaxaca; Coahuila to Tamaulipas and
south to Chiapas and Yucatán; favors lower elevation than last
species; migratory) to Argentina and Bolivia; casual or accidental
in s. Texas.

BROWN-CHESTED MARTIN, *Phaeoprogne tapera.* 6½   Plate 31
RANGE: South America; birds in southern part of range migrate in
summer as far as Panama.

CLIFF SWALLOW, *Petrochelidon pyrrhonota.* 5
RANGE: North America to Mexico (Sinaloa to Tamaulipas and south to Oaxaca and Veracruz); on migration to s. South America.

CAVE SWALLOW, *Petrochelidon fulva.* 5
FIELD MARKS: Similar to Cliff Swallow, but forehead is darker than throat.
RANGE: W. Texas, Mexico (Coahuila to Chiapas and Yucatán).

BARN SWALLOW, *Hirundo rustica.* 6
RANGE: North America to Mexico (Sonora across to Coahuila and south to Michoacán; large numbers migrate along coastal lowlands of Tamaulipas and Veracruz and a smaller number through Yucatán); Eurasia; winters south to Tierra del Fuego.

ROUGH-WINGED SWALLOW, *Stelgidopteryx serripennis.* 5
(Listed as a race of *S. ruficollis* by others.) Plate 31
RANGE: North America from British Columbia to Mexico (mostly in arid interior at 6000 to 8000 ft.; Baja California to Tamaulipas and south to Oaxaca); winters south to Panama.

SALVIN'S SWALLOW, *Steligidopteryx fulvipennis.* 5 Plate 31
(Considered a race of *S. ruficollis* by some.)
FIELD MARKS: Crown distinctly darker than back, tertials edged with white, and throat pale cinnamon-buff. These features make this form "intermediate" between *serripennis* and *uropygialis.*
RANGE: C. Mexico (s. Guerrero to Chiapas; Veracruz to Chiapas; coastal lowlands up to about 5000 ft) to Costa Rica (subtropical regions at 5000 to 6000 ft.) and adjacent w. Panama.

PANAMA SWALLOW, *Stelgidopteryx uropygialis.* 4½ Plate 31
(Considered a race of *S. ruficollis* by some.)
FIELD MARKS: Rump is pale grayish brown or grayish white, in distinct contrast to back.
RANGE: S.e. Nicaragua to n.w. Peru; from coastal lowlands up to 6000 ft. where it overlaps range of previous species in Central America.

RIDGWAY'S SWALLOW, *Stelgidopteryx ridgwayi.* 5 Plate 31
(Considered a race of *S. ruficollis* by some.)
FIELD MARKS: Has black under tail-coverts.
RANGE: The Yucatán peninsula of Mexico.

COBAN SWALLOW, *Notiochelidon pileata.* 5 Plate 31
FIELD MARKS: Rather similar to Salvin's Swallow, but crown is darker (black) and contrasts plainly with the brown back; tail black and

plainly forked (may not show except when banking); under tail-coverts black.
RANGE: Highlands of s. Mexico (s.c. Chiapas), Guatemala, and El Salvador; 5000 to 9000 ft.

WHITE-THIGHED SWALLOW, *Neochelidon tibialis.*   4   Plate 31
FIELD MARKS: Tail less deeply forked than last species; thighs white.
RANGE: C. Panama to Peru.

BLUE-AND-WHITE SWALLOW, *Pygochelidon cyanoleuca.*   5
Plate 31
FIELD MARKS: Like Tree Swallow with black under tail-coverts.
RANGE: Mexico (s. Chiapas where possibly a straggler) to Patagonia.

BANK SWALLOW, *Riparia riparia.*   5
RANGE: North America to Mexican border; southward on migration to South America.

TREE SWALLOW, *Iridoprocne bicolor.*   5
RANGE: North America; in winter as far south as n. South America. (Hundreds of thousands winter in marshes near Tampico and Alvarado, Mexico.)

MANGROVE SWALLOW, *Iridoprocne albilinea.*   5   Plate 31
FIELD MARKS: Whole rump bright white.
RANGE: Mexico (Sonora to Chiapas; Tamaulipas to Yucatán; in coastal marshes and along lagoons and up rivers to as much as a hundred miles inland and up to 300 ft. elevation) to w. Peru.

VIOLET-GREEN SWALLOW, *Tachycineta thalassina.*   5   Plate 31
FIELD MARKS: A white spot on each side of rump.
RANGE: W. North America and Mexico (as far south as Oaxaca and Veracruz; breeding in highlands only in southern part of range); in winter south to w. Panama.

CROWS: Corvidae

AMERICAN RAVEN, *Corvus sinuatus.*   21
   (Considered a race of *C. corax* by others.)
RANGE: North America, Mexico (Baja California and Sonora to Tamaulipas and south to Chiapas; in west from mts. down to sea level; in east confined to pine-oak association in mts. at 3000 to 9000 ft.), Guatemala, El Salvador, Honduras, and Nicaragua.

WHITE-NECKED RAVEN, *Corvus cryptoleucus.*   17½
RANGE: W. United States and Mexico (n. Sonora to Tamaulipas; in

the central plateau as far south as Guanajuato; in semi-desert lowlands in Tamaulipas and in arid plateaus in the central part of the
range).

AMERICAN CROW, *Corvus brachyrhynchos.* 17
RANGE: North America to n.w. Mexico (Baja California and extreme
n. Sonora).

TAMAULIPAS CROW, *Corvus imparatus.* 14   Plate 32
VOICE: Usually a frog-like *gurrrr.* The pitch is somewhat variable in
different calls and varies from about D^1 up to G^1; the volume is
rather low.
RANGE: Mexico (from China, Nuevo León to the Rio Grande Delta
and southward via Linares to the area about 15 miles south of
Valles, San Luis Potosí, across to n. Veracruz in the vicinity of
Tampico).

SINALOA CROW, *Corvus sinaloae.* 14   Plate 32
(Considered identical to the last species by some.)
FIELD MARKS: Similar to last species but has a slightly longer tail and a
slightly shorter wing; the voice is quite different.
VOICE: A relatively shrill *ceow.* The highest part is about B^2, and the
pitch slurs down one or one and a half tones. The call sounds very
much like that of the Brown Jay of e. Mexico.
RANGE: Mexico (Pacific slope of s. Sonora to Colima; from sea level
up to about 1000 ft. or more.).

CLARK NUTCRACKER, *Nucifraga columbiana.* 11
RANGE: W. North America to n.w. Mexico (n. Baja California and
occasionally in northern part of other border states; in mts.).

PIÑON JAY, *Gymnorhinus cyanocephalus.* 9
RANGE: Mts. of w. United States to n. Baja California; in winter occasionally in mts. of other n. Mexican states.

WHITE-THROATED MAGPIE-JAY, *Calocitta formosa.* 20
Plate 32
FIELD MARKS: Narrow black collar below white throat.
VOICE: A great variety of figures and phrases. These vary from soft,
mellow, liquid, or tinkling calls all the way to loud, harsh squawks.
Occasionally loud calls of other birds, such as Parrots, are imitated.
RANGE: S.w. Mexico (Colima to Chiapas; up to 3000 ft. in semi-arid
woods and savannas) to n.w. Costa Rica.

BLACK-THROATED MAGPIE-JAY, *Calocitta colliei.* 27   Plate 32
(Considered a race of *C. formosa* by some.)
FIELD MARKS: Throat black (occasionally in any part of the range

there are birds with pale blue spots on the throat that by contrast appear almost white).

VOICE: Loud, rather harsh calls, one of which sounds very similar to that of the Sinaloa Crow.

RANGE: N.w. Mexico (s. Sonora to Jalisco along the Pacific slope; mostly from 100 to 2000 ft.).

BROWN JAY, *Psilorhinus morio.*   17   Plate 32

FIELD MARKS: Belly grayish white; tail dark brownish gray.

VOICE: A slightly nasal *peow,* sometimes so loud and explosive that it almost sounds like *pow.* The highest pitch reached in any of the calls is about D^4. Less excited calls may be softer and accented differently.

RANGE: E. Mexico (s.e. Nuevo León and Tamaulipas to e. Oaxaca, n. Tabasco, and n.e. Chiapas).

WHITE-TIPPED JAY, *Psilorhinus mexicanus.*   17½   Plate 32

(Considered a color phase of *P. morio* by some.)

FIELD MARKS: Belly white; end of tail white.

RANGE: S.e. Mexico (c. Veracruz to Chiapas and Yucatán) to n.w. Panama.

DICKEY JAY, *Cyanocorax dickeyi.*   15   Plate 32

FIELD MARKS: Forehead, crest, and throat black.

RANGE: Sinaloa and adjacent Durango and Nayarit, Mexico; in oak-pine forests at about 5000 ft.; local; family groups range together.

BLACK-CHESTED JAY, *Cyanocorax affinis.*   14   Plate 32

FIELD MARKS: Crown and nape purplish blue.

RANGE: S.e. Costa Rica to w. Venezuela and Colombia .

GREEN JAY, *Xanthoura luxuosa.*   10

(Listed as *X. yncas* by some; placed in genus *Cyanocorax* by some.)

FIELD MARKS: No crest and no noticeable nasal plumes. In the northeastern part of range the eyes are brown; elsewhere they are yellow. Birders may accordingly treat Green-Jay as a genus and list one population as the Northern, or Brown-eyed, Green-Jay and the other as the Yellow-eyed Green-Jay.

VOICE: More nearly like *Cyanocitta* Jays than *Cyanocorax.*

RANGE: S. Texas, Mexico (Colima, Jalisco, Nayarit, and Guanajuato to Chiapas; Nuevo León and Tamaulipas to Chiapas and Yucatán; from sea level up to about 6000 ft. but most abundant at about 3000 ft.; avoids virgin rain forest), Guatemala, British Honduras, and Honduras.

BLUE JAY, *Cyanocitta cristata.* 10
RANGE: E. North America to Texas; rare fall visitor to n.e. Tamaulipas, Mexico.

STELLER'S JAY, *Cyanocitta stelleri.* 11½
FIELD MARKS: Conspicuous long crest.
RANGE: W. North America to mts. of c. Mexico (Baja California, Sonora, and Chihuahua to Oaxaca; e. San Luis Potosí to Puebla and Veracruz; mostly in pine and fir forests from 8000 to 10000 ft., but lower in extreme n.w.).

SHORT-CRESTED JAY, *Cyanocitta ridgwayi.* 11   Plate 32
(Considered a race of *C. stelleri* by others.)
FIELD MARKS: Crest short and blue, usually decumbant (seldom if ever raised in full in manner of Steller's Jay); unless the observer is close enough to notice the white spots above and below the eye, he may mistake this bird for the Unicolored Jay.
RANGE: Pine forests in mts. of Chiapas, Mexico, through Guatemala, El Salvador, and Honduras to Nicaragua.

UNICOLORED JAY, *Aphelocoma unicolor.* 12   Plate 32
FIELD MARKS: Immatures are largely grayish brown.
VOICE: Usual call is rather similar to that of the Mexican Jay. There is a shrill, short "whistle," *O'Ink* (or *O'Weet*) and a lower pitched *wert.* The first is pitched about F^4 and the last B^3. The calls may be given singly or in series. Three such calls might be sounded in one sec. or a bit less. The higher one might be confused with one call of the Azure-hooded Jay, but the latter will almost certainly also use his low-pitched call, which is different.
RANGE: Mexico (pine-oak woods and cloud forests in mts. of Guerrero, Veracruz, Puebla, Oaxaca, and Chiapas), Guatemala, El Salvador, and Honduras.

MEXICAN JAY, *Aphelocoma ultramarina.* 11
RANGE: Mts. of s.w. United States and Mexico (Sonora across to Nuevo León and Veracruz; in pine-oak woods from 4000 to 8000 ft.).

SCRUB JAY, *Aphelocoma coerulescens.* 10   Plate 32
RANGE: Florida, w. United States, and Mexico (Baja California, Sonora, Chihuahua, and Coahuila to Guerrero, Oaxaca, Puebla, and Veracruz; in scrubby oak woods, shrubby slopes, or "succulent desert" at from 5000 to 6000 ft.).

SILVER-THROATED JAY, *Cyanolyca argentigula.* 10   Plate 32
FIELD MARKS: Throat patch silver or pale lavender.
RANGE: Mts. of Costa Rica and w. Panama; cloud forests 4000 ft. up.

BLACK-THROATED JAY, *Cyanolyca pumilo.*   10   Plate 32
RANGE: Mts. of s. Mexico (s.w. Chiapas in dense underbrush of humid
   forests), Guatemala, El Salvador, and Honduras.

DWARF JAY, *Cyanolyca nana.*   9   Plate 32
RANGE: Mts. of e.c. Mexico (Mexico, Veracruz, and Oaxaca).

OMILTEME JAY, *Cyanolyca mirabilis.*   9½   Plate 32
RANGE: Oak-pine forest on mt. at Omilteme, Guerrero, Mexico.

AZURE-HOODED JAY, *Cyanolyca cucullata.*   11½   Plate 32
   (Considered a race of *C. pulchra* by some.)
FIELD MARKS: Patch on back of crown light blue bordered on each side
   by a narrow white line.
VOICE: A somewhat raspy *ur'Rank* that is very similar to the call of a
   Steller's Jay. At the highest part, the pitch is about D^2. There is also
   a call of much higher pitch that may be shown as *wike*. In this, the
   top pitch is E^4. The calls may be given singly or in series so that
   three would require one sec.
RANGE: Mts. of e. Mexico (e. San Luis Potosí to Chiapas; cloud forests
   at 3000 to 5000 ft.), Guatemala, and Honduras.

SAN BLAS JAY, *Cissilopha sanblasiana.*   12½   Plate 32
FIELD MARKS: A small frontal crest is formed by straight and somewhat elongated feathers in the middle of the forehead; eyes dull
   yellow or brown depending upon age of individual; bill black in
   adults and yellow in immatures.
RANGE: W. Mexico (Pacific slope in Nayarit and south to Guerrero; the
   mangrove association and woods just back of it are favored, but
   range extends up slope for several hundred feet at least).

BEECHEY JAY, *Cissilopha beecheii.*   15   Plate 32
FIELD MARKS: No frontal crest; eyes bright yellow.
VOICE: A rather soft *jaay* call is so nasal and burry that it is probably
   better represented as *jerrr* or *jurrr,* according to the pitch, which
   varies with different individuals from F^1 up to A^1. The sound is almost like that of a fly buzzing under a piece of paper. A single call
   or a slow or fast series (up to ten in five sec.) is used.
RANGE: W. Mexico (s.e. Sonora, Sinaloa, and Nayarit; up to 1500 ft.).

YUCATAN JAY, *Cissilopha yucatanica.*   13   Plate 32
   (Considered a race of *C. sanblasiana* by some.)
FIELD MARKS: Similar to the Beechy Jay but lacks the bright yellow
   iris. No frontal crest; however, at times all feathers of the head are
   erected, giving the head a slightly fuzzy look. Immatures have white
   spots at the tip of the outside tail feathers.

VOICE: There are numerous and varied calls, including a loud, harsh clatter or rattle and a rather loud, sharp *pip*; also a series of *che* figures, which brings to mind a Titmouse song and which might be mistaken for a song of the Peten Vireo or of the Orange Oriole.

RANGE: Yucatán peninsula of Mexico and adjacent "mainland" Campeche, Peten district of Guatemala and British Honduras.

HARTLAUB JAY, *Cissilopha melanocyanea.* 12

FIELD MARKS: Similar to Yucatan Jay but with a yellow iris (immatures, brown iris); belly, sides, and flanks are grayish blue; feathers of crown are longer and capable of being erected into a bushy crest, although this is seldom done.

RANGE: Highlands of Guatemala, El Salvador, Honduras, and Nicaragua; in pine association largely; from 3000 to 8000 ft.

TITMICE: Paridae

MEXICAN CHICKADEE, *Parus sclateri.* 4½

RANGE: Mts. of s.w. United States and Mexico (Sonora to Chihuahua and south to Oaxaca and Veracruz; in pine-oak and fir regions).

MOUNTAIN CHICKADEE, *Parus gambeli.* 4½

RANGE: Mts. of w. North America to n. Baja California.

BLACK-CRESTED TITMOUSE, *Parus atricristatus.* 4½

RANGE: Texas and n.e. Mexico (Coahuila, Nuevo León, and Tamaulipas to c. Veracruz; lowlands up to 3000 ft.; dry woods or brush up to 3000 ft.)

PLAIN TITMOUSE, *Parus inornatus.* 5

RANGE: W. United States to Baja California and n.e. Sonora, Mexico.

BRIDLED TITMOUSE, *Parus wollweberi.* 4½

RANGE: Mts. of s.w. United States and n. Mexico (Sonora to Tamaulipas and south to Oaxaca; in pine-oak regions).

VERDIN, *Auriparus flaviceps.* 3½

RANGE: S.w. United States and n. Mexico (Baja California to Tamaulipas and south to Sinaloa and Hidalgo; in semi-deserts and dry brushy woods from lowlands up to 8000 ft.).

PLAIN BUSHTIT, *Psaltriparus minimus.* 3½

RANGE: W. United States and n.w. Mexico (Baja California and Sonora; highlands).

BLACK-EARED BUSHTIT, *Psaltriparus melanotis.* 3½
(Considered a race of *P. minimus* by some.)
RANGE: Highlands of s.w. United States, Mexico (w. Sonora to w. Nuevo León and south to Chiapas and Veracruz; in higher pine and fir forests), and Guatemala.

NUTHATCHES: Sittidae

WHITE-BREASTED NUTHATCH, *Sitta carolinensis.* 5
RANGE: North America to Mexico (Baja California to Nuevo León and south to Guatemalan border of Chiapas; pine regions).

RED-BREASTED NUTHATCH, *Sitta canadensis.* 4
RANGE: North America to Mexico (Guadalupe Island; occasional or rare in border states in the north, at least in winter).

PYGMY NUTHATCH, *Sitta pygmaea.* 3½
RANGE: W. North America to Mexico (mts. of Baja California to Nuevo León and south to Puebla and Veracruz).

CREEPERS: Certhiidae

BROWN CREEPER, *Certhia americana.* 5
(Considered a race of *C. familiaris* by some.)
RANGE: North America, Mexico (Sonora to Tamaulipas and south to Veracruz and Chiapas; in higher pine and fir forests), Guatemala, Honduras, and Nicaragua.

WREN-TITS: Chamaeidae

WREN-TIT, *Chamaea fasciata.* 5½
RANGE: Pacific coast of United States to n. Baja California.

DIPPERS: Cinclidae

AMERICAN DIPPER, *Cinclus mexicanus.* 6
RANGE: W. North America and Mexico (Chihuahua to Oaxaca, Puebla, and Veracruz; along rapid mountain streams) to w. Panama.

WRENS: Troglodytidae

SHORT-BILLED MARSH-WREN, *Cistothorus stellaris*.   4
   (Considered a race of *C. platensis* of South America by some.)
RANGE: E. North America; winters to n.e. Mexico (Tamaulipas and e. San Luis Potosí).

GUATEMALAN MARSH-WREN, *Cistothorus elegans*.   4
   (Considered a race of *C. platensis* by some.)
FIELD MARKS: Similar to Short-billed Marsh-Wren.
RANGE: Mexico (Michoacán, Veracruz, and Chiapas; highland grassy marshes) and south to w. Panama.

LONG-BILLED MARSH-WREN, *Telmatodytes pulustris*.   4½
RANGE: North America to n. Sonora, Mexico; in winter to Jalisco and Veracruz.

GRAY CACTUS-WREN, *Campylorhynchus megalopterus*.   7
                                                            Plate 33
RANGE: Mexico (Michoacán, Morelos, Mexico, Veracruz and Oaxaca; humid pine and fir forests; 5000 to 10000 ft.).

BANDED CACTUS-WREN, *Campylorhynchus zonatus*.   7   Plate 33
FIELD MARKS: No bars on belly. Young have black crowns.
VOICE: A series of low-pitched, somewhat Jay-like sounds, one of which might be shown as *churr, rurrr,* or *jurr,* and another as *rahay.* The pitch is about D^1 or E^1. Since two birds usually sing at the same time it makes quite a jumble, although there is some rhythm on account of the repetition of accented figures.
RANGE: Mexico (c. Veracruz and e. Oaxaca to Chiapas; from cactus and brush patches in the lowlands up to 8000 ft. or more in pine-oak woods) and south to w. Ecuador.

NORTHERN CACTUS-WREN, *Campylorhynchus brunneicapillus*.
                                                            6½   Plate 33
VOICE: The "song" phrase is a series of rapid figures all on the same pitch, as *churr-churr-churr,* delivered at such a rate that twelve may be given in three sec.; or a more hurried *chu-chu-chu-chu,* given at such a rate that there will be twelve in two sec.
RANGE: S.w. United States and Mexico (Baja California across to Tamaulipas and south to Jalisco and Hidalgo; semi-desert regions up to 5000 ft. or more).

YUCATAN CACTUS-WREN, *Campylorhynchus yucatanicus.*   6½
Plate 33

(Considered a race of *C. brunneicapillus* by some.)

FIELD MARKS: Similar to last species (both have streaks on the back rather than bars), but the crown is grayer and the under tail-coverts are barred rather than spotted.

VOICE: The song is a series of slow, deliberate motifs and might be said to be intermediate in effect between that of the Chiapas Cactus-Wren and the Rufous-backed Cactus-Wren, as it is low pitched like the first and phrased like the last. The motifs are usually relatively long, which makes it awkward to suggest the form and accent by use of words. However, one might say it is something like *Who'l watch-a-clock* and *huert ja-weet-jah.* Either would require about one sec. or slightly more time, and three of them could be given in five sec. The pitch varies through D^1, E^1, and F^1. The female scolds (presumably her "song") at the same time.

RANGE: Northern part of Yucatán peninsula in arid region.

BOUCARD CACTUS-WREN, *Campylorhynchus jocosus.*   6½
Plate 33

FIELD MARKS: Similar to Northern Cactus-Wren but without spots on the white throat and with much shorter black and white marks on the back. Adults have dusky brown crown, while that of immature is black.

VOICE: Most often heard is a call that sounds like scolding. It is frequently given in rapid series, *chu-chu-chu-chu.* The song is a series of figures or motifs, such as *wEurrr-wEurrr-wEurrr.* This is at such a tempo that seven figures will require five sec.

RANGE: C. Mexico (s. Jalisco through Morelia and Guerrero to w. Puebla and Oaxaca; most common in high "succulent deserts" and semi-deserts, but also into pines; mostly from 4000 to 8000 ft.).

SPOTTED CACTUS-WREN, *Campylorhynchus gularis.*   6½   Plate 33

(Considered a race of *C. jocosus* by some.)

FIELD MARKS: Similar to previous species, but crown is brown (not dusky brown), and the line over the eye is buff or buffy white. The immatures have spots on the breast.

VOICE: The song phrase is made up of a series of motifs or figures that may be different in different phrases. It may be represented as *haltepec-haltepec-haltepec.* It is relatively soft compared to the song of Sclater's Cactus-Wren, and the tempo is such that four figures such as the three shown would be sounded in five sec.

RANGE: N.w. Mexico from s.e. Sonora and Chihuahua to Jalisco, Michoacán, and San Luis Potosí; mostly in rather open oak or oak-pine woods (seems to avoid succulent desert and arid plains which are frequented by the Boucard Cactus-Wren and the Northern Cactus-Wren); from 1500 to 8000 ft.

RUFOUS-NAPED CACTUS-WREN, *Campylorhynchus rufinucha.*
6¼   Plate 33

FIELD MARKS: Crown and line back of eye black; underparts white, speckled with black.

RANGE: S.e. Mexico (Veracruz, e. Puebla, and e. Oaxaca).

SCLATER'S CACTUS-WREN, *Campylorhynchus humilis.*   6
Plate 33

(Considered a race of *C. rufinucha* by some.)

FIELD MARKS: Similar to last species, but the crown is dusky brown to rufous and the line back of eye is chestnut; the under tail-coverts are speckled with black; sometimes the sides and flanks have a few black specks, but usually the underparts are largely white.

VOICE: Loud calls (usually two-figure motifs) are repeated as a series. These may sound something like *Pa-Key* or *Pe-Chark.* The pitch varies from about A^3 to D^4.

RANGE: Mexico (Colima and Michoacán and south through Guerrero and Oaxaca to the arid Pacific slope of Chiapas as far south as Tonalá; from sea level up to about 2000 ft.).

RUFOUS-BACKED CACTUS-WREN
Campylorhynchus capistratus.   7   Plate 33

(Considered a race of *C. rufinucha* by some.)

FIELD MARKS: Crown black; back chestnut or rufous, sometimes with some streaks of buffy white or black; below white or pale buffy white (no black spots).

VOICE: The song is rather similar to that of the last species but is somewhat softer and the motifs are longer, such as *Wait be-careful.* Five such motifs could be delivered in a space of six sec. The female usually sings shorter motifs at the same time.

RANGE: Mexico (Pacific slope of Chiapas below Tonalá) to n.w. Costa Rica; lowlands up to about 4000 ft. in semi-arid brushland.

CHIAPAS CACTUS-WREN, *Campylorhynchus chiapensis.*   7½
Plate 33

(Considered a race of *C. rufinucha* by some.)

FIELD MARKS: Crown black; back bright chestnut; below white; no barring on wings.

VOICE: Lower pitched than other Cactus-Wrens. The song consists of short motifs repeated in series. One such motif may be shown as *Look-out-now.* This would require one sec. for delivery, but there would be only a fraction of a sec. before it was repeated. The pitch of this would be about F^1, F^1 sharp, E^1. Since both members of a pair almost invariably sing at the same time, the combined output often sounds like a guttural jumble.

RANGE: Coastal lowlands in semi-arid brushy areas from Tonalá, Chiapas, Mexico, to the Guatemalan border; local.

WHITE-HEADED CACTUS-WREN
  Campylorhynchus albobrunneus. 7   Plate 33
  (Considered a race of *C. turdinus* by some.)
  RANGE: C. Panama to n.w. (Pacific) Colombia.

RUFOUS-AND-WHITE WREN, *Thryothorus rufalbus.* 5½   Plate 33
FIELD MARKS: Under tail-coverts barred; flanks not barred.
VOICE: The song might be likened to a recording of a Banded Wren
  played at half speed: it is slow and low pitched, making it "alto."
RANGE: Mexico (s.w. Chiapas) to Venezuela and Colombia; favors
  dry creek beds in the lowlands but may rise into humid subtropics.

CAROLINA WREN, *Thryothorus ludovicianus.* 5
RANGE: E. and s. United States and n.e. Mexico (Tamaulipas to e.
  San Luis Potosí).

SINALOA WREN, *Thryothorus sinaloa.* 5   Plate 33
VOICE: The song is loud, and the quality and pitch are about the same
  as in the Banded Wren. The phrases are usually of two- to five-sec.
  duration and are composed of a great variety of motifs. The pitch
  varies from A^3 to B^4, but most of the figures range between A^3
  and E^4. A majority of the phrases end with a sudden single high
  figure (B^4) that is strongly accented but may not seem as loud as
  some others, because it is so shrill. A similar high figure may be
  interposed in the middle of the phrase where it seems completely
  out of place. A four-and-a-quarter-sec. song phrase might be represented as *perteek-hur caWeeo-Weeo tEEt che wit-wit-wit-wit-
  wit-wit-wit-wit chEEt*. The *tEEt* and *chEEt* are the shrill figures;
  the *Weeo-Weeo* (D^4) is quite loud; and the *wit* series is a rattle
  of the type that some will be inclined to call a "trill." A somewhat
  different type of song phrase may be shown as *Wot-cheebur wit-wit
  a'chit-yeeh cheo che-r-r-r-r-r-r-r-r-r-r-r chEEt*. The final *chEEt* is as
  high as before, the *r-r-r* series is a repercussion (roll) lasting about
  a half sec., the *yeh* is a weak, nasal figure something like some
  efforts of a White-eyed Vireo, and the other parts are the usual loud,
  mellow figures and motifs. The whole phrase requires about three
  sec.
RANGE: N.w. Mexico (s.e. Sonora and Chihuahua to Guerrero; from
  sea level up to about 2000 ft.)

STRIPED-BREASTED WREN, *Thryothorus thoracicus.* 4¼
                                                        Plate 33
FIELD MARKS: Crown not black; under tail-coverts barred. Immatures
  have throat brown without black stripes.
RANGE: Nicaragua to w. Panama; restricted to Caribbean slope except

at a few spots where it spills over slightly at some gap in the continental divide; favors underbrush in humid forest.

STRIPED-THROATED WREN, *Thryothorus leucopogon.* 4½
(Considered a race of *T. thoracicus* by some.) Plate 33
RANGE: E. Panama to w. Ecuador.

SALVIN'S WREN, *Thryothorus semibadius.* 5 Plate 33
(Considered a race of *T. atrogularis* by some.)
FIELD MARKS: Crown chestnut, bordered at side by a narrow line of black; underparts (except throat) barred with black.
RANGE: S.w. Costa Rica and adjacent Panama; tropical zone from the mangroves up to humid woods at 3000 ft; favors edge underbrush.

BANDED WREN, *Thryothorus pleurostictus.* 5½ Plate 33
VOICE: Soft calls are shown as *queek* and *querk*, which may be given alternately. The songs are loud, clear, and mellow for the most part. Some motifs are of Cardinal-like quality, but some figures are very shrill (these seem to be weak and unaccented.). The pitch varies from G^3 up to B^4, but most of the figures do not go above D^4. The song phrases vary in duration from two to twelve sec. One phrase may be represented as *chur re-e-e-e-e-e-e-e-e-e-e-e Sweet-weet-weet-weet-weet.* This lasts three sec.; the *re-e-e* is a repercussion. Another type lasting about four sec. may be shown as *rre Seeeewa ChaChe wheo-weo-weo-weo-weo.* The introductory *rre* is quite weak and a bit buzzy; the other parts are loud and clear.
RANGE: Pacific slope of Mexico (Morelos and Guerrero to Chiapas; semi-arid brushland and dry woods) to n.w. Costa Rica.

BUFF-BELLIED WREN, *Thryothorus leucotis.* 5 Plate 33
RANGE: C. Panama and n. Colombia.

MODEST WREN, *Thryothorus modestus.* 5 Plate 33
FIELD MARKS: No barring on under parts; flanks cinnamon-buff.
RANGE: Mexico (w. Chiapas and possibly Oaxaca and Guerrero) to c. Panama; thickets in semi-open country (avoids interior of forest).

ZELEDON'S WREN, *Thryothorus zeledoni.* 5¼ Plate 33
(Considered a race of *T. modestus* by some.)
FIELD MARKS: Larger and grayer than Modest Wren; has relatively larger bill and shorter tail.
RANGE: Caribbean lowlands of Nicaragua, Costa Rica, and w. Panama.

WHITE-BROWED WREN, *Thryothorus albinucha.* 5 Plate 34
FIELD MARKS: Similar to Carolina Wren, but tail is more like that of Bewick Wren, although shorter.

RANGE: Mexico (Campeche, Yucatán, and Quintana Roo; favors dry woods and semi-arid brushland but is also present in some humid woods), Guatemala (Peten district), and Nicaragua.

HAPPY WREN, *Thryothorus felix.* 5   Plate 34
FIELD MARKS: Conspicuous black and white stripes on cheeks; under tail-coverts barred with black.
VOICE: The song is made up of several short phrases that may be represented by *Chu-Wit Chur-r-r-r-r.* This requires one and a half sec.; the pitch of the first three figures is about E⁴, F⁴, D⁴. The *Chur-r-r-r* is a rattle, and the *Wit* is more strongly accented than the other parts. The phrase is repeated a number of times with only a short rest between each.
RANGE: W. Mexico (s. Sonora and w. Durango and south to w. Puebla and Oaxaca; lowlands to 4000 ft.; avoids extremely arid regions).

SPOTTED-BREASTED WREN, *Thryothorus maculipectus.* 5
(Considered a race of *T. rutilus* by some.)   Plate 34
VOICE: The call is a short, soft musical figure that has a rising inflection, *pleeet;* it sounds as though the bird were "trilling" its tongue. The structure of the song phrase varies from place to place, but the quality, style, pitch, and approximate length remain the same so that when one is learned the others will be recognized. The phrases are loud, clear, and ringing; they are repeated so that four will be given in about seven sec. The pitch varies from D⁴ up to G⁴. Some phrases may be paraphrased as *Skip-teer Rea-cheer-forYou, Cheet-weigh get-yuWhip, You-can't-hear-me-can-you, ReeChee-raVeer-chWoo.*
RANGE: Mexico (c. Tamaulipas and e. San Luis Potosí to Chiapas and Yucatán; sea level up to 3000 ft. or more), Guatemala, British Honduras, El Salvador, Honduras, and Nicaragua.

RUFOUS-BREASTED WREN, *Thryothorus rutilus.* 5   Plate 34
RANGE: Costa Rica (Pacific slope) to Venezuela and Colombia.

BLACK-CAPPED WREN, *Thryothorus nigricapillus.* 5   Plate 34
RANGE: E. Panama to w. Ecuador.

BAY WREN, *Thryothorus castaneus.* 5   Plate 34
(Considered a race of *T. nigricapillus* by some.)
RANGE: Caribbean slope of Nicaragua, Costa Rica, and both slopes of w. Panama.

NORTHERN BLACK-THROATED WREN, *Thryothorus atrogularis.*
5¼ Plate 34
RANGE: Caribbean slope in Nicaragua, Costa Rica, and w. Panama; favors low brushy thickets in semi-open areas near woods.

SOUTHERN BLACK-THROATED WREN, *Thryothorus spadix.*

5½   Plate 34

FIELD MARKS: Crown black (not brown); tail black barred with rufous; breast rufous.

RANGE: Highlands of e. Panama and n.w. Colombia.

BLACK-BELLIED WREN, *Thryothorus fasciatoventris.*   5½   Plate 34

RANGE: S.w. Costa Rica to Colombia; humid tropics; favors the densest thickets along streams or in cutover areas.

BEWICK WREN, *Thryomanes bewickii.*   4½

RANGE: United States and Mexico (Baja California to Tamaulipas and south to Oaxaca and Veracruz); favors semi-desert regions.

NORTHERN HOUSE-WREN, *Troglodytes aedon.*   4½

RANGE: North America to n.w. Mexico (mts. of Baja California; in winter to s. Mexico).

SOUTHERN HOUSE-WREN, *Troglodytes musculus.*   4½   Plate 34

(Considered a race of *T. aedon* by some.)

FIELD MARKS: Similar to Northern House-Wren, but tail is relatively shorter, and the underparts are washed with buff.

RANGE: Mexico (s.e. Tamaulipas to Oaxaca, Chiapas, and Yucatán) to South America.

COZUMEL HOUSE-WREN, *Troglodytes beani.*   4½   Plate 34

(Considered a race of *T. musculus* by some.)

RANGE: Cozumel Island off coast of Quintana Roo, Mexico.

BROWN-THROATED HOUSE-WREN, *Troglodytes brunneicollis.*

(Considered a race of *T. aedon* by some.)   4½   Plate 34

RANGE: Mts. of s. Arizona to Isthmus of Tehuantepec in Mexico.

RUFOUS-BROWED HOUSE-WREN, *Troglodytes rufociliatus.*   4

Plate 34

RANGE: Mts. of s. Mexico (s.c. Chiapas at 8000 to 10000 ft.), Guatemala, El Salvador, and Honduras.

OCHRACEOUS HOUSE-WREN, *Troglodytes ochraceus.*   4   Plate 34

(Considered a race of *T. solstitialis* by some.)

RANGE: Highlands of Costa Rica and w. Panama.

TIMBERLINE WREN, *Thryorchilus browni.*   3½   Plate 34

RANGE: Mt. peaks in Costa Rica and w. Panama; from a little below to a little above timber line; frequents impenetrable "dwarf bamboo" thickets and tangles of brush at forest edge.

WHITE-BREASTED WOOD-WREN, *Henicorhina leucosticta.* 4

Plate 34

FIELD MARKS: Tail quite short; face and side of neck streaked with black and white.

VOICE: The song phrases are short, lasting about one sec. and are usually repeated a number of times before another is taken up, although two are sometimes used alternately. The rest between the phrases is usually about one sec., but in some songs the pause may be as long as three sec. The phrases are loud and clear and almost liquid. One phrase may be represented as *three-for-free*; the pitch is about E^4 (the phrase being E^4, E^4 flat, E^4). Most similar song phrases, such as *cherie-cherie-been, cherie ch-ee, a-wee ah-la-ee,* and *ah we-we,* are all pitched in the range E^4 to F^4. A somewhat lower type is *worl-may-play,* which varies from B^3 to D^4.

RANGE: Mexico (e. San Luis Potosí and south through Veracruz, e. Puebla, e. Oaxaca to Chiapas, Campeche, and Quintana Roo; sea level up to 4000 ft. in extreme south; stays low in underbrush of humid tropical woods) to Brazil and Peru. Not in El Salvador.

GRAY-BREASTED WOOD-WREN, *Henicorhina leucophrys.* 4

Plate 34

VOICE: Short song phrases are repeated in series. The pitch varies from D^4 to C^5. Most of the phrases require about one sec.; these may be represented by *tic-Cheek-aWee* or *a'cauit ch-weigh-hec.* A phrase requiring two sec. may be given as *weo Teesee Cleo-ha-weechy.*

RANGE: Highlands of Mexico (humid pine-oak forests and cloud forests from e. San Luis Potosí, e. Puebla, and Veracruz to e. Oaxaca and Chiapas; mostly from 4000 to 8000 ft.) to Venezuela and Bolivia.

WHITE-BELLIED WREN, *Uropsila leucogastra.* 4   Plate 34

VOICE: The song is sweet and much softer than that of most Wrens. The pitch ranges from A^3 to E^4, but the range in a given phrase is limited, as B^3, B^3 flat, B^3, C^4 for the phrase *plicaree turk.* Other phrases may be represented as *p'Tur-r-dle-turk* and *plicaRee-Eeo.*

RANGE: Mexico (Colima to Guerrero; Tamaulipas and e. San Luis Potosí through Veracruz, Puebla, Oaxaca, and Chiapas to Yucatán; lowlands up to about 2000 ft.), British Honduras, and Guatemala.

ROCK WREN, *Salpinctes obsoletus.* 5

RANGE: W. North America, Mexico (Baja California to Nuevo León and south to Chiapas; in semi-deserts and rocky cañons or mts.), Guatemala, El Salvador, Honduras, Nicaragua, and n.w. Costa Rica.

CAÑON WREN, *Catherpes mexicanus.* 4½

RANGE: Highlands of w. North America and Mexico (Baja California across to Tamaulipas and south to Chiapas; mostly in high basins and rocky cañons, at times in humid cañons and towns; from 500 to 7000 ft.).

SUMICHRAST WREN, *Hylorchilus sumichrasti.*   5¼   Plate 34
FIELD MARKS: Bill as long as head, straight and slender; throat pale gray or grayish brown.
RANGE: Veracruz, Mexico; in humid woods or rocky slopes at 1500 to 2000 ft.; very local in region south of Córdoba.

NORTHERN NIGHTINGALE-WREN, *Microcerculus philomela.*   4
Plate 34

(Considered a race of *M. marginatus* by some.)
FIELD MARKS: Bill about as long as head and straight; throat white; breast and belly brownish gray; these color features are, however, variable, so that there is overlapping with the following species; hence, the birds are best separated by the song.
VOICE: The song phrase is made up of a long series of figures that slowly move up and down the scale at random and resemble notes of a fife.
RANGE: S. Mexico (e. Chiapas) to c. Costa Rica; humid, tall forest in tropical and subtropical regions.

SOUTHERN NIGHTINGALE-WREN, *Microcerculus luscinia.*   4
(Considered a race of *M. marginatus* by some and of *M. philomela* by others.)   Plate 34
FIELD MARKS: Underparts white in adults, brown in young.
RANGE: C. Costa Rica to Panama.

NORTHERN MUSICAL-WREN, *Cyphorhinus phaeocephalus.*   4¼
Plate 34

(Considered a race of *C. arada* by some.)
FIELD MARKS: Bill almost as long as head and wedge-shaped; tail about half as long as wing; no line over eye; breast chestnut; a small area of bare skin around eye.
RANGE: Honduras to w. Ecuador; favors tropical forest along the Caribbean and is semiterrestrial.

MOCKINGBIRDS: Mimidae

BLACK CATBIRD, *Melanoptila glabirostris.*   8   Plate 35
RANGE: Mexico (Campeche, Yucatán, and Quintana Roo), British Honduras, and Honduras; in thickets in semi-arid regions or thickets that have sprung up in partially cleared areas.

NORTHERN CATBIRD, *Dumetella carolinensis.* 8
RANGE: North America; winters to Panama.

NORTHERN MOCKINGBIRD, *Mimus polyglottos.* 9
RANGE: United States and Mexico (Baja California to Tamaulipas and south to Oaxaca and Veracruz; confined to semi-desert and savanna regions or areas of open woods).

GRACEFUL MOCKINGBIRD, *Mimus gilvus.* 9   Plate 35
FIELD MARKS: No white patches show on wings in flight; tail feathers (except middle pair) tipped with white.
RANGE: Mexico (extreme s. Oaxaca to Chiapas; extreme s. Veracruz to Chiapas and Yucatán; semi-desert or savanna regions) to Honduras; Panama Canal Zone; Colombia to Brazil.

MEXICAN BLUE-MOCKINGBIRD, *Melanotis caerulescens.* 10
                                                              Plate 35
VOICE: The calls are varied and frequently loud. The pitch varies from D^2 up to A^4 or higher. At times one figure will be very high and thin, and the next one nearly three octaves lower and so startlingly different as to suggest it was made by a different bird. Some motifs resemble those of a Yellow-breasted Chat and some are more like those of other Thrashers but generally louder and more disjointed or haltingly given. The same song phrase or series of motifs will frequently be repeated a number of times. There are liquid vibratos and dry (bonelike) rattles, full rich figures, and thin squeaky or buzzy ones.
RANGE: Mexico (cloud forest and oak woods for the most part, but on the Pacific slope occasionally down to sea level; from Sonora to Tamaulipas and south to the Isthmus of Tehuantepec; favors thick low cover in underbrush mostly from 3000 to 6000 ft.).

WHITE-BREASTED BLUE-MOCKINGBIRD
Melanotis hypoleucus. 10½   Plate 35
(Considered a race of *M. caerulescens* by some.)
RANGE: Highlands of Mexico south of Isthmus of Tehuantepec (4000 to 8000 ft.), Guatemala, El Salvador, and Honduras.

LONG-BILLED THRASHER, *Toxostoma longirostre.* 10
RANGE: S. Texas and e. Mexico (Coahuila, Nuevo León, and Tamaulipas south to Querétaro, Puebla, and Veracruz).

BROWN THRASHER, *Toxostoma rufum.* 10
RANGE: E. North America; winters south to Rio Grande region of Tamaulipas; rare.

COZUMEL THRASHER, *Toxostoma guttatum.*   9½   Plate 35
RANGE: Cozumel Island.

OCELLATED THRASHER, *Toxostoma ocellatum.*   11   Plate 35
VOICE: There are short, halting phrases that sound like an effort of a
  Mexican Blue-Mockingbird, such as represented by *torbit torbit-jay
  torbit chur torbit torbit-jay.* Figures or motifs are frequently repeated
  twice and sometimes three times, and there may be a pause of a
  sec. or more between motifs. When in "full song" this species sounds
  more like the Curve-billed Thrasher.
RANGE: Mexico (Hidalgo, Mexico, Morelos, Puebla, and Oaxaca; in
  rather dry, open oak woods or in regions of low scrubby oaks mixed
  with other scattered shrubs; from 4000 to 7000 ft.).

GRAY THRASHER, *Toxostoma cinereum.*   9½   Plate 35
RANGE: Baja California.

BENDIRE THRASHER, *Toxostoma bendirei.*   8½
RANGE: S.w. United States and n.w. Mexico (Sonora; northern arid
  areas; to Sinaloa in winter).

CURVE-BILLED THRASHER, *Toxostoma curvirostre.*   10
FIELD MARKS: The eye is orange or yellow.
RANGE: S.w. United States and Mexico (Sonora to Tamaulipas and
  south to Oaxaca and Veracruz; in semi-desert regions; sea level up to
  7000 ft.).

CALIFORNIA THRASHER, *Toxostoma redivivum.*   10
RANGE: California and Baja California.

LECONTE THRASHER, *Toxostoma lecontei.*   9½
RANGE: S.w. United States and n.w. Mexico (Baja California and n.w.
  Sonora).

CRISSAL THRASHER, *Toxostoma dorsale.*   10½
RANGE: S.w. United States and n.w. Mexico (Baja California and
  Sonora to Coahuila and south to Hidalgo).

SOCORRO THRASHER, *Mimodes graysoni.*   9½   Plate 35
RANGE: Socorro Island off western coast of Mexico.

SAGE THRASHER, *Oreoscoptes montanus.*   7½
RANGE: W. North America; winters to n. Mexico (Baja California to
  Tamaulipas).

BLACK-CAPPED MOCKINGTHRUSH, *Donacobius atricapillus.*   9
Plate 35
FIELD MARKS:Tail graduated, ends of feathers white.
RANGE: E. Panama to Argentina and Bolivia.

THRUSHES: Turdidae

AMERICAN ROBIN, *Turdus migratorius.*   8½
RANGE: North America to highlands of Mexico (e. Sonora and Durango
to Guerrero; w. Tamaulipas and south to Veracruz, Puebla, and
Oaxaca; in oak-pine forest; 8000 to 10000 ft.; in winter to sea
level in various regions) and south in winter to Guatemala.

SAN LUCAS ROBIN, *Turdus confinis.*   9   Plate 36
(Considered a race of *T. migratorius* by some.)
FIELD MARKS: Crown same shade as back (not darker); white line
over eye continuous (not broken).
RANGE: Mts. at southern extremity of Baja California.

RUFOUS-COLLARED ROBIN, *Turdus rufitorques.*   9   Plate 36
FIELD MARKS: Under tail-coverts largely brownish gray; male has black
belly.
RANGE: Highlands of extreme s. Mexico (mts. of c. and s. Chiapas;
oak-pine region from 5000 to 10000 ft.), Guatemala, and El
Salvador.

RUFOUS-BACKED ROBIN, *Turdus rufopalliatus.*   9   Plate 36
RANGE: W. Mexico (Sonora to the Isthmus of Tehuantepec in Oaxaca;
east to Distrito Federal; lowlands up to 7000 ft, tends to stay below
the range of the American Robin).

WHITE-THROATED ROBIN, *Turdus assimilis.*   8½   Plate 36
(Considered a race of *T. albicollis* by some.)
VOICE: Calls may be represented as *swee, tseet,* or a heavier *seeerp,
turp,* or *trup.* At a distance one call may sound like *beep-beep-beep.*
The song phrases vary in composition from place to place and also
individually, but the quality, form, and tempo are the same, and,
hence, the song may be recognized. It is usually loud and clear and
made up of a series of short figures or motifs (many of them double)
that are delivered in a staccato manner with about one per sec. A
typical phrase may be shown as *wheewa chipcheree chur-chur twe-
twe turi-turi cheo-cheo.* This requires six sec. Also, *treetreeo wheeo
where truly-truly cheewee weo-weo wehere truly-truly*; this requires
eight sec.
RANGE: Mexico (s.e. Sonora to Durango and south to Oaxaca; w.

Tamaulipas and e. San Luis Potosí south to Chiapas; usually from 3000 to 7000 ft. but locally lower in west; on Atlantic slope favors cloud forest) to Ecuador.

GRAY'S ROBIN, *Turdus grayi.* 9   Plate 36
VOICE: Calls of clear "whistled" quality that require about one sec. for delivery may be shown as *meeoo* and *meeert.* A lower-pitched *cut-cut* possibly indicates worry or alarm. The song is smoother and usually more melodious than that of the previous species. A number of figures or motifs are doubled in a given phrase, and some are used several times and are varied in arrangement in succeeding phrases. Such composition gives the melody, and the more accomplished singers attain a perfect measured rhythm. (In some areas the dawn song is somewhat different from that heard later in the day.) The tempo may be illustrated by *wher-hee-cutcut-chitery churr-churr whit-cheur-chee-chewit cherrt-weeoo-chitery,* which requires seven and a half sec. The measured rhythm is possibly better shown with a shorter phrase, such as *farmer-farmer feed-that-cow feed-it feed-it feed-it now.* The pitch varies mostly from C^4 up to E^4.
RANGE: Extreme s. Texas, Mexico (Nuevo León and Tamaulipas to Chiapas and Yucatán; lowlands up to 5000 ft. or more but more common below 4000 ft.; tends to avoid virgin cloud forest or dense tall humid forest) and south to n. Colombia.

PALE-VENTED ROBIN, *Turdus obsoletus.* 8   Plate 36
(Considered a race of *T. fumigatus* by some.)
RANGE: Costa Rica to w. Ecuador; humid forest edge; 3000 to 7000 ft.

MOUNTAIN ROBIN, *Turdus plebejus.* 9   Plate 36
(Considered a race of *T. ignobilis* by some.)
VOICE: Song is very high pitched and fast, so that it might be mistaken for sound produced by an insect, but the jerky rhythm will identify it if one listens carefully.
RANGE: Mts. of s. Mexico (Chiapas) to w. Panama; from upper subtropical zone up to timber line; favors forest edge and mountain meadows.

BLACK ROBIN, *Turdus infuscatus.* 9   Plate 36
RANGE: Mts. of e. Mexico (s.w. Tamaulipas and e. San Luis Potosí to Chiapas; mostly in cloud forest and beech association; 3000 to 6000 ft.), Guatemala, El Salvador, and Honduras.

SOOTY ROBIN, *Turdus nigrescens.* 9½   Plate 36
RANGE: Mts. of Costa Rica and w. Panama; favors high meadows and pastures near timber line.

VARIED THRUSH, *Ixoreus naevius.*   8
RANGE: North America; winters to n. Baja California.

TOWNSEND SOLITAIRE, *Myadestes townsendi.*   7
RANGE: W. North America to Mexico (pine region in mts. of Chihuahua
   and Durango; straggles into e. Sonora and sometimes a bit farther
   south in winter).

BROWN-BACKED SOLITAIRE, *Myadestes obscurus.*   7½   Plate 36
FIELD MARKS: Back brown; throat white bordered by narrow black line.
VOICE: The call is a high-pitched, metallic *wenk*. This is also used as
   an introductory figure in the song phrase. It is slurred very steeply
   upward, beginning at D⁴ and reaching to C⁵, but is so quick that
   one cannot follow its progress. The song is so fast and high pitched
   that the effect is often called squeaky. After the preliminary figures
   the song phrase begins with bugle notes, *dah-dee-day-dah* (D⁴-
   B⁴-G⁴-D⁴), which is no doubt the reason the bird is called "The
   Bugler." A full song phrase with all the preliminary figures may be
   represented by *wenk wenk wenk wenk wenk-wenkdah-dee-day-dah-
   cherkee-werhee-churchur-che-wer-but-but-reeba chip*. The first two
   wenk figures require one sec.; then there is a rest of one and a half
   sec., followed by the next four *wenk* figures (the last one runs into
   the first figure of the phrase proper), which take up one and a
   quarter sec.; the remaining part is crowded into about two and three
   fourths sec. All this makes it too fast to really distinguish the details
   of the figures and therefore makes it impossible to give a very good
   representation.
RANGE: Mts. of Mexico (Chihuahua to Nuevo León and w. Tamaulipas
   and south to Chiapas; mostly in oak-pine woods from 3000 to 7000
   ft. (avoids virgin cloud forest and heavy, humid woods that are
   frequented by the Slate-colored Solitaire; in winter may descend
   into lower areas), Guatemala, El Salvador, and Honduras.

SLATE-COLORED SOLITAIRE, *Myadestes unicolor.*   7   Plate 36
VOICE: The songs are made up of a great variety of figures and motifs,
   most of which are quite liquid and flutelike, but some are rattles
   and some are vibrato figures. The pitch ranges mostly from G³ to
   G⁴. The tempo is unhurried and may be estimated from a representative   phrase—*cheeehee-turtle-eeegypt-rererere-Weeoo-teedeedee-
   dee-WheoWheo-Churrrrr*, which last for five sec.
RANGE: Highlands of e. Mexico (e. San Luis Potosí and Veracruz to
   Chiapas; in cloud forests or similar humid woods in the mts.; mostly
   from 3000 to 5000 ft. but at times down to 2000 ft. in the north)
   to n. Nicaragua.

BLACK-FACED SOLITAIRE, *Myadestes melanops.* 7 Plate 36
(Considered a race of *M. ralloides* by some.)
RANGE: Mts. of Costa Rica and w. Panama; favors cool, wet forest from 3000 to 6000 ft.

VARIED SOLITAIRE, *Myadestes coloratus.* 7 Plate 36
RANGE: Mts. of e. Panama.

WOOD THRUSH, *Hylocichla mustelina.* 7
RANGE: E. North America; in winter as far south as Panama.

HERMIT THRUSH, *Hylocichla guttata.* 7
RANGE: North America to n.w. Mexico (mts. of Baja California); in winter as far south as Guatemala.

OLIVE-BACKED THRUSH, *Hylocichla ustulata.* 6¼
RANGE: N. North America, in winter as far south as Argentina.

GRAY-CHEEKED THRUSH, *Hylocichla minima.* 6¼
RANGE: N. North America; reported on migration in British Honduras, Guatemala, Honduras, Costa Rica, and Panama.

WILSON'S THRUSH, *Hylocichla fuscescens.* 6
RANGE: North America; on migration in Mexico, Honduras, Costa Rica, and Panama.

SPOTTED NIGHTINGALE-THRUSH, *Catharus dryas.* 6¼
Plate 36
RANGE: S. Mexico (cloud forests on mts. of s.w. Chiapas), Guatemala, Honduras, Colombia, Venezuela, Ecuador, Peru, and Bolivia.

BLACK-HEADED NIGHTINGALE-THRUSH, *Catharus mexicanus.*
5½ Plate 36
VOICE: Thin, weak but somewhat liquid, and with a Thrush-like quality. The song phrases are made up of closely joined figures or motifs. One may be repeated a number of times, and then an entirely different one will be used; there may be a pause of six or seven seconds between phrases in a song period. The pitch usually ranges from F^4 up to C^5, and the phrase is usually about one and a half sec. long. At times the bird snaps its bill twice just before it sings so that a "click-click" precedes the vocalization. Song phrases may be represented by *ptChor-ptchrre-a-prricket, plick-a-chee-rurrr-chee-plicket,* and *p'Tay-Cheeter-chay-Reter-chree.*
RANGE: E. Mexico (s.w. Tamaulipas and e. San Luis Potosí to Chiapas; at 3000 to 5000 ft. in cloud forest and brushy areas formerly occupied by cloud forest, and rarely in humid woods at somewhat higher

elevation; favors thicket underbrush) to w. Panama (not in British Honduras or El Salvador).

BLACK-BACKED NIGHTINGALE-THRUSH, *Catharus hellmayri.*
6   Plate 36

(Considered a race of *C. fuscater* by some.)

RANGE: Costa Rica and w. Panama; subtropical areas at 3000 to 6000 ft.

RUSSET NIGHTINGALE-THRUSH, *Catharus occidentalis.* 6
Plate 36

VOICE: The song is similar to that of the Hermit Thrush, and some of the motifs are almost the same.

RANGE: Highlands of n. and c. Mexico (mts. of Chihuahua to w. Tamaulipas and s. to Oaxaca and Veracruz; underbrush in oak-pine and fir forest, mostly from 8000 to 10000 ft. but locally down to 5000 ft. on some humid Atlantic slopes).

FRANTZIUS' NIGHTINGALE-THRUSH, *Catharus frantzii.* 6
Plate 36

(Considered a race of *C. occidentalis* by some.)

FIELD MARKS: Similar to the preceding species, but lower bill is entirely pinkish yellow; throat and belly white (not buffy white).

RANGE: Mexico (s. Jalisco to Chiapas; s.e. San Luis Potosí to Chiapas; cloud forests and humid mountain woods; mostly at 5000 to 9000 ft.) and south to w. Panama.

ORANGE-BILLED NIGHTINGALE-THRUSH
Catharus aurantiirostris. 6   Plate 36

VOICE: Most of the song phrases are stronger and louder than those of the Black-headed Nightingale-Thrush, and many have something of the quality and manner of delivery of the White-eyed Vireo. As in the Vireo, the phrases are frequently somewhat jerky and are repeated a number of times with slight changes here and there or with an added figure or motif at the end, such as may be represented by *Ge-Erick Stig-Roo, Ge-Erick Stig-roo Tic, Ge-Erick Stig-a-Roo Cheer,* and *Ge-Erick Stig-Roo Che-wheerrzie.* Or the phrase may suddenly change, with only a small part of the preceding one retained or to something entirely different, as *Ge-Erick Sie-Beree Churrr-bert* or *Chip Sie-brew che-rragedy.* Some phrases are as weak as those of the Black-headed Nightingale-Thrush, but these are usually short, such as *Chee-rt Wicket.* Most of the phrases vary in length from one to one and a half sec. The pitch is about the same as that used by the Black-headed. Rests between phrases within a period vary mostly from two to five sec.

RANGE: Highlands of Mexico (in thickets in mt. forests or brushy pastures from Sinaloa and Chihuahua south to Guerrero and Puebla;

from s.w. Tamaulipas, e. San Luis Potosí, and Hidalgo south to Veracruz, Oaxaca, and Chiapas; favors subhumid woods and avoids heavy humid woods and cloud forests, but when present in a transition area may venture at times a short distance within an adjoining cloud forest; from 3000 to 8000 ft.) to c. Costa Rica; Venezuela, and n.e. Colombia.

GRAY-HEADED NIGHTINGALE-THRUSH
Catharus griseiceps. 6   Plate 36
(Considered a race of *C. aurantiirostris* by some.)
FIELD MARKS: Head slate gray, contrasting with the tawny olive back; bill orange yellow.
RANGE: Mts. of s.w. Costa Rica and w. Panama.

SLENDER-BILLED NIGHTINGALE-THRUSH
Catharus gracilirostris. 5½   Plate 36
RANGE: Mts. of Costa Rica and w. Panama; 8000 to 10000 ft.

AZTEC THRUSH, *Ridgwayia pinicola.* 8   Plate 36
RANGE: High mts. of Mexico (Chihuahua and Durango south to Guerrero and Veracruz; pine-fir forest at 8000 to 10000 ft.).

EASTERN BLUEBIRD, *Sialia sialis.* 5½
RANGE: North America to highlands of Mexico (mt. forests and high savannas but not deserts, from Sonora to Tamaulipas and south to Chiapas; in lowlands on migration), Guatemala, El Salvador, Honduras, and Nicaragua; near pines.

MEXICAN BLUEBIRD, *Sialia mexicana.* 5½
FIELD MARKS: Throat blue.
RANGE: W. North America to highlands of n.w. Mexico (Baja California and e. Sonora to Nuevo León and south to Zacatecas, Puebla, and Veracruz; mostly from 7000 to 9000 ft.; more widespread in winter).

MOUNTAIN BLUEBIRD, *Sialia currucoides.* 6
RANGE: W. North America; winters to n.w. Mexico (Baja California, Sonora, and occasionally in states to the east).

WREN-THRUSHES: Zeledoniidae

CROWNED WREN-THRUSH, *Zeledonia coronata.* 4   Plate 34
RANGE: Mts. of Costa Rica and w. Panama; favors wet forest from 5000 ft. to timber line, where found on or near the ground in dense thickets.

GNATCATCHERS: Sylviidae

BLUE-GRAY GNATCATCHER, *Polioptila caerulea.* 4
RANGE: United States, Mexico (Baja California to Tamaulipas and south to Chiapas and Yucatán; mostly from 1000 to 5000 ft.; not likely to be found below 1000 ft. in breeding season except in the Yucatán peninsula; local in summer but mostly in savannas and open woods; more widespread in winter), and Guatemala.

WHITE-LORED GNATCATCHER, *Polioptila albiloris.* 4 Plate 35
(Considered a race of *P. plumbea* by some.)
FIELD MARKS: Male—Cap (extending down to upper part of ear region) shining blue black; tertials conspicuously edged with white (this may decrease with wear and be much less noticeable just before moult); cheek (area just below ear) brilliant white. Female —Similar to male, but cap slate instead of black; jaw patch not quite so snowy white; lores white at all seasons instead of just in winter, as in male. Immatures may have a white superciliary line.
RANGE: Mexico (semi-arid regions of Pacific slope from Nayarit to Chiapas; sea level up to 2000 ft.), Guatemala, El Salvador, and n.w. Costa Rica.

YUCATAN GNATCATCHER, *Polioptila albiventris.* 4   Plate 35
(Considered a race of *P. albiloris* by some, of *P. bilineata* by others, and of *P. plumbea* by still others.)
FIELD MARKS: No conspicuous white jaw patch and no faint gray wash on breast as in White-lored Gnatcatcher and has a faint brown wash on the primaries that the White-lored lacks.
VOICE: The song phrase begins with some thin, high-pitched figures and after about four of these becomes clearer and a bit louder. It may be shown as *che-che-chay-chay-Chee-Chee-Chee-Chee.*
RANGE: Arid portions of n. Yucatán.

WHITE-BROWED GNATCATCHER, *Polioptila bilineata.* 4
Plate 35
(Considered a race of *P. plumbea.*)
FIELD MARKS: Black of crown does not extend down to the eye (a white area is left above the eye), and the cap then curves down back of the ear. Sometimes there is a short black line through the eye that will cause the white to appear as a superciliary line (both sexes).
VOICE: The song phrase is a thin, shrill rattle, as *te-te-te-te-te-te,* of about fifteen figures, which lasts about two sec. It is repeated after a pause of some eight sec. The pitch is about B[4].
RANGE: Mexico (lowland humid forests and wet savannas in extreme s. Veracruz to Chiapas, s. Campeche, and Quintana Roo) to w. Colombia.

BLACK-CAPPED GNATCATCHER, *Polioptila nigriceps.* 4

Plate 35

(Considered a race of *P. albiloris* by some and a race of *P. plumbea* by others.)

FIELD MARKS: No bright white cheek patch; there is a faint brown wash on the wings; in winter plumage the male has the eyelids partly white (not a complete eye ring); the outside tail feathers have somewhat more than the terminal half white. Female lacks the black cap.

RANGE: Mexico (s. Sonora to Nayarit).

BLACK-TAILED GNATCATCHER, *Polioptila melanura.* 4

RANGE: S.w. United States and n. Mexico (Baja California, n. Sonora, Chihuahua, and across to w. Nuevo León and w. Tamaulipas; south through Coahuila to w. San Luis Potosí).

SLATE-THROATED GNATCATCHER, *Polioptila schistaceigula.* 4

Plate 35

RANGE: E. Panama to n.w. Ecuador.

KINGLETS: Regulidae

GOLDEN-CROWNED KINGLET, *Regulus satrapa.* 3½

RANGE: North America through highlands of Mexico to Guatemala; favors fir forests at 10000 to 12000 ft. but descends to lowlands in winter.

RUBY-CROWNED KINGLET, *Regulus calendula.* 4

RANGE: North America to Guadalupe Island, Mexico; in winter as far south as Guatemala.

PIPITS: Motacillidae

AMERICAN PIPIT, *Anthus rubescens.* 5½

(Considered a race of *A. spinoletta* by some.)

RANGE: N.e. Siberia and n. North America; winters to El Salvador.

SPRAGUE PIPIT, *Anthus spragueii.* 5½

RANGE: Great Plains of North America; winters to s. Mexico.

PANAMA PIPIT, *Anthus parvus.* 4½

Plate 27

(Considered a race of *A. lutescens* by some.)

RANGE: Savanna regions of c. and w. Panama.

WAXWINGS: Bombycillidae

CEDAR WAXWING, *Bombycilla cedrorum.*   6
RANGE: North America; winters to c. Panama.

SILKY-FLYCATCHERS: Ptilogonatidae

MEXICAN PTILOGONYS, *Ptilogonys cinereus.*   8   Plate 39
FIELD MARKS: Eye ring and patches in wings and tail white.
VOICE: The fast call may be represented as *Itsa-Hit* or *Plicka-It*. This
   requires slightly over a half sec. Sometimes it may be even more
   hurried or clipped off and will sound more like *Plick-It* or *Che-Wit*.
RANGE: Highlands of Mexico (pine-oak forests from Sinaloa and Chihuahua to s.w. Tamaulipas and south to Chiapas; 4000 to 8000
   ft.) and Guatemala.

LONG-TAILED PTILOGONYS, *Ptilogonys caudatus.*   9¼   Plate 39
RANGE: Mts. of Costa Rica and w. Panama.

CRESTED PHAINOPEPLA, *Phainopepla nitens.*   6½
RANGE: S.w. United States and Mexico (Baja California, Sonora, Chihuahua, and Coahuila south to Puebla and Veracruz; arid regions).

SALVIN'S PHAINOPTILA, *Phainoptila melanoxantha.*   8   Plate 39
FIELD MARKS: Crown black; rump yellow (male) or olive-green (female).
RANGE: Mts. of Costa Rica and w. Panama; favors underbrush and
   edge.

SHRIKES: Laniidae

LOGGERHEAD SHRIKE, *Lanius ludovicianus.*   7
RANGE: North America to Mexico (savannas and arid basins mostly at
   4000 to 8000 ft. from Baja California to Tamaulipas and south to
   the Isthmus of Tehuantepec; in other regions in winter).

STARLINGS: Sturnidae

COMMON STARLING, *Sturnus vulgaris.*   6
RANGE: Eurasia and North America; in winter south as far as n.
   Veracruz.

PEPPERSHRIKES: Cyclarhidae

MEXICAN PEPPERSHRIKE, *Cyclarhis flaviventris.* 5½   Plate 37
(Considered a race of *C. gujanensis* by some.)
VOICE: The song is loud and clear but mellow and has a recitative form
that brings to mind that of a White-eyed Vireo. The pitch varies
mostly from G³ up to D⁴. The phrases are from one- to two-sec. duration. One of two sec. may be represented as *There's enough here
for each of us.* A given phrase will be repeated a number of times
before another is taken up. Various other calls are quite different but
seldom heard.
RANGE: Mexico (s. Tamaulipas and e. San Luis Potosí to Chiapas and
Yucatán), e. Guatemala, and Honduras.

COZUMEL PEPPERSHRIKE, *Cyclarhis insularis.* 5½   Plate 37
(Considered a race of *C. gujanensis* by some.)
RANGE: Cozumel Island.

YELLOW-BREASTED PEPPERSHRIKE, *Cyclarhis flavipectus.* 5½
Plate 37
(Considered a race of *C. guajanensis* by some.)
RANGE: W. Guatemala and south to Venezuela and Colombia.

SHRIKE-VIREOS: Vireolaniidae

CHESTNUT-SIDED SHRIKE-VIREO, *Vireolanius melitophrys.* 8
Plate 37
VOICE: A shrill call something like that of the Olivaceous Flycatcher
but less plaintive (possibly like a distant scream of a Buteo). It
might be written as *meeu* or *queeu.*
RANGE: Mexico (Michoacán to Morelos and Mexico; e. San Luis Potosí to Puebla and Veracruz; pine-oak or cloud forests; 5000 to 9000
ft.) and Guatemala.

EMERALD SHRIKE-VIREO, *Smaragdolanius pulchellus.* 5¼
Plate 37
VOICE: The song phrase is a series of short figures, usually three but
sometimes four and rarely two. The tempo is such that a three-
figure phrase will have a duration of one half sec. After a rest of
about two and a half sec. the phrase is repeated. It is usually likened
to *che-che-che* because it is so fast; however, the second and third
figures really slur downward a bit at the end so that the phrase is
better represented as *che-chea-chea.* The bird is a persistent singer,
and the loud clear song rings through the tree tops in tall wet forest.
Both the Golden Vireo and the Peten Vireo sing songs made up of a

series of *che* figures; however, in both cases more than four figures are used in a phrase.

RANGE: S. Mexico (s. Veracruz and Oaxaca and south) to Panama.

BAIRD'S SHRIKE-VIREO, *Smaragdolanius eximius.*   5¼   Plate 37
(Considered a race of *S. pulchellus* by some.)
FIELD MARKS: Similar to last species, but has a yellow line over the eye as in the Chestnut-sided Shrike-Vireo.
RANGE: E. Panama and Colombia.

VIREOS: Vireonidae

BLACK-CAPPED VIREO, *Vireo atricapillus.*   4
RANGE: S.w. United States; winters in n. Mexico to Sinaloa and San Luis Potosí.

COZUMEL VIREO, *Vireo bairdi.*   4¼   Plate 37
RANGE: Cozumel Island.

WHITE-EYED VIREO, *Vireo griseus.*   4¼
RANGE: E. United States and n. Mexico (Coahuila, Nuevo León, Tamaulipas, San Luis Potosí, and Hidalgo); south in winter to Honduras.

VERACRUZ VIREO, *Vireo perquisitor.*   4¼   Plate 37
(Considered a race of *V. griseus* by some.)
FIELD MARKS: Similar to White-eyed Vireo, but underparts are dirty yellow instead of plainly bicolored.
RANGE: Coastal lowlands of c. Veracruz, Mexico.

PETEN VIREO, *Vireo semiflavus.*   4¼   Plate 37
(Considered a race of *V. griseus* by some and of *V. pallens* by others.)
FIELD MARKS: Underparts are all yellow (not bicolored), and eye is not white.
VOICE: The "song" phrase consists of a series of identical figures, such as *che*, repeated at a rate of eight in two sec. In this case the tones are clear and the pitch is about G^4. Other phrases are somewhat nasal in quality. There is a series of *weo* figures and a series of *chu* figures that are given at the same rate. There is also a much faster song in which the phrase is a rattle of some twenty *chu* figures in two sec. The warning or alarm call is a slightly nasal, vibratory *queeee* that lasts about one sec.
RANGE: Atlantic lowlands from Yucatán peninsula of Mexico to Nica-

ragua; common in regions of scrubby growth both inland and near the coast, but also present in second-growth areas in humid woods.

MANGROVE VIREO, *Vireo ochraceus.* 4¼   Plate 37
(Considered a race of *V. griseus* by some and of *V. pallens* by others.)
FIELD MARKS: Similar to Peten Vireo but less gray above and a paler, dull creamy yellow below.
VOICE: The song is a series of *che* figures like that of Peten Vireo.
RANGE: Pacific mangroves from Mexico (s. Sonora to Chiapas; apparently never out of sight of mangroves) to El Salvador.

PALE VIREO, *Vireo pallens.* 4½   Plate 37
(Considered a race of *V. griseus* by some.)
FIELD MARKS: Similar to last species but dull white below.
RANGE: Pacific coastal mangroves from southern border of El Salvador to n.w. Costa Rica.

HUTTON VIREO, *Vireo huttoni.* 4
FIELD MARKS: Similar to Ruby-crowned Kinglet, but has a heavier bill and does not flick wings so nervously.
RANGE: W. North America to mts. of Mexico and Guatemala.

CARMIOL'S VIREO, *Vireo carmioli.* 4   Plate 37
FIELD MARKS: Greener above than last species; light yellow below; line over eye pale yellow.
RANGE: Costa Rica and w. Panama; favors forest edge and pastures at high elevation in mts.

GOLDEN VIREO, *Vireo hypochryseus.* 5   Plate 37
FIELD MARKS: Line over eye and cheeks yellow.
VOICE: The song is a series of *chea* figures that are pitched at E^4. There are usually from five to ten of these in a phrase, and they are given at such a rate that nine figures would require two sec.
RANGE: W. Mexico (s.e. Sonora and Chihuahua to Oaxaca; Tres Marias Islands); up to 5000 ft.; more common in wooded cañons and along arroyos.

GRAY VIREO, *Vireo vicinior.* 5
RANGE: S.w. United States and n.w. Mexico (Baja California, Sonora, and Durango).

DWARF VIREO, *Vireo nelsoni.* 4   Plate 37
FIELD MARKS: Whole bill is black (lower one not gray); a grayish white line over eyes; two narrow wing bars.

VOICE: Song gives impression of being a combination of that of the White-eyed Viero and the Hutton Vireo.
RANGE: W. Mexico (Michoacán to Oaxaca; very rare).

BELL VIREO, *Vireo belli.* 4¼
RANGE: W. United States and w. Mexico (Baja California to Tamaulipas and south to Guanajuato and San Luis Potosí); winters to Nicaragua.

YELLOW-THROATED VIREO, *Vireo flavifrons.* 5
RANGE: E. North America; winters through Mexico to Venezuela and Colombia.

SOLITARY VIREO, *Vireo solitarius.* 5
RANGE: North America to Mexico (Baja California to Coahuila and south to Oaxaca and Veracruz; in pine-oak woods, mostly from 6000 to 8000 ft. but down to 600 ft. locally in Baja California) and south to Honduras; winters through Mexico to n. Nicaragua.

RED-EYED VIREO, *Vireo olivaceus.* 5
RANGE: North America to s. United States; winters mainly in South America.

YELLOW-GREEN VIREO, *Vireo flavoviridis.* 5
(Considered a race of V. *olivaceus* by some.)
RANGE: Extreme s. Texas, Mexico (Sonora to Chiapas; Nuevo León and Tamaulipas to Chiapas and Yucatán; Tres Marias Islands; lowlands up to 4000 ft. but more common below 2000 ft.; open woods; migratory), and south to Brazil and Bolivia.

YUCATAN VIREO, *Vireo magister.* 5½   Plate 37
FIELD MARKS: Similar to Philadelphia Vireo, but line over eye is buffy yellow instead of white.
RANGE: Mexico (Yucatán peninsula and adjacent islands) and British Honduras; coastal regions.

BLACK-WHISKERED VIREO, *Vireo altiloquus.* 5
RANGE: Caribbean coast or offshore islands in Honduras and Panama; winters to South America.

PHILADELPHIA VIREO, *Vireo philadelphicus.* 5
RANGE: E. North America; winters from s. Mexico to Colombia.

WARBLING VIREO, *Vireo gilvus.* 5
RANGE: North America to mts. of n.w. Mexico (Baja California, s.e. Sonora, Chihuahua, and south to Guerrero; in oak and pine-oak woods; widespread on migration); winters to El Salvador.

BROWN-CAPPED VIREO, *Vireo leucophrys.* 4½   Plate 37
(Considered a race of *V. gilvus* by some.)
RANGE: E. Mexico (s.w. Tamaulipas and e. San Luis Potosí through Veracruz to Chiapas; largely restricted to cloud forests from 3000 to 5000 ft.) to Venezuela and Bolivia.

GREEN-WINGED VIREO, *Vireo brevipennis.* 4½   Plate 37
FIELD MARKS: Crown, wings, and tail, bright olive-green; bend of wing yellow; iris white.
RANGE: Mexico (mts. of Guerrero, Oaxaca, and Veracruz; 5000 to 7000 ft.).

GOLDEN-FRONTED HYLOPHILUS, *Hylophilus aurantiifrons.* 4
Plate 37
RANGE: C. Panama to Venezuela and Colombia.

YELLOW-GREEN HYLOPHILUS, *Hylophilus viridiflavus.* 4
Plate 37
(Considered a race of *H. flavipes* by some.)
FIELD MARKS: Side of head gray; breast and belly clear yellow.
RANGE: Costa Rica and Panama; coastal lowlands; avoids forest.

TAWNY-CROWNED HYLOPHILUS, *Hylophilus ochraceiceps.* 4¼
Plate 37
RANGE: Mexico (humid forests of s. Veracruz and e. Oaxaca to Chiapas and Campeche) to Panama, w. Colombia, and n.w. Ecuador.

GRAY-HEADED HYLOPHILUS, *Hylophilus decurtatus.* 4 Plate 37
FIELD MARKS: In this genus the bill is shorter than the head and somewhat more slender than in Vireos, but it does have a slight Vireo hook at the end. In this species the crown and hindneck are mousegray, contrasting plainly with the yellowish olive-green back.
VOICE: The usual "song" is a short three-figure motif that is so high pitched that it may not be noticed as the bird sings in the tree top. It may be represented by *re-chawik.* It requires about a half sec. and is pitched about B⁴. The second figure drops down about one tone at the lowest part. It is repeated after a short rest and is occasionally repeated immediately as a double motif. At a distance it is difficult to make out all the parts of so quick a motif, and it may sound more like *weechee.*
RANGE: Mexico (e. San Luis Potosí south to Chiapas and Yucatán; favors tree tops in humid forest; lowlands up to 5000 ft.) to w. Panama.

LESSER HYLOPHILUS, *Hylophilus minor.* 3½   Plate 37
(Considered a race of *H. decurtatus* by some.)
RANGE: E. Panama to w. Ecuador.

WEAVERS: Ploceidae

HOUSE SPARROW, *Passer domesticus.* 5¼
RANGE: Old World; introduced into North and South America; at present common over most of North America to southern Mexico.

BLACKBIRDS: Icteridae

WAGLER'S OROPENDOLA, *Zarhynchus wagleri.* 12½   Plate 38
VOICE: The call is a loud, harsh croak; the song sounds somewhat like that of the following species, but is less elaborate.
RANGE: Mexico (s. Veracruz to Chiapas) to w. Ecuador.

MONTEZUMA OROPENDOLA, *Gymnostinops montezuma.* 17
                                                                 Plate 38
VOICE: The various calls are mostly Grackle-like. There is a harsh *crack* and a somewhat softer *cluck;* also a low-volume call that sounds like the breaking of a bundle of small dry twigs or the ripping of cloth. The song is a liquid gurgle or possibly better described as being between a gurgle and a gobble. It bubbles up the scale and then down rapidly, beginning at low volume and getting louder throughout. Although different phrases vary somewhat, all have the same general pattern and effect; they last from one to one and a half sec. The pitch varies from A^1 up to about F^5 (the last, to take in some squeaky sounds). A phrase might be represented by *cadink-adink-cadonk-awonk* or *caduink-caduink-caduink-cadaiEachYou.* The last requires one and a half sec. (the speed explains the "gobble" effect).
RANGE: Mexico (extreme s. Tamaulipas south to Chiapas and Quintana Roo; mostly in humid regions up to 2000 ft. but at times up to 4000 ft.) and along Caribbean slope to c. Panama.

BLACK OROPENDOLA, *Gymnostinops guatimozinus.* 17   Plate 38
RANGE: E. Panama and Colombia.

GLOSSY OROPENDOLA, *Psarocolius melanterus.* 16   Plate 38
(Considered a race of *P. decumanus* by some; listed in genus *Ostinops* by some and in *Xanthornus* by others.)
RANGE: Panama and w. Colombia.

LAWRENCE'S CACIQUE, *Cacicus vitellinus.* 10   Plate 38
(Considered a race of *C. cela* by some.)
FIELD MARKS: Small patch on wing and rump orange yellow; very short space at base of tail feathers, covered by tail-coverts, yellow.
RANGE: C. Panama to n.w. Colombia.

SMALL-BILLED CACIQUE, *Cacicus microrhynchus.* 8 Plate 38
(Considered a race of *C. uropygialis* by some.)
RANGE: Nicaragua to Panama and adjacent Caribbean lowlands of
Colombia; humid lowlands up to about 3000 ft.

PACIFIC CACIQUE, *Cacicus pacificus.* 9 Plate 38
(Considered a race of *C. uropygialis* by some.)
RANGE: Pacific lowlands of extreme e. Panama and adjacent Colombia.

PREVOST CACIQUE, *Amblycercus holosericeus.* 8 Plate 38
VOICE: The usual call is a rather loud and somewhat nasal *aurk* or
aurk-aurk. The song consists of a series of loud, mellow figures or
motifs. Some of these may be represented by *reechOver, white-wite,*
and *donKey* or *wonKey.* The duration of a motif is about a half sec.
and the motifs are separated by a rest of between a half and one sec.
A given motif is usually repeated a number of times to form a
phrase, but at times two different ones are used alternately, as
WhiteWite WonKey. The pitch varies from G³ up to C⁴. The female
frequently joins in with a loud, dry rattle that may last for one or
two sec. At times she will begin her rattle first, and the male will
answer with his song.
RANGE: Mexico (e. Tamaulipas, e. San Luis Potosí, Distrito Federal,
Puebla, and Veracruz south to Atlantic and Pacific slopes of Chiapas
and Yucatán; favors dense underbrush in rather humid woods or
bamboo thickets along rivers in drier areas; lowlands up to 5000
ft., but more common in lowlands) and south to Venezuela and
Bolivia.

MEXICAN CACIQUE, *Cassiculus melanicterus.* 11 Plate 38
VOICE: The calls are usually loud and of a nasal quality. One sounds
something like the *aurk* call of Prevost Cacique and may be represented as *caaeck.* There is also a sharp *klacKit.* The song phrase is
loud and sounds a bit like a heavy barn door swinging on a rusty
hinge. It is usually preceded by one or two preliminary figures of
quite low volume that might be thought of as a gasp for breath before
the bird bursts out with the song. The preliminary figures are likely
of the same type as the *glub-glub* of a Cowbird and may be shown
as *wump* or *wump-wump.* The remainder of the phrase that follows
immediately may be indicated by *Klee Klaaa Eee.* The preliminary
figure is so different that some may not realize that it is made by the
same bird. The loud portion of the phrase lasts about one sec. or a
a fraction longer; in it the pitch of the first figure is G⁴, and the *klaaa*
drops down to A³ while the final shriek is again almost as high as the
klee. Variations of the phrase appear in different parts of the country,
such as *Wump Klaackee-Klackee* and *Wump ceeKlackee,* but all are
easily recognized if one is known.
RANGE: W. Mexico from Sonora to Chiapas (in Chiapas crosses over

the continental divide into the interior basin); favors semi-arid regions where there are large trees along streams; avoids both humid forest and arid regions.

GIANT COWBIRD, *Scaphidura oryzivorus.* 13   Plate 38
FIELD MARKS: Immatures have a white iris.
RANGE: Mexico (Veracruz to Chiapas), Central America (except El Salvador and British Honduras), and south to Argentina and Bolivia.

RED-EYED COWBIRD, *Tangavius aeneus.* 7¼   Plate 38
FIELD MARKS: Male—greenish bronze on back and rump, the plumage somewhat uneven. Female—black; wings and tail glossed with bluish green.
RANGE: S. Texas, Mexico (Tamaulipas and e. San Luis Potosí to Chiapas and Yucatán), and south to w. Panama; sea level up to 7500 ft.

BRONZED COWBIRD, *Tangavius assimilis.* 7½   Plate 38
(Considered a race of *T. aeneus* by some.)
FIELD MARKS: Male—similar to preceding species, but the rump is violet instead of being the same color as the back, and the plumage is smooth. Female—sooty gray, paler below.
RANGE: S. Arizona and Mexico (Pacific slope from Sonora to Oaxaca).

BROWN-HEADED COWBIRD, *Molothrus ater.* 7
RANGE: North America to Mexico (Baja California to Tamaulipas and south to Oaxaca).

SHINY COWBIRD, *Molothrus bonariensis.* 9   Plate 38
RANGE: E. Panama to Argentina and Chile.

BRONZED GRACKLE, *Quiscalus aeneus.* 11
(Considered a race of *Q. quiscula* by others.)
RANGE: Canada and c. United States; in winter rarely to n.e. Tamaulipas, Mexico.

GREAT-TAILED GRACKLE, *Cassidix mexicanus.* 17 (♀ 13)
                                        Plate 38
FIELD MARKS: Tail plainly longer than wing in both sexes.
VOICE: There are a great number of calls; they vary from loud, harsh clatters and rattles to shrill shrieks, and down to soft rolls, wheezy noises, and smooth, clear "whistles." The alarm call is a loud cluck. Some calls may be represented as *clackit-clackit-clackit* (harsh), which lasts about one sec., a drawn-out, sweeter *ah-weet*, and a fast *tee-te-te-te-te.* Figures shown as *tee* are pitched about G⁴. The song is quite elaborate and lasts from ten to fifteen sec., according to the number of times the middle motif is repeated. It starts out like the

slow breaking of a bundle of small dry twigs; it then runs into a low, soft, but fast, roll or repercussion (*rrrrr*) that probably continues on throughout the remainder of the phrase, although it is drowned out at times. Upon this is superimposed a louder, but still relatively soft, spiral (*chewey-chewey-chewey-chewey*) that is broken into by a loud, harsh *KlickaKLACKIT*; the spiral, however, continues on again with the *Chewey* motif until interrupted by a second *Klicka-KLACKIT*; it continues once again with the *Chewey* motif until a third *KlickaKLACKIT* breaks in, this time to be followed by a terminal series of *chewey* figures given at about twice the tempo of the previous ones and also somewhat louder (the faster *chewey* may sound more like *che* to some). The whole phrase requires fifteen sec.; however it may be shortened by exclusion of one or two of the middle motifs; also the *KlickaKLACKIT* may be shortened to *Klee-KLACKIT*, or it may be softened.

RANGE: S.e. Arizona, s. New Mexico, s. Texas, Mexico (the Atlantic slope and interior basins) and south to Peru; sea level up to 8000 ft.

PACIFIC GRACKLE, *Cassidix graysoni.*   13   (♀ 11)   Plate 38
(Considered a race of *C. mexicanus* by some.)

FIELD MARKS: Tail shorter than wing in both sexes (in the southern part of the range some birds have tails that are equal to the wing or barely longer—they are usually considered hybrids or "intergrades"); the bill is relatively shorter and thicker than in the Great-tailed Grackle; the female is darker, especially the throat.

RANGE: S.w. Arizona and Mexico (Pacific slope Sonora to Guerrero).

NICARAGUAN GRACKLE, *Cassidix nicaraguensis.*   11   Plate 38
FIELD MARKS: Female is grayish white below, the breast darker.

RANGE: Marshes around Lake Managua and Lake Nicaragua in Nicaragua, and in n. Costa Rica near Lake Nicaragua.

RUSTY BLACKBIRD, *Euphagus carolinus.*   8
RANGE: North America; rare or accidental in n.w. Mexico in winter.

BREWER'S BLACKBIRD, *Euphagus cyanocephalus.*   8
RANGE: W. North America to n. Baja California; winters to Guatemala.

SUMICHRAST'S BLACKBIRD, *Dives dives.*   10   Plate 38
VOICE: The calls are many and varied, mostly loud and clear, often quite liquid, sometimes mellow, and sometimes shrill. One of the commonest may be shown as *wot cheer;* this requires about one sec.; the pitch of the *wot* is E^3, and the beginning of the *cheer* is one octave higher (it slurs downward after the start). There is a metallic *cleek* and a thin, high-pitched *sspeeeeeee* that is like a soft whistle through the teeth.

RANGE: S.e. Mexico (extreme s. Tamaulipas and e. San Luis Potosí

south to Chiapas and Yucatán; favors edge; sea level up to 5000 ft.
but more common below 3000 ft. and in moist regions) to n. Nicaragua.

ORCHARD ORIOLE, *Icterus spurius*.   6

RANGE: E. United States and south to c. Mexico (except in the Rio
Grande Delta of n.e. Tamaulipas, confined to high tableland from
Coahuila south through Jalisco and Michoacán to Oaxaca; more
widespread on migration); winters from Tamaulipas to Venezuela
and Colombia.

FUERTES ORIOLE, *Icterus fuertesi*.   6   Plate 39
(Considered a race of *I. spurius* by some.)

FIELD MARKS: Similar to Orchard Oriole in pattern (has all-black tail),
but the male is burnt orange and black, so that at first glance it looks
like a Baltimore Oriole.

VOICE: Quality is the same as in Orchard Oriole; each individual has
a slightly different song phrase.

RANGE: S. Texas (Rio Grande Delta; rare) and Mexico (lowlands of
Tamaulipas, e. San Luis Potosí and south to s. Veracruz; migratory
and has straggled as far w. as Guerrero; local; edge habitat).

LESSON'S ORIOLE, *Icterus prosthemelas*.   7   Plate 39
FIELD MARKS: Black of throat extends down onto the chest.

RANGE: Mexico (c. Veracruz and e. Oaxaca to Chiapas and Yucatán;
lowlands to 3000 ft.; favors edge, especially areas where there are
clumps of bananas or bamboo) to n.w. Panama; Caribbean Islands.

WAGLER'S ORIOLE, *Icterus wagleri*.   8   Plate 39
FIELD MARKS: No black on chest. Possibly three years are required to
attain full adult plumage. First year birds have no black on throat.

VOICE: The call is a short, weak, nasal *dur* or *nur*. It is somewhat insectlike and since the bird usually calls while low in the brush it may be
passed by for an insect.

RANGE: Highlands of Mexico (semi-desert, brushy regions from s. Sonora across to Nuevo León and south to Chiapas; usually from 3000
to 7000 ft., rarely lower; migratory) to n. Nicaragua.

SCOTT'S ORIOLE, *Icterus parisorum*.   7

FIELD MARKS: Wing bar white; upper back not black; yellow in tail.
Streaked-back immature has side of head and throat grayish yellow
and olive-yellow.

RANGE: S.w. United States and Mexico (Baja California across to Coahuila and south to Michoacán, Puebla, and extreme w.c. Veracruz;
in high interior basins in arid brushland or scrub pines in mts.; migratory in north where it descends into arid tropical regions in winter.

BAR-WINGED ORIOLE, *Icterus maculialatus*.   7½   Plate 39
FIELD MARKS: One large yellow wing bar, one narrow white wing bar,
and one white bar running along the primaries.
VOICE: The song is somewhat variable as to phrasing but is usually
slowly "whistled" after the fashion of the Underwood and Black-
headed Orioles. The tones are of moderate volume and most are mellow. A common song phrase may be shown as *ah tea-cher tea-cher
dont go-way*. This requires a total of five sec.; the starting pitch of
each figure is B³-E⁴-C⁴ sharp E⁴-C⁴ sharp E⁴ A³-A³. If those notes are
whistled and slurred a bit, as suggested by the words used to denote
the motifs, and if the timing is watched, a good approximation of
the song can be given even though one has never heard the bird.
Other songs have the same range of pitch and same quality but may
be faster, such as *tulee-a-feature-too-a-chuchay a-woo-Chwooo-
aoochay-Wheeeeoo-wope-Cheewoo*. Although this has more than
twice as many figures as the other phrase, it requires only six sec.
RANGE: S. Mexico (s. Oaxaca and Chiapas; favors semi-arid woods
from 2000 to 5000 ft.; local), Guatemala, and El Salvador.

HOODED ORIOLE, *Icterus cucullatus*.   7
VOICE: The usual song is weak and so fast that it is a hurried jumble.
RANGE: S.w. United States, Mexico (Baja California, Sonora, and Chi-
huahua south to Guerrero; Nuevo León and Tamaulipas south to
Veracruz, Yucatán, and Quintana Roo; favors semi-desert regions or
savannas or open areas in more humid regions, especially in those
containing groves of palms; lowlands up to 2000 ft.), and British
Honduras.

ORANGE-CROWNED ORIOLE, *Icterus auricapillus*.   8   Plate 39
RANGE: E. Panama, Venezuela, and Colombia.

YELLOW-TAILED ORIOLE, *Icterus mesomelas*.   8   Plate 39
VOICE: The song consists of a series of loud, mellow motifs. A given one
may be short and may be represented by *Be careful* (may be repeated
five times in four sec.); by somewhat longer *The-world-is-FAIR-
today*; or by *KICK-a-pokey-bear* (repeated seven times in seven
sec.); or still longer, as *Look-there-the-loop-hole-CATALPA*, which
is repeated six times in eleven sec. The pitch varies from D³ up to
E⁴. At times a given motif will be repeated six or seven times, after
which there will be a short roll (*trrrr*) followed by a different motif
that will in turn be repeated five or six times; these make the song
more interesting. Quite short motifs (probably sung by the female)
make a somewhat more jerky song (might be confused with song of
Rufous-naped Cactus-Wren).
RANGE: Mexico (s. Veracruz and e. Oaxaca south to Chiapas and Yucatán; favors edge or open places where there is dense low growth,

for instance, marshy pastures in tropical zone, but is found up to about 4000 ft. at times) to n.w. Panama; Bahamas.

GIRAUD'S ORIOLE, *Icterus giraudii.*   8   Plate 39
(Considered a race of *I. chrysater* by others.)
FIELD MARKS: Crown does not show greenish yellow wash in either sex.
RANGE: Panama to Venezuela and Colombia.

UNDERWOOD ORIOLE, *Icterus chrysater.*   8½   Plate 39
FIELD MARKS: Most individuals show a greenish yellow crown patch (in some old males this may not be distinct).
VOICE: The song is made up of mellow phrases, slowly delivered after the fashion of the Bar-winged and Black-headed Orioles. In the pine region of the mountains of central Chiapas, where the species is common, the song dominates the dawn chorus. In this dawn song all individuals sing the same phrase with only slight variations and continue repeating it for fifteen to thirty minutes. This phrase may be represented as *How-will-I-meet-you Oh how-will-I-meet-you.* It requires a total of seven sec., and the pitch varies from A^3 to D^4 (the basic tones of the *How-will-I-meet-you* are D^4-B^3flat-A^3-D^4-B^3 flat). Daytime songs are shorter and more varied but of the same quality.
RANGE: Mts. of s. Mexico (Chiapas) and south to n. Nicaragua; mostly at 6000 to 8000 ft. in pine-oak woods.

MAYAN ORIOLE, *Icterus mayensis.*   8½   Plate 39
(Considered a race of *I. chrysater* by others.)
FIELD MARKS: Crown not greenish yellow.
RANGE: Mexico (northern part of Yucatán peninsula).

BLACK-HEADED ORIOLE, *Icterus graduacauda.*   8
VOICE: The song is similar in quality to that of the Underwood and Bar-winged Orioles, but the slowly "whistled" phrases are apt to be a bit more disjointed.
RANGE: S. Texas, Mexico (Nayarit to Guerrero and Oaxaca; Nuevo León and Tamaulipas to Chiapas; lowlands up to 7000 ft.; local and scarce except in northeastern states where it is more common below 4000 ft.; nonmigratory) to n.e. Guatemala.

SPOTTED-BREASTED ORIOLE, *Icterus pectoralis.*   7½   Plate 39
FIELD MARKS: Similar to Altamira Oriole but with a different wing pattern (it lacks a complete white wing bar). It takes several years to develop the spots fully; hence, many do not have them.
VOICE: The tones are somewhat liquid and flutelike. The style of the song is intermediate between that of the Altamira and Underwood Oriole.

RANGE: Mexico (semi-arid Pacific lowlands of Oaxaca and Chiapas) to n.w. Costa Rica.

ALTAMIRA ORIOLE, *Icterus gularis.* 8½ Plate 39
VOICE: The song phrases vary in different areas, but the tones are loud, clear, and flutelike, and the quality is the same everywhere. Often the figures are at melodic intervals (one phrase frequently heard in n.e. Mexico is practically identical to the first eight or nine notes of the "Donkey Serenade"). This bird sometimes imitates the songs of other Orioles.
RANGE: Rio Grande Delta region of Texas, Mexico (Guerrero to Chiapas; Tamaulipas and San Luis Potosí to Chiapas and Yucatán; favors semi-arid regions or more open places in humid areas; lowlands up to 4000 ft. but more common below 3000 ft.), and South to Nicaragua.

BALTIMORE ORIOLE, *Icterus galbula.* 6½
FIELD MARKS: Small dusky spots on crown and back of female.
RANGE: E. North America; winters from e. Mexico to Colombia.

BULLOCK ORIOLE, *Icterus bullockii.* 7
(Considered a race of *I. galbula* by some.)
FIELD MARKS: Intermediate between the Baltimore Oriole and the Abeille Oriole and thought by some to be a hybrid species. Male—side of neck, rump, and upper tail-coverts orange. Female—belly grayish white; sides and flanks pale olive-gray.
RANGE: W. North America to n. Mexico (n. Baja California, Sonora, and Sinaloa and east to Tamaulipas; in semi-desert brushland and in highland basins); winters south to Guatemala (rarely further south).

ABEILLE ORIOLE, *Icterus abeillei.* 7 Plate 39
(Considered a race of *I. bullockii* by some.)
FIELD MARKS: Male—side of neck, rump, and upper tail-coverts black. Female—belly dull white; sides and flanks gray.
RANGE: Arid interior plateaus of Mexico from Jalisco to San Luis Potosí and south to Morelos, Puebla, and Veracruz; occasionally up into the pines, at least in winter.

ORANGE ORIOLE, *Icterus auratus.* 7½ Plate 39
VOICE: The song phrase consists of a thin introductory figure followed by a series of *che* figures.
RANGE: The Yucatán peninsula of Mexico and adjacent islands; favors edge and second-growth woods.

SCARLET-HEADED ORIOLE, *Icterus pustulatus.* 7½ Plate 39
FIELD MARKS: The back is streaked with short, narrow black marks. Several years are required for males to develop intense colors.

VOICE: Aside from "scolding" that sounds almost like a rattle, the most frequently heard vocalization is a series of high-pitched figures hesitantly joined into a phrase, *chip chip cheet cher.* There is a seldom heard song phrase that may be indicated by *wert-che-boo cheerful-cher-cher-cher-cher-cher-peet.*

RANGE: Mexico (Sonora to Chihuahua and south to Guerrero, n. Oaxaca, Morelos, Puebla, and w. Veracruz; in the tropical zone up to 3000 ft.; favors semi-desert or subhumid wooded areas, but avoids "desert" growth.

TRES MARIAS ORIOLE, *Icterus graysonii.*   8
(Considered a race of *I. pustulatus* by some.)

FIELD MARKS: Similar to last species but paler and with very few, if any, black streaks on the back.

RANGE: Tres Marias Islands, Mexico.

SCLATER'S ORIOLE, *Icterus sclateri.*   7½   Plate 39
(Considered a race of *I. pustulatus* by some.)

FIELD MARKS: Paler than the Scarlet-headed Oriole, with much wider black streaks on the back (back appears mostly black); more white in the wings.

VOICE: A shrill, almost metallic *peet;* also a low-pitched rattle.

RANGE: Mexico (Pacific slope of Oaxaca and Chiapas and semi-arid interior basin on east side of continental divide in Chiapas; lowlands up to 3000 ft.; in subhumid woods and savannas; partly migratory) and south to n.w. Costa Rica.

TRICOLORED BLACKBIRD, *Agelaius tricolor.*   7½
RANGE: Oregon and south to n. Baja California.

RED-WINGED BLACKBIRD, *Agelaius phoeniceus.*   7¼
FIELD MARKS: There is considerable plumage variation, especially in the amount of streaking on the breast of the females in some regions, which may be due to hybridization with Bicolored Blackbird.

RANGE: North America, Mexico (Baja California to Tamaulipas and south to Chiapas and Yucatán; avoids heavy forest and also non-irrigated semi-desert regions), and south to n.w. Costa Rica.

BICOLORED BLACKBIRD, *Agelaius gubernator.*   8   Plate 40
(Considered a race of *A. phoeniceus* by some.)

FIELD MARKS: Black with poppy-red lesser wing-coverts (female has only a small amount of red and sometimes none). In various regions of Mexico hybridization with the previous species occurs, but in several local areas it breeds side by side with the Red-winged Blackbird with no interbreeding.

RANGE: Mexico (San Luis Potosí, Mexico, and Morelos); local. (There are hybrid populations in many areas in n.w. Mexico and in California that some will regard as Red-winged Blackbirds or as belonging to neither species.)

YELLOW-HEADED BLACKBIRD, *Xanthocephalus xanthocephalus.*
8½
RANGE: W. North America to Mexico (n. Baja California to Jalisco; in winter as far as s. Tamaulipas and Puebla).

RED-BREASTED BLACKBIRD, *Leistes militaris.* 5½   Plate 40
FIELD MARKS: Bill shorter than head; tail a bit more than half as long as wing.
RANGE: Panama to Brazil and Peru.

EASTERN MEADOWLARK, *Sturnella magna.* 8½
RANGE: E. and s. North America to Mexico (Sonora across to Tamaulipas and south to Chiapas and Yucatán; in savannas and broad cultivated areas) and south to n.e. Brazil and Colombia.

WESTERN MEADOWLARK, *Sturnella neglecta.* 8½
RANGE: W. North America to Mexico (Baja California and Sonora across to Nuevo León and south to Jalisco; winters east to Tamaulipas).

BOBOLINK, *Dolichonyx oryzivorus.* 6
RANGE: North America; migrates through West Indies, across Yucatán peninsula of Mexico, and through Central America (except Guatemala and El Salvador) to South America as far as Argentina and Bolivia.

WOOD-WARBLERS: Parulidae

BLACK-AND-WHITE WARBLER, *Mniotilta varia.* 4½
RANGE: E. North America; winters to Mexico and south to Venezuela and Ecuador.

PROTHONOTARY WARBLER, *Protonotaria citrea.* 5
RANGE: S.e. United States; migrates to Mexico (rare in eastern maritime states; a few winter in Campeche) and Venezuela.

SWAINSON WARBLER, *Limnothlypis swainsonii.* 5
RANGE: S.e. United States; winters in West Indies and Mexico (some migrate through eastern maritime states and a few winter in Quintana Roo) to Honduras.

WORM-EATING WARBLER, *Helmitheros vermivorus.* 4½
RANGE: E. United States; winters in Mexico (migrates through eastern

maritime states and a few winter in Chiapas and Quintana Roo) and south to Panama.

GOLDEN-WINGED WARBLER, *Vermivora chrysoptera.* 4¼
RANGE: E. North America; migrates through eastern states of Mexico to Venezuela and Colombia.

BLUE-WINGED WARBLER, *Vermivora pinus.* 4¼
RANGE: E. United States; winters in Mexico (migrates through eastern states and a few winter from e. San Luis Potosí south) and south to Venezuela and Colombia.

TENNESSEE WARBLER, *Vermivora peregrina.* 4¼
RANGE: E. North America; winters to Mexico (eastern states) and south to Venezuela and Colombia.

ORANGE-CROWNED WARBLER, *Vermivora celata.* 4¼
RANGE: North America to Todos Santos islands off coast of Baja California; winters through Mexico to Guatemala.

NASHVILLE WARBLER, *Vermivora ruficapilla.* 4
RANGE: N. North America; winters to Mexico and Guatemala.

VIRGINIA WARBLER, *Vermivora virginiae.* 4¼
RANGE: Mts. of w. United States; winters to Oaxaca, Mexico.

COLIMA WARBLER, *Vermivora crissalis.* 5
RANGE: Chisos mts. of w. Texas, and Coahuila, Mexico; in pine-oak regions from 6000 to 8000 ft.; winters in w. Mexico.

LUCY'S WARBLER, *Vermivora luciae.* 4¼
RANGE: S.w. United States and n.w. Mexico (n. Baja California and Sonora); winters in w. Mexico.

IRAZU WARBLER, *Vermivora gutturalis.* 4¼   Plate 43
FIELD MARKS: No white on side of head; throat orange; belly white.
RANGE: Mts. of Costa Rica and w. Panama.

HARTLAUB WARBLER, *Vermivora superciliosa.* 4¼   Plate 43
VOICE: A high-pitched *t'cherrrr.*
RANGE: Highlands of Mexico (Sinaloa and Chihuahua across to Nuevo León and Tamaulipas and south to Chiapas; mainly in oak-pine regions and cloud forests), Guatemala, El Salvador, Honduras, and Nicaragua.

PARULA WARBLER, *Parula americana.* 4
RANGE: E. North America; winters in Mexico, Guatemala, El Salvador, and rarely a bit further south.

SENNETT WARBLER, *Parula insularis.* 4   Plate 43
(Considered a race of *P. pitiayumi* by some.)
FIELD MARKS: Two distinct white wing bars; no white eye ring.
RANGE: S. Texas and Mexico (s.e. Sonora and Chihuahua, south to Jalisco and Colima; Tres Marias Islands; Nuevo León and Tamaulipas south through e. San Luis Potosí to Veracruz; from sea level up to about 4000 ft.; local in areas of good tree growth; partially migratory).

SOCORRO WARBLER, *Parula graysoni.* 4   Plate 43
(Considered a race of *P. pitiayumi* by some.)
RANGE: Socorro Island off western coast of Mexico and southern tip of Baja California.

CHIRIQUI WARBLER, *Parula inornata.* 3½   Plate 43
(Considered a race of *P. pitiayumi* by some.)
FIELD MARKS: Does not have two white wing bars (may have one partial bar or none).
RANGE: Mexico (Chiapas) and south to w. Panama; favors rather open humid woods above 2000 ft.

OLIVE WARBLER, *Peucedramus taeniatus.* 4½
RANGE: Mts. of s.w. United States, Mexico (e. Sonora to Tamaulipas and south to Chiapas; in pine forests), Guatemala, El Salvador, south to Nicaragua.

YELLOW WARBLER, *Dendroica aestiva.* 4
(Considered a race of *D. petechia* by some.)
RANGE: North America to c. Mexico (strictly a temperate-zone bird; 5000 to 8000 ft.; n. Sonora to Coahuila and w. Tamaulipas, and south to Mexico and Morelos; local, frequently breeding in city parks; widespread in lowlands in winter); in winter south to n. South America.

CHESTNUT-CROWNED WARBLER, *Dendroica rufivertex.* 4
Plate 43
(Considered a race of *D. petechia* by some.)
RANGE: Cozumel Island off coast of Quintana Roo, Mexico.

MANGROVE WARBLER, *Dendroica erithachorides.* 4   Plate 43
(Considered a race of *D. petechia* by some.)
RANGE: Mexico (Baja California and Sonora south along coast in man-

groves; s. Tamaulipas and south to Yucatán), south to Panama and Colombia.

MAGNOLIA WARBLER, *Dendroica magnolia.* 4¼
RANGE: North America; winters south to c. Panama.

CAPE MAY WARBLER, *Dendroica tigrina.* 4¼
RANGE: N. North America; winters in West Indies, and casually in Mexico (Yucatán peninsula), British Honduras, and Honduras; at times to Panama.

BLACK-THROATED BLUE WARBLER, *Dendroica caerulescens.*
4½
RANGE: N.e. North America; winters in West Indies and occasionally in Mexico (Cozumel Island), Guatemala, and Colombia.

MYRTLE WARBLER, *Dendroica coronata.* 5
RANGE: N. North America; winters south to Colombia.

AUDUBON WARBLER, *Dendroica auduboni.* 5
RANGE: Mts. of w. North America to w. Mexico (pine-oak regions in Chihuahua and Durango, and locally to Guanajuato and possibly Guerrero); widespread in winter south to Guatemala and very rarely to Costa Rica.

GOLDMAN WARBLER, *Dendroica goldmani.* 5   Plate 44
(Considered a race of *D. auduboni* by some and *D. coronata* by others.)
FIELD MARKS: Similar to Audubon Warbler but much richer in color; adult male has back black instead of gray with black streaks, and the more golden yellow crown patch is bordered by white, as is the yellow throat patch; there is no white line or mark above the eye; female is browner.
RANGE: Cloud forest area in mts. of s.w. Chiapas, Mexico, and adjacent Guatemala.

BLACK-THROATED GRAY WARBLER, *Dendroica nigrescens.* 4
RANGE: Mts. of w. North America to Baja California and n.e. Sonora, Mexico; in winter south to Oaxaca and Veracruz.

TOWNSEND WARBLER, *Dendroica townsendi.* 4¼
RANGE: Mts. of n.w. North America; winters south to Nicaragua.

BLACK-THROATED GREEN WARBLER, *Dendroica virens.* 4¼
RANGE: E. North America; in winter south to Colombia.

GOLDEN-CHEEKED WARBLER, *Dendroica chrysoparia.* 4¼
RANGE: C. Texas; winters in Mexico, Guatemala, Honduras, and Nicaragua.

HERMIT WARBLER, *Dendroica occidentalis.* 4¼
RANGE: Mts. of w. North America; winters in Mexico, Guatemala, El Salvador, Honduras and n. Nicaragua.

CERULEAN WARBLER, *Dendroica cerulea.* 4
RANGE: E. North America; in winter south as far as Bolivia.

BLACKBURNIAN WARBLER, *Dendroica fusca.* 4¼
RANGE: E. North America; winters from Guatemala to Peru.

YELLOW-THROATED WARBLER, *Dendroica dominica.* 4½
RANGE: E. United States; winters to Costa Rica.

GRACE'S WARBLER, *Dendroica graciae.* 4¼
VOICE: The song is clear but fast and high pitched. It may be represented by *chea-chea-chea-chea-chea-chea-chea-chea-chea-chea-chea-chea-cheechee.* The pitch varies slightly but is around C^5; the whole phrase as shown lasts only two sec. The *chea* figures are so fast that they sound more like *chip* to some; at the start they are relatively soft and the tempo is fast; the tempo is retarded slightly after about five figures are delivered, and the volume increases; finally the phrase ends with the quick *cheechee.*
RANGE: Mts. of s.w. United States, Mexico (in pine-oak regions, mostly at 7000 to 9000 ft. in e. Sonora, Chihuahua, Durango, Oaxaca, and Chiapas; more widespread in winter), Guatemala, El Salvador, British Honduras, and n. Nicaragua.

CHESTNUT-SIDED WARBLER, *Dendroica pensylvanica.* 4¼
RANGE: E. North America; winters from Nicaragua to Colombia.

BAY-BREASTED WARBLER, *Dendroica castanea.* 5
RANGE: N.e. North America; winters in Panama and Colombia.

BLACKPOLL WARBLER, *Dendroica striata.* 4¼
RANGE: N. North America; winters from Colombia to Brazil; stragglers or accidentals appear here and there in Mexico.

PINE WARBLER, *Dendroica pinus.* 5
RANGE: E. North America; in winter south as far as Tamaulipas, Mexico.

PRAIRIE WARBLER, *Dendroica discolor.* 4
RANGE: E. United States; winter visitor on Cozumel Island, Mexico, and occasionally farther south in Central America.

PALM WARBLER, *Dendroica palmarum.* 4½
RANGE: N. North America; winters in Mexico (Tamaulipas, Veracruz, and Yucatán), British Honduras, Honduras, and the West Indies.

NORTH AMERICAN OVENBIRD, *Seiurus aurocapillus.* 5
RANGE: E. North America; winters through Mexico and south to Colombia.

LOUISIANA WATERTHRUSH, *Seiurus motacilla.* 5¼
RANGE: E. United States; winters in Mexico and south to Colombia.

NORTHERN WATERTHRUSH, *Seiurus noveboracensis.* 5
RANGE: N. North America; winters in Mexico and south to n. South America.

KENTUCKY WARBLER, *Oporornis formosus.* 4½
RANGE: E. United States; winters in s.e. Mexico and south to Colombia.

MOURNING WARBLER, *Oporornis philadelphia.* 4½
RANGE: E. North America; migrates through Mexico to n.w. South America.

MACGILLAVRAY WARBLER, *Oporornis tolmiei.* 4½
RANGE: W. North America; winters in Mexico and south to Colombia.

NORTHERN YELLOWTHROAT, *Geothlypis trichas.* 4¼
RANGE: North America to c. Mexico; winters south to Panama.

BELDING YELLOWTHROAT, *Geothlypis beldingi.* 5   Plate 43
FIELD MARKS: The male lacks a white border to black mask.
RANGE: S. Baja California, Mexico.

ALTAMIRA YELLOWTHROAT, *Geothlypis flavovelata.* 4½
                                                    Plate 43
(Considered a race of *G. beldingi* by some.)
FIELD MARKS: In winter plumage the yellow of crown of male is reduced to a narrow border to the black mask.
VOICE: Similar in quality to the song of the Northern Yellowthroat but different in phrasing, such as *chea-chea-cheety chea-chea-cheety chee-chee.*
RANGE: Mexico (fresh water ponds and waterways in s. Tamaulipas, adjacent Veracruz, and extreme e. San Luis Potosí).

CHAPALA YELLOWTHROAT, *Geothlypis chapalensis.* 5 Plate 43
(Considered a race of *G. trichas* by some and of *G. beldingi* by others.)
FIELD MARKS: Similar to Altamira Yellowthroat, but yellow on crown of male much more restricted.
VOICE: Quality similar to that of Northern Yellowthroat; the phrasing may be indicated by *cheety-upee cheety-upee cheety-upee cheety-up.* Sometimes it will end with the *upee.*
RANGE: C.w. Mexico around Lake Chapala and lower Rio Lerma in Jalisco.

HOODED YELLOWTHROAT, *Geothlypis nelsoni.* 4½ Plate 43
FIELD MARKS: Black mask of male relatively broad and bordered above by gray; tail longer than wing.
VOICE: Similar in quality to that of Northern Yellowthroat but with shorter figures in the song phrase, as *witchy-witchy.*
RANGE: Mexico (mts. of s.e. Coahuila, s.w. Tamaulipas, e. San Luis Potosí, and south to Oaxaca; from 4000 to 8000 ft. in grassy openings or fields; in the north found on humid side of mts. for the most part; seems to avoid marshy places).

ORIZABA YELLOWTHROAT, *Geothlypis speciosa.* 4½ Plate 43
RANGE: Mexico (mts. of c. states from Michoacán to Veracruz; favors wet meadows).

BAIRD'S YELLOWTHROAT, *Geothlypis semiflava.* 4½ Plate 43
FIELD MARKS: Male has no light border to the wide black mask.
VOICE: The song phrase is composed of some fifteen to seventeen smoothly flowing, warbled figures or very short motifs of about equal length and equally spaced (space between figures is about the same as the length of the figures, which is roughly 0.2 sec.) throughout the 3.5-sec. duration. Although the pitch and quality is about the same, the effect is quite different from a song of a bird of the species group of the Northern Yellowthroat, because a given motif is not repeated in series in each phrase (such as *witchity-witchity-witchity*) and because the phrase is longer. (This species is the northernmost representative of the South American species group of the genus, which uses this distinctive phrase structure.) The pitch varies from C^4 to C^5, and almost every figure is warbled up and down through this whole range; however, no two adjoining figures are alike although they are similar in structure. There is usually (perhaps always) a single vibrato figure interposed near the end of the phrase. This is about 0.1 sec. in length and contains about seven warble cycles with an average pitch of G^4; hence, some will think of it as a very short buzz.
RANGE: Honduras to n.w. Panama; w. Colombia and w. Ecuador;

favors bushy or grassy thickets in semi-open areas up to subtropical zone.

CHIRIQUI YELLOWTHROAT, *Geothlypis chiriquensis.* 4½

Plate 43

(Considered a race of *G. aequinoctialis* by some.)

RANGE: Volcán Chiriquí in w. Panama.

GRAY-HEADED GROUNDCHAT, *Chamaethlypis poliocephala.* 5

Plate 43

(Placed in genus *Geothlypis* by some.)

FIELD MARKS: This genus has a thicker, Chat-like bill and a relatively longer tail than *Geothlypis*; also in this genus the sexes are almost alike (lores in female not really black).

VOICE: Most of the song phrases are like those of a Bunting in quality, style, pitch, and length; however, at rare intervals there may be a song that sounds more like a Sparrow. One phrase may be represented by *cher if-you-will-sur if-you-able-if-you-will-sur if-you-will.* This requires about three sec. for delivery; the highest pitch is about F^4, and the lowest A^3. Variations of the same phrase will be given after short pauses; these will vary in length from two to four sec. for the most part. The Sparrow-type song may be represented by the phrase *chip-chip-chip-chip-chip-Cheert Chip Chip.* This is a series of rapidly delivered figures followed by some louder, more deliberate ones.

RANGE: Mexico (Sinaloa south to Morelos; s. Tamaulipas and e. San Luis Potosí south to e. Oaxaca, Chiapas, and Yucatán; favors savannas, either humid, subhumid, or dry; from sea level up to 8000 ft., but more common below 5000 ft.) and south to w. Panama.

YELLOW-BREASTED CHAT, *Icteria virens.* 6½

RANGE: North America to n. Mexico (Baja California to Tamaulipas and south to Jalisco and Guanajuato; sea level up to 5000 ft.; usually near small streams in semi-arid regions or in irrigated basins); south in winter to w. Panama.

RED-BREASTED CHAT, *Granatellus venustus.* 5   Plate 44

VOICE: A song phrase may be represented by *toweet toweet toweet toweet toweet weeche-weeche-weeche.* This requires a total time of about four sec.; the slower *toweet* series takes three sec., and the faster *weeche* portion only one sec. The highest part of the *toweet* is pitched about B^4 and the other parts a bit lower.

RANGE: W. Mexico (s. Sinaloa to Chiapas; favors subhumid regions, mainly cañons and foothills from sea level up to 4000 ft. or more; in Chiapas occurs on the eastern side of the continental divide in the interior basin).

TRES MARIAS CHAT, *Granatellus francescae.* 5½   Plate 44
(Considered a race of *G. venustus* by some.)
RANGE: Tres Marias Islands, Mexico.

GRAY-THROATED CHAT, *Granatellus sallaei.* 4½   Plate 44
FIELD MARKS: Outside tail feathers in female not extensively white.
VOICE: The song is thin and plaintive, and the phrase is a bit drawn
out at the end, such as *seeoo seeoo seeoo seeoo seeee sue.*
RANGE: E. Mexico (s. Veracruz, e. Oaxaca, and south to Chiapas and
Yucatán and Quintana Roo; favors subhumid, brushy woods; quite
local in the more humid areas).

HOODED WARBLER, *Wilsonia citrina.* 4½
RANGE: E. United States; winters through Mexico to Panama.

WILSON WARBLER, *Wilsonia pusilla.* 4¼
RANGE: North America, winters in Texas, Mexico, and south to w.
Panama.

CANADA WARBLER, *Wilsonia canadensis.* 5
RANGE: N. North America; migrates through Mexico to Colombia and
Peru.

RED-FACED WARBLER, *Cardellina rubrifrons.* 4½
RANGE: Mts. of s.w. United States, Mexico, and Guatemala; local in
high pine forests.

AMERICAN REDSTART, *Setophaga ruticilla.* 4½
RANGE: North America; winters in Mexico and south to Brazil and
Peru.

PAINTED REDSTART, *Setophaga picta.* 4½   Plate 43
RANGE: Mts. of s.w. United States, Mexico (Sonora to Nuevo León
and Tamaulipas south to Chiapas; oak-pine regions from 3000 to
8000 ft.; favors less humid woods than the following species),
Guatemala, El Salvador, Honduras, and Nicaragua.

RED-BELLIED REDSTART, *Myioborus miniatus.* 5   Plate 43
VOICE: The songs are thin and shrill; a phrase may be represented as
seet-seet-seet-seet-seet.
RANGE: Highlands of Mexico (mts. of Chihuahua and into adjacent
Sonora, at least in winter, south to Oaxaca; from e. San Luis Potosí
through Veracruz to Chiapas; favors cloud forests in east and the
more humid oak-pine forest in west; 4000 to 8000 ft.), Guatemala,
El Salvador, and n. Nicaragua.

YELLOW-BELLIED REDSTART, *Myioborus aurantiacus.*   4½

Plate 43

(Considered a race of *M. miniatus* by some.)
RANGE: Costa Rica to Brazil and Bolivia.

COLLARED REDSTART, *Myioborus torquatus.*   4½   Plate 43
RANGE: Mts. of Costa Rica and w. Panama; mostly above 5000 ft.
where it favors edge in humid areas.

FAN-TAILED WARBLER, *Euthlypis lachrymosa.*   5½   Plate 43
FIELD MARKS: Partially hidden yellow crown spot.
VOICE: The song phrase begins with some thin, fast figures and then
becomes somewhat louder and more deliberate, which may be illustrated by *che-che-che awee wee che cheer.* This requires one
and a half sec. for delivery, and the pitch varies around B⁴. At a
distance most of the phrase may be missed, and it may seem more
like *che che cheche.*
RANGE: Mexico (Baja California, Sonora, and Chihuahua south to
Guerrero and w. Chiapas; s. Tamaulipas and e. San Luis Potosí to
Veracruz; favors rocky slopes with ample shrubby cover and ravines
that are forest-covered; 500 to 4000 ft.), Guatemala, El Salvador,
Honduras, and Nicaragua.

RED WARBLER, *Ergaticus ruber.*   4½   Plate 43
FIELD MARKS: Ear patch usually silver-white but sometimes silver-gray
or brown. Juveniles are russet with silver-gray ear patch.
VOICE: The thin, high-pitched call is not readily suggested by a word,
but various listeners have suggested *p'zeet, pleet, clink,* and *pink.*
RANGE: Mts. of Mexico from Sinaloa and Chihuahua south to Oaxaca
and Veracruz; in pine-fir regions from 8000 to 10000 ft.

PINK-HEADED WARBLER, *Ergaticus versicolor.*   4¼   Plate 43
(Considered a race of *E. ruber* by some.)
FIELD MARKS: Similar to Red Warbler but without the ear patch. Instead, this species has the whole head pink with a silver gloss to the
feathers that so reflects the light that it makes them appear almost
white at some angles.
RANGE: Mts. of s. Mexico (Chiapas) and Guatemala; 7000 to 11000
ft.

BLACK-EARED WARBLER, *Basileuterus melanotis.*   4½   Plate 43
(Considered a race of *B. tristriatus* by some.)
FIELD MARKS: Middle of crown grayish buff with a black stripe on each
side; line over eye pale buffy gray.
RANGE: Costa Rica and w. Panama; humid woods; 3000 to 7000 ft.

TACARCUNA WARBLER, *Basileuterus tacarcunae.* 4½ Plate 43
(Considered a race of *B. tristriatus* by some.)
FIELD MARKS: Middle of crown orange; line over eye olive; ear patch olivaceous.
RANGE: Mt. Tacarcuna in e. Panama.

LICHTENSTEIN'S WARBLER, *Basileuterus culicivorus.* 4½
Plate 43
FIELD MARKS: Resembles a female Nashville Warbler except for the black stripes along the side of the crown.
VOICE: A phrase of the lively song may be represented as *here how now Peechie.* This requires about one and a half sec. or a bit less; the pitch is about G^4. The *here* begins with G^4 and slurs down to F^4. The next two figures hold the F^4, and the *Peechie,* which is strongly accented, begins at G^4 and, after slurring down to F^4, ends up at A^4. At a distance only the *Peechie* may be noticed.
RANGE: Mexico (humid woods or along streams in drier areas; rare in Nayarit and Jalisco; from Nuevo León and Tamaulipas south to Chiapas; from lowland humid forest to mountain cloud forest) to w. Panama. On fall migration stragglers sometimes appear in the Rio Grande Delta of Texas.

BLACK-CHEEKED WARBLER, *Basileuterus melanogenys.* 4½
Plate 44
(Considered a race of *B. tristriatus* by some.)
RANGE: Highlands of Costa Rica and w. Panama; mostly from 5000 ft. up to timber line; favors thickets and scrub along edge.

PIRRE WARBLER, *Basileuterus ignotus.* 4½ Plate 44
FIELD MARKS: Similar to last species but with line over eye light yellow instead of white, and side of head green, mottled with dusky.
RANGE: Mt. Pirre in e. Panama.

BELL WARBLER, *Basileuterus belli.* 4½ Plate 43
RANGE: Mexico (Sinaloa through Michoacán to Guerrero; Nuevo León and Tamaulipas south to Chiapas; mostly in pine-oak regions and cloud forests but sometimes down cañons and out into somewhat drier basins; 3000 to 8000 ft.), Guatemala, El Salvador, and Honduras.

RUFOUS-CAPPED WARBLER, *Basileuterus rufifrons.* 4½ Plate 44
FIELD MARKS: Line over eye and belly white; jaw and lower portion of ear region white.
RANGE: Mexico (Sonora and Chihuahua south to Oaxaca; Nuevo León and Tamaulipas south to Veracruz and Chiapas; favors edge or shrubby or weedy savannas or shrubby streamsides in drier areas; sea level to 7000 ft.) and n.c. Guatemala.

SALVIN WARBLER, *Basileuterus salvini.* 4½   Plate 44
(Considered a race of *B. rufifrons* by some.)
FIELD MARKS: Similar to last species but sides of neck and hindneck
olive like back instead of gray; belly entirely yellow.
RANGE: Mexico (e. Chiapas), n. Guatemala, and Honduras. (Northern
limit of range unknown on account of reported hybridization with
previous species.)

DELATTRE WARBLER, *Basileuterus delattrii.* 4½   Plate 44
(Considered a race of *B. rufifrons* by some.)
FIELD MARKS: Crown and whole ear region chestnut; no white line
below ear patch; entire belly yellow.
RANGE: S. Chiapas, Mexico, and south to Colombia

BUFF-RUMPED WARBLER, *Basileuterus fulvicauda.* 4½ Plate 44
RANGE: Honduras to Brazil and Peru; semiterrestial like the North
American Ovenbird or N. Waterthrush; favors areas along wet trails
or small streams in humid tropical woods.

HONEYCREEPERS: Coerebidae

COZUMEL BANANAQUIT, *Coereba caboti.* 4   Plate 37
(Considered a race of *C. bahamensis* by some and *C. flaveola* by
others).
FIELD MARKS: Similar to Mexican Bananaquit but has dull white
throat; breast yellow; sides and flanks grayish yellow.
RANGE: Islands of Cozumel and Holbox off coast of Quintana Roo.

MEXICAN BANANAQUIT, *Coereba mexicana.* 4   Plate 37
(Considered a race of *C. flaveola* by some.)
VOICE: The "song" is a very shrill "buzz" (thin and insectlike) that
ends with a still higher-pitched figure. It usually sounds like *churr-
we-eet* but is too fast to hear the parts clearly and is usually thought
of as *ssss-eet*. It takes only a half sec., and the pitch is about A^5. It
is frequently repeated immediately, making a couplet, but is otherwise repeated after a short rest.
RANGE: Mexico (s. Veracruz, e. Oaxaca, and south; lowlands up to
3500 ft.; favors humid woods) and south to Ecuador.

WHITE-EARED CONEBILL, *Ateleodacnis leucogenys.* 3½
(Listed as *Conirostrum leucogenys* by some.)   Plate 31
RANGE: E. Panama to n. Venezuela and Colombia.

SCARLET-THIGHED DACNIS, *Dacnis venusta.* 4½   Plate 31
RANGE: Costa Rica to w. Ecuador; favors semi-open areas in humid
subtropics, but descends into lowlands at times.

VIRIDIAN DACNIS, *Dacnis viguieri.* 4½　　　　Plate 31
RANGE: E. Panama and Colombia.

BLUE DACNIS, *Dacnis cyana.* 4　　　　Plate 31
RANGE: Nicaragua to Argentina and Bolivia; lowland humid forest.

SHINING HONEYCREEPER, *Cyanerpes lucidus.* 4　　Plate 31
　(Considered a race of *C. caeruleus* by some.)
FIELD MARKS: Black of throat extends down onto chest in male; in
　female the throat is buff and chest is streaked blue; legs yellow.
RANGE: S. Mexico (cloud forests of s. Chiapas) and south to Colombia.

BLUE HONEYCREEPER, *Cyanerpes cyaneus.* 4　　Plate 31
FIELD MARKS: Throat of female pale olive-yellow to almost white.
VOICE: There is a thin *chee,* or *thee,* rather like the call of a Blue-gray
　Gnatcatcher.
RANGE: Mexico (e. San Luis Potosí and Veracruz south to Chiapas
　and Yucatán; also on the Pacific slope of Chiapas; sea level up to
　4000 ft. but mostly below 2000 ft.; open woods or edge) to Brazil
　and Bolivia.

GREEN HONEYCREEPER, *Chlorophanes spiza.* 5　　Plate 31
VOICE: A weak, shrill *chip,* sometimes given in series at a rate of about
　eight in five sec. Pitch about C^5.
RANGE: Mexico (humid lowlands of s. Veracruz and e. Oaxaca to
　Chiapas and Campeche; at times upwards into humid savannas or
　open wooded country to about 5000 ft.) to Brazil and Bolivia.

SLATY DIGLOSSA, *Diglossa plumbea.* 4　　　　Plate 35
　(Considered a race of *D. baritula* by some.)
RANGE: High mts. of Costa Rica and w. Panama; 7000 ft. up to above
　timber line; favors open shrubby areas or edge.

MEXICAN DIGLOSSA, *Diglossa baritula.* 4　　　Plate 35
RANGE: Mexico (n. of Isthmus of Tehuantepec in states of Colima,
　Jalisco, Michoacán, Morelos, Guanajuato, Distrito Federal, Hidalgo,
　Puebla, Veracruz, and Oaxaca; 5000 to 10000 ft. in rather open
　woods or clearings where it works the flowers at any level from tree
　tops to low weeds on the ground).

MOUNTAIN DIGLOSSA, *Diglossa montana.* 4　　Plate 35
　(Considered a race of *D. baritula* by some.)
FIELD MARKS: Similar to Mexican Diglossa, but male has the head
　more slate (less black), the whole throat is slate gray instead of just
　the upper part, and the breast and belly are darker cinnamon; fe-
　male is light cinnamon below instead of brownish buff.

RANGE: Mexico (mts. of s. Chiapas), Guatemala, and El Salvador; 5500 to 11000 ft.

SWALLOW-TANAGERS: Tersinidae

GREEN SWALLOW-TANAGER, *Tersina viridis.*   5   Plate 35
RANGE: E. Panama to Argentina and Bolivia.

TANAGERS: Thraupidae

While some tropical members of this family resemble Tanagers of the United States in size, shape, and general appearance, there are other groups that at first glance may not seem to a novice to be Tanagers at all. The Euphonias are short birds with stubby tails and short thick bills; when one bird of this group is learned, others will be readily recognized by their similar shape and behavior. The Euphonias, Chlorospinguses, and Chlorophonias might be confused with Manakins, Finches, and Shrike-Vireos and are best placed in their proper family by reference to the plates.

BLUE-CROWNED CHLOROPHONIA, *Chlorophonia occipitalis.*   5
                                                            Plate 40
RANGE: Mts. of s. Mexico (cloud forests of s. Veracruz and Chiapas; uncommon) to n. Nicaragua; favors edge.

GOLDEN-BROWED CHLOROPHONIA, *Chlorophonia callophrys.*
5   Plate 40
(Considered a race of *C. occipitalis* by some.)
FIELD MARKS: Forehead and area over eye bright yellow in male; female has blue collar across hindneck.
RANGE: Costa Rica and w. Panama.

BLUE-HOODED EUPHONIA, *Euphonia elegantissima.*   4
                                                            Plate 40
(Considered a race of *E. musica* by some.)
RANGE: Mexico (highlands; mixed oak woods and cloud forests; chiefly 3000 to 5000 ft., but may wander seasonally in search of food either higher or lower; s. Sonora to Guerrero; s. Tamaulipas to Chiapas) to w. Panama.

ORANGE-BELLIED EUPHONIA, *Euphonia xanthogaster.*   4
                                                            Plate 40
RANGE: E. Panama to Brazil and Bolivia.

TAWNY-CAPPED EUPHONIA, *Euphonia anneae.* 4   Plate 40
RANGE: Costa Rica to n.w. Colombia; humid subtropics.

FULVOUS-VENTED EUPHONIA, *Euphonia fulvicrissa.* 3½
                                           Plate 40
FIELD MARKS: Male has the throat blue black and the belly tawny;
female has the midline of belly tawny.
RANGE: Panama to w. Ecuador.

WHITE-VENTED EUPHONIA, *Euphonia minuta.* 3½   Plate 40
FIELD MARKS: Female has the lower throat pale gray.
RANGE: S.e. Mexico and Guatemala to w. Ecuador; open woods in
humid regions; lowlands.

GODMAN EUPHONIA, *Euphonia godmani.* 3½   Plate 40
(Considered a race of *E. affinis* by some.)
FIELD MARKS: Female has crown and hindneck gray; belly white.
RANGE: Mexico (semi-arid, tropical, and subtropical regions in Sonora,
Sinaloa, Nayarit, and Colima; uncommon).

LESSON EUPHONIA, *Euphonia affinis.* 3½   Plate 40
VOICE: The call is rather similar to that of a Goldfinch. The song is a
shrill squeak followed by a thin rattle of lower pitch—*sweet che-e-e-
e-e-e.* The rattle is like the thinner ones of a Towhee.
RANGE: Mexico (Tamaulipas and e. San Luis Potosí south to Chiapas
and Yucatán; semi-arid regions or partially cleared areas or pastures
in more humid regions) to n.w. Costa Rica.

YELLOW-CROWNED EUPHONIA, *Euphonia luteicapilla.* 3½
                                           Plate 40
FIELD MARKS: Female—yellow below; yellowish-olive-green above.
RANGE: Nicaragua to Panama; favors open areas in humid regions.

THICK-BILLED EUPHONIA, *Euphonia crassirostris.* 3½
                                           Plate 40
(Considered a race of *E. laniirostris* by some.)
FIELD MARKS: Yellow of forehead extends back over half of crown in
male; entire underparts yellow in both sexes.
RANGE: Costa Rica to n. Venezuela and Colombia.

BONAPARTE'S EUPHONIA, *Euphonia lauta.* 3½   Plate 40
FIELD MARKS: Similar to preceding species, but male has smaller yellow
spot on forecrown (does not extend past eye) and the female has
the median portion of the breast and belly pale grayish white instead of yellow.
VOICE: There is a shrill *squeek* and a thin, rapid *chip-chip-chip*; also

a "fussing" call, *tut-a-tut-ta*, of Nuthatch quality. The song phrase is rather insectlike: *squeek-a-cheeky*.

RANGE: Mexico (humid tropical and subtropical woods or along streams in somewhat drier areas from s. Tamaulipas south on the Atlantic slope to w. Panama; favors open areas with scattered tall trees.

GOULD'S EUPHONIA, *Euphonia gouldi.* 3½   Plate 40
FIELD MARKS: Forehead yellow in male and chestnut in female.
RANGE: Mexico (tropical rain forest; s. Veracruz to Quintana Roo) to n.w. Panama.

TAWNY-BELLIED EUPHONIA, *Euphonia imitans.* 3½   Plate 40
FIELD MARKS: Male similar to Lesson Euphonia but has the crown yellow as well as the forehead, and the yellow feathers have a small dot of black; female appears like the male of Gould's Euphonia with the whole belly tawny, but has the forehead chestnut.
RANGE: S.w. Costa Rica and adjacent Panama; humid forest.

EMERALD TANAGER, *Tangara florida.* 4½   Plate 40
RANGE: Costa Rica to w. Colombia; humid tropics.

SPECKLED TANAGER, *Tangara chrysophrys.* 4½   Plate 40
RANGE: Costa Rica to w. Ecuador; favors wet subtropics.

SILVER-THROATED TANAGER, *Tangara icterocephala.*   4½
                                                                              Plate 40
RANGE: Costa Rica to w. Ecuador; favors edge in subtropics.

GOLDEN-MASKED TANAGER, *Tangara larvata.* 4½   Plate 41
   (Considered a race of *T. nigrocincta* by some.)
RANGE: Mexico (tropical wet forest edge; s. Veracruz to e. Chiapas) to n.w. Ecuador.

CABANIS TANAGER, *Tangara cabanisi.* 5   Plate 41
RANGE: S.w. Mexico (high mts. of s.w. Chiapas) and adjacent Guatemala.

PALMER TANAGER, *Tangara palmeri.* 5½   Plate 41
RANGE: E. Panama to n. w. Ecuador.

GRAY TANAGER, *Tangara inornata.* 4½   Plate 41
RANGE: Costa Rica to Colombia.

BAY-AND-BLUE TANAGER, *Tangara gyroloides.* 4½   Plate 41
   (Considered a race of *T. gyrola* by some.)

RANGE: Costa Rica to Brazil and Ecuador; humid subtropics, but may extend into lowlands at times.

LAVINIA'S TANAGER, *Tangara lavinia.* 4½   Plate 41
FIELD MARKS: Similar to last species, but color of head lighter, and rump is green instead of blue.
RANGE: Guatemala to w. Ecuador; favors habitats similar to previous species but on the average at a bit lower elevation.

DOW TANAGER, *Tangara dowii.* 5   Plate 41
RANGE: Costa Rica and w. Panama; mt. forests up to timber line.

GREEN-NAPED TANAGER, *Tangara fucosa.* 5   Plate 41
RANGE: Mts. of e. Panama.

ARCE'S TANAGER, *Bangsia arcaei.* 5½   Plate 41
RANGE: Wet foothills of e. Costa Rica and adjacent Panama.

BLUE TANAGER, *Thraupis cana.* 5½   Plate 41
(Considered a race of *T. episcopus* by some; others say *T. virens.*)
FIELD MARKS: Adults have bright blue wings, but in some lights a few individuals (possibly immature) appear to have green wings.
VOICE: A thin, shrill *squeet.*
RANGE: Mexico (tropical woods on Atlantic slope from e. San Luis Potosí south; favors edge and open areas) to Venezuela, n. and w. Colombia, w. Ecuador, and n.w. Peru.

ABBOT TANAGER, *Thraupis abbas.* 6   Plate 41
VOICE: A thin, shrill *weet* or a series of Sparrow-like chips.
RANGE: Mexico (tropical woods and less common in subtropical oak woods or cloud forest; s. Tamaulipas south) to Nicaragua.

PALM TANAGER, *Thraupis palmarum.* 6   Plate 41
RANGE: Nicaragua to Brazil and Bolivia.

CRIMSON-BACKED TANAGER, *Ramphocelus dimidiatus.* 6
     Plate 41
RANGE: Panama to w. Venezuela and Colombia.

PLUSH TANAGER, *Ramphocelus passerinii.* 6   Plate 41
VOICE: The call is something like the clucking of the tongue against the jaw teeth. The song, which is usually given only at dawn, is composed of a long series of two-figure motifs.
RANGE: Mexico (s. Veracruz and south; favors open areas grown over with dense low growth or marsh plants) to n.w. Panama; in humid regions from sea level up to the subtropical zone.

YELLOW-RUMPED TANAGER, *Ramphocelus icteronotus.* 6

Plate 41

RANGE: Panama to w. Colombia and Ecuador.

CRIMSON-COLLARED TANAGER, *Phlogothraupis sanguinolenta.*

6½   Plate 41

VOICE: A shrill *t'wee* or *tze tze tsweze* or *tswe tswe.*

RANGE: Mexico (humid tropical woods; s. Veracruz south; favors dense underbrush or thickets in openings) to n.w. Panama; Caribbean slope.

SUMMER TANAGER, *Piranga rubra.* 6½

RANGE: S. United States and n. Mexico (Baja California to Tamaulipas and south to Durango); in winter south to Brazil and Bolivia.

HEPATIC TANAGER, *Piranga hepatica.* 7

(Considered a race of *P. flava* by some.)

RANGE: Highlands of s.w. United States and Mexico, south to n. Nicaragua.

BRICK-RED TANAGER, *Piranga lutea.* 7

(Considered a race of *P. flava* by some.)

FIELD MARKS: Similar to Hepatic Tanager, but ear region not gray.

RANGE: Mts. of Costa Rica (Caribbean slope) to Venezuela and Bolivia.

ROSE-THROATED TANAGER, *Piranga roseogularis.* 5½

Plate 41

RANGE: Mexico (Yucatán peninsula and adjacent islands) and the Peten district of Guatemala.

SCARLET TANAGER, *Piranga olivacea.* 6¼

RANGE: E. North America; migrates through Central America to winter in South America.

WHITE-WINGED TANAGER, *Piranga leucoptera.* 5   Plate 41

FIELD MARKS: Female is yellow below; one wing bar is indistinct.

RANGE: Mexico (e. San Luis Potosí and south on Atlantic slope; favors cloud forests, but may be found in mixed woods down to about 1500 ft. and occasionally down to sea level) and south to Guiana and Bolivia; humid subtropics.

WESTERN TANAGER, *Piranga ludoviciana.* 6¼

RANGE: W. North America to n. Baja California and n.e. Sonora, Mexico; south in winter as far as Panama.

STRIPED-BACKED TANAGER, *Piranga bidentata.* 6½   Plate 41
VOICE: The calls and song bring to mind those of a Scarlet Tanager or Summer Tanager.
RANGE: Mexico (Sinaloa to Mexico; Nuevo León to Chiapas; cloud forests and oak-pine woods in mts.) to w. Panama.

RED-HEADED TANAGER, *Piranga erythrocephala.* 5½   Plate 41
RANGE: Mexico (oak-pine and oak woods in mts. of Sonora to Chihuahua and south to Oaxaca; uncommon.).

OLIVACEOUS TANAGER, *Chlorothraupis olivacea.* 5½   Plate 41
RANGE: E. Panama to Ecuador.

CARMIOL TANAGER, *Chlorothraupis carmioli.* 6   Plate 41
RANGE: Nicaragua to Bolivia; favors understory in tropical woods and moves about in flocks.

BODDAERT'S TANAGER, *Tachyphonus rufus.* 6   Plate 41
RANGE: Costa Rica to Argentina and Peru; favors semi-open habitat in humid tropics (on Caribbean slope in Central America).

WHITE-SHOULDERED TANAGER, *Tachyphonus luctuosus.* 4½   Plate 42
RANGE: E. Panama to Brazil and Bolivia.

COSTA RICAN TANAGER, *Tachyphonus axillaris.* 5   Plate 42
(Considered a race of *T. luctuosus* by some.)
FIELD MARKS: Male has a small concealed crown spot of yellow; female is yellow below.
RANGE: Caribbean slope of s.e. Honduras to n.w. Panama; edge.

CHIRIQUI TANAGER, *Tachyphonus nitidissimus.* 5   Plate 42
(Considered a race of *T. luctuosus* by some.)
FIELD MARKS: Male has an exposed orange rufous crown patch; female has yellowish olive chest.
RANGE: S.w. Costa Rica and adjacent Panama.

TAWNY-CRESTED TANAGER, *Tachyphonus delattrii.* 5½   Plate 42
RANGE: Caribbean slope of Nicaragua and Costa Rica south to Ecuador.

LAWRENCE'S TANAGER, *Heterospingus rubrifrons.* 5½   Plate 41
(Considered a race of *H. xanthopygius* by some.)
FIELD MARKS: Yellow spot on rump and white spot at side of breast.
RANGE: Caribbean slope in extreme s.e. Costa Rica and Panama.

GRAY-HEADED TANAGER, *Eucometis spodocephala.*   6   Plate 42
(Considered a race of *E. penicillata* by some.)
RANGE: Mexico (s. Veracruz, Campeche, Quintana Roo, and Yucatán)
to w. Panama; favors dense underbrush in humid forest.

GRAY-CRESTED TANAGER, *Eucometis penicillata.*   7   Plate 42
RANGE: E. Panama to Paraguay and Bolivia.

CASSIN'S TANAGER, *Mitrospingus cassinii.*   6½   Plate 41
RANGE: Costa Rica to w. Ecuador; tropical woods; thickets in edge.

YELLOW-BACKED TANAGER, *Hemithraupis flavicollis.*   5
Plate 42
RANGE: E. Panama to Brazil and Bolivia.

BLACK-AND-YELLOW TANAGER, *Chrysothlypis chrysomelas.*   4
Plate 42
FIELD MARKS: Female is yellowish olive-green above and yellow below.
RANGE: Costa Rica and Panama; wet foothill regions on Caribbean
slope; favors upper parts of trees where it acts somewhat like a
Warbler.

RED-CROWNED ANT-TANAGER, *Habia rubica.*   6½   Plate 42
FIELD MARKS: Male has a black or dark brown stripe down center of
crown that is separated to form a dark border to the base of the
crest (which is usually hidden) when the crest is erected. Female
crest ochraceous.
VOICE: The dawn song is composed of a long series of short motifs.
It may be represented by *tee-cher tee-cher tee-cher* or *chin-choppa
chin-choppa chin-choppa-chin.* These may be repeated for thirty
minutes or more while the crest is displayed. The second example
described above would require about seven sec. During the day
there may be irregular or short phrases that seem to be variants of
the first example of song, such as *cher tee tee cher.* There is also
a soft call that might be likened to *chook.*
RANGE: Mexico (Nayarit to Chiapas; s. Tamaulipas and e. San Luis
Potosí south to Chiapas and Yucatán; favors humid lowland forest
but sometimes found in drier woods up to 3000 ft. to Argentina
and Bolivia.

DUSKY-TAILED ANT-TANAGER, *Habia fuscicauda.*   7   Plate 42
(Considered a race of *H. gutturalis* by some.)
FIELD MARKS: Male has a red crown patch that is mostly concealed
and is not erected while the dawn song is given. The throat of female is yellow and set off from the tawny olive chest.
VOICE: There are some harsh scolding calls that are usually given in
short series; such as *zurr-zurr-zurr.* The dawn song, which is

delivered from a perch some ten or fifteen feet up from the ground, may be represented by *be-care-ful be-care-ful* and so on, or the three-figure motif may sound more like *get-care-ful*. Each figure is rather deliberately accented. Daytime phrases are faster and usually somewhat disjointed, as *careful ceerful keerful carful*.

RANGE: Mexico (semi-arid and humid woods up to 4000 ft.; s. Tamaulipas south on Atlantic slope; avoids mature rain forest) to n. Colombia.

BLACK-CHEEKED ANT-TANAGER, *Habia atrimaxillaris.*   7
Plate 42

(Considered a race of *H. gutturalis* by some.)

FIELD MARKS: Sexes appear alike. Male exposes red crown spot while singing dawn song, but the crest feathers are not erected.

RANGE: S.w. Costa Rica in lowland rain forest; ranges low in underbrush and frequently sings from a stump or log on ground.

ROSE-BREASTED THRUSH-TANAGER, *Rhodinocichla rosea.*   7½
Plate 42

RANGE: Mexico (tropical woods in Sinaloa, Nayarit, Colima, and Jalisco) to n. Venezuela and Colombia; favors dense thickets.

BLACK-THROATED SHRIKE-TANAGER, *Lanio aurantius.*   7
Plate 42

RANGE: Mexico (humid tropical forests in Veracruz, Oaxaca, Tabasco, Chiapas, and Quintana Roo) to n. Honduras.

WHITE-THROATED SHRIKE-TANAGER, *Lanio leucothorax.*   7
Plate 42

(Considered a race of *L. aurantius* by some.)

FIELD MARKS: Male throat white or buffy white; lower back yellow. Female throat brown.

RANGE: S.e. Honduras and e. Costa Rica.

BLACK-RUMPED SHRIKE-TANAGER, *Lanio melanopygius.*   7
Plate 42

(Considered a race of *L. aurantius* by some.)

RANGE: Pacific slope of s. Costa Rica and w. Panama.

COZUMEL SPINDALIS, *Spindalis benedicti.*   6   Plate 42
(Considered a race of *S. zena* by some.)

RANGE: Cozumel Island off coast of Quintana Roo, Mexico.

BROWN-HEADED CHLOROSPINGUS, *Chlorospingus ophthalmicus.*
5   Plate 44

FIELD MARKS: Crown brown contrasting with the olive-green back;

white area around and back of eye relatively large; throat white tinged with brownish buff.

RANGE: Mexico (e. San Luis Potosí, e. Puebla, e. Oaxaca, and Veracruz; cloud forests mostly at 4000 to 5000 ft.).

WHITE-FRONTED CHLOROSPINGUS, *Chlorospingus albifrons.* 5

Plate 44

(Considered a race of *C. ophthalmicus* by some.)

FIELD MARKS: White area back of eye relatively small.

RANGE: Mexico (cloud forests in Guerrero).

CHIRIQUI CHLOROSPINGUS, *Chlorospingus novicius.* 5

Plate 44

(Considered a race of *C. ophthalmicus* by some.)

FIELD MARKS: Throat buffy white, more or less speckled with black.

RANGE: Nicaragua, Costa Rica, and extreme w. Panama; humid subtropics.

DWIGHT'S CHLOROSPINGUS, *Chlorospingus dwighti.* 5

Plate 44

(Considered a race of *C. ophthalmicus* by some.)

FIELD MARKS: Crown slate gray, becoming black at the sides and producing two broad, indistinct stripes.

RANGE: Cloud forests on Atlantic slope in Mexico (Chiapas) and Guatemala.

DUSKY-HEADED CHLOROSPINGUS, *Chlorospingus postocularis.*

5   Plate 44

(Considered a race of *C. ophthalmicus* by some.)

FIELD MARKS: Similar to last species but has a smaller white spot back of eye and lacks the black stripes on the crown.

RANGE: Subtropical zone on Pacific slope of Mexico (Chiapas), Guatemala, El Salvador, and Honduras.

PILEATED CHLOROSPINGUS, *Chlorospingus pileatus.* 5

Plate 44

RANGE: Mt. zone 6000 ft. to timber line; Costa Rica and w. Panama.

ZELEDON'S CHLOROSPINGUS, *Chlorospingus zeledoni.* 5

Plate 44

FIELD MARKS: Similar to last species but has much shorter white line over the eye and less contrast to the underparts.

RANGE: High mts. up to timber line on volcanoes of c. Costa Rica.

PIRRE CHLOROSPINGUS, *Chlorospingus inornatus.* 5   Plate 44

RANGE: Mt. Pirre in e. Panama at 3000 to 4000 ft.

DOTTED CHLOROSPINGUS, *Chlorospingus punctulatus.* 5
Plate 44

(Considered a race of *C. ophthalmicus* by some.)
RANGE: Subtropical zone in w. Panama.

OLIVE-CROWNED CHLOROSPINGUS, *Chlorospingus olivaceiceps.*
5 Plate 44

(Considered a race of *C. canigularis* by some.)
RANGE: Wet subtropics of Caribbean slope of c. Costa Rica; scarce.

DRAB-BREASTED CHLOROSPINGUS, *Chlorospingus hypophaeus.*
5 Plate 44

(Considered a race of *C. flavigularis* by some.)
FIELD MARKS: Crown olive-green; throat yellow; chest and flanks
buffy brown.
RANGE: Upper tropical zone in w. Panama.

TACARCUNA CHLOROSPINGUS, *Chlorospingus tacarcunae.* 5
Plate 44

(Considered a race of *C. ophthalmicus* by some.)
RANGE: Upper tropical zone on Mt. Tacarcuna in e. Panama and adjacent Colombia.

FINCHES: Fringillidae

BLACK-HEADED SALTATOR, *Saltator atriceps.* 9½ Plate 45
FIELD MARKS: Back, wings, and tail olive-green, changeable in some
lights to bright yellowish green; throat white (in s. Veracruz
sometimes brownish buff) and bordered by a black line (birds in
Costa Rica and south sometimes lack the black border).
VOICE: The call is short and almost explosive and might be said to
resemble a kissing or smacking noise, or it may sometimes be a
sharp *chuck* or *chuh*. The song phrase begins with one or two
preliminary figures and ends with a hurried chuckle: *chuck chuck-
weet-ta-cuckweer-heh-heh-heh-heh-huh-huh-huh-huh-heh.* The
phrase as shown requires two sec.
RANGE: Mexico (Guerrero to Chiapas; s. Tamaulipas and e. San Luis
Potosí to Chiapas and Yucatán; from sea level up to 4000 ft. but
more common below 3000 ft.; favors dense shrubby edge in humid
tropics, but at times goes into semi-arid areas and up into lower part
of oak region) and south to c. Panama.

BUFF-THROATED SALTATOR, *Saltator maximus.* 7½ Plate 45
FIELD MARKS: Similar to the brown-throated phase of the preceding
species but has a more restricted throat patch (at least in the area

where the two occur together); also lacks the abrupt change of color from head to back.

VOICE: The song is made up of a series of rather soft, mellow phrases of short motifs that are hesitantly delivered (after the fashion of a Red-eyed Vireo). A phrase may be shown as *try-lay think-o-it thinky-you*; this requires two and a half sec. The pitch varies around D^4 (up a half tone to one tone and down a half tone to one tone); the quality is something like that of an Eastern Bluebird. The phrase may be repeated over and over with only short intervening rests, or a new period may be started with a somewhat different phrase.

RANGE: Mexico (c. Veracruz south through e. Oaxaca to Chiapas, Campeche, and Quintana Roo) to Brazil and Bolivia.

LICHTENSTEIN'S SALTATOR, *Saltator grandis.* 7½   Plate 45
   (Considered a race of *S. coerulescens* by others.)

FIELD MARKS: Under tail-coverts cinnamon-buff.

VOICE: Commonly there is a clear, mellow, "whistled" phrase that may be paraphrased as *its-a-boid*. This is drawn out so as to require one sec.; it begins about E^4, drops down to B^3, and then the *boid* begins with B^3 and slurs up to D^4. Sometimes the phrase is lengthened by adding a second motif that is softer, more hurried, and bubbling; it may be shown as *would-you-like-to-see* (C^4 sharp-D^4-D^4 sharp-E^4-F^4sharp). When this is added the whole phrase then requires about two sec. Pairs frequently sing duets (may be antiphonal).

RANGE: Mexico (s. Tamaulipas to Chiapas and Yucatán; mostly in tropical regions but up into the edge of the oak association at times) to Costa Rica; favors rather open country.

VIGORS' SALTATOR, *Saltator vigorsii.* 8   Plate 45
   (Considered a race of *S. coerulescens* by others.)

FIELD MARKS: Similar to last species but larger and much paler.

RANGE: Mexico (Pacific slope from Sinaloa to Oaxaca).

STREAKED SALTATOR, *Saltator albicollis.* 6   Plate 45

RANGE: S.w. Costa Rica to Venezuela and Peru; from sea level up to 4000 ft.; favors rather open areas.

NORTHERN CARDINAL, *Richmondena cardinalis.* 8

RANGE: E. and s. United States, Mexico (Tres Marias Is., Baja California, and Sonora across to Tamaulipas, southward to Sinaloa, Durango, n.e. Jalisco, Hidalgo, Tabasco, Quintana Roo, and Yucatán; from sea level up to about 5000 ft.), and British Honduras.

LONG-CRESTED CARDINAL, *Richmondena carnea.* 7   Plate 45
   (Considered a race of *R. cardinalis* by some.)

FIELD MARKS: Similar to preceding species, but crest longer and stiffer (feathers not blended); rump lighter in color than back; bill shaped somewhat differently; the folded wing of female has the same color as the back with little or no red color showing.

RANGE: Mexico (Pacific coastal lowlands from Colima to the Isthmus of Tehuantepec).

GRAY PYRRHULOXIA, *Pyrrhuloxia sinuata.* 7½

FIELD MARKS: Yellow bill.

RANGE: S.w. United States and w. Mexico (Baja California to Tamaulipas and south to Michoacán and San Luis Potosí; arid brushland up to 7000 ft.).

EVENING GROSBEAK, *Hesperiphona vespertina.* 7¼

RANGE: N. North America and mts. of Mexico (Durango, Mexico, Puebla, Veracruz, and Oaxaca; mostly from 8000 to 10000 ft.).

ABEILLE GROSBEAK, *Hesperiphona abeillei.* 6   Plate 45

FIELD MARKS: Female has crown, part of face, wings, and tail black.

VOICE: There are several short calls of which one of the most noticeable is a burry *jerr.* The song is composed of short phrases; a typical one may be represented as *be-be jerr chee* (F^4-F^4 D^4 G^4), or it may be rearranged as *be-be chee jerr.* It may also be shortened to *be-be jerr* or *be-be chee.* The longest one shown requires one sec. for delivery and is repeated after a rest of about one sec.

RANGE: Mexico (Tamaulipas, e. San Luis Potosí, Puebla, Veracruz, and Oaxaca; cloud forests and humid oak woods from 3000 to 6000 ft.) and Guatemala.

YELLOW GROSBEAK, *Pheucticus chrysopeplus.* 8   Plate 45

FIELD MARKS: Except for bill, looks like an Oriole.

VOICE: The song is rich and mellow and somewhat similar to that of the Black-headed Grosbeak. Short phrases might be confused with some given by the Mexican Peppershrike.

RANGE: Mexico (Sonora and Chihuahua and south to Chiapas; from sea level up to about 5000 ft.; favors open woods in subhumid regions or wooded cañons in arid regions) and Guatemala.

BLACK-THIGHED GROSBEAK, *Pheucticus tibialis.* 8   Plate 45

(Considered a race of *P. chrysopeplus* by some.)

RANGE: Costa Rica and w. Panama; humid mt. belt to timber line.

ROSE-BREASTED GROSBEAK, *Pheucticus ludovicianus.* 7¼

RANGE: W. North America; winters from e. Mexico to Colombia.

BLACK-HEADED GROSBEAK, *Pheucticus melanocephalus.* 7½

RANGE: W. North America and Mexico (pine-oak forests and high arid basins from Baja California to Tamaulipas and south to Oaxaca and Veracruz).

CRIMSON-COLLARED GROSBEAK, *Rhodothraupis celaeno.* 7½
Plate 45

FIELD MARKS: Female has head (except nape), throat, and chest black; back, wings, and tail olive-green.

VOICE: The quality is rich and mellow and brings to mind that of a Cardinal. A song phrase may be represented as *twit-twert-teer-twerty-dur.* The pitch varies mostly from C⁴ up to F⁴. The call is a shrill, thin "whistle" very much like that produced by an old-fashioned disc-like "tin whistle."

RANGE: Mexico (s. Nuevo León, Tamaulipas, e. San Luis Potosí, and n. Veracruz; lowlands up to 3000 ft.; in semi-desert woods, edge habitats in more humid woods, and open areas in lower part of oak association; most common in semi-arid brushy regions from 500 to 1000 ft.).

GREEN GROSBEAK, *Caryothraustes canadensis.* 7   Plate 45
RANGE: E. Panama to n.e. Brazil and Colombia.

BISHOP GROSBEAK, *Caryothraustes poliogaster.* 6½   Plate 45
VOICE: The two most commonly heard song phrases may be shown as *prrrt Sweet Sweet,* which is a low buzz followed by two high, clear, slurred figures (the *Sweet* begins at G⁴ and goes up to D⁵) and is so fast that the whole phrase requires slightly less than one sec.; and *chu weet-chu chur-chur-chur,* which requires one and a half sec. (the loudest parts of this phrase are the *chur* figures, which are just the opposite of the *sweet* in the first example and which slur downward from D⁵ to G⁴). The last phrase is frequently shortened or simplified, but the important part is always the *chur* of which there are always at least two in a phrase.

RANGE: Mexico (c. Veracruz and e. Oaxaca to Chiapas; in humid tropical forests) to c. Panama.

SLATE-COLORED GROSBEAK, *Pitylus grossus.* 7   Plate 45
RANGE: Nicaragua to w. Ecuador; favors tree tops in heavy wet forest (Caribbean slope in Central America) from lowlands into foothills.

BLUE GROSBEAK, *Guiraca caerulea.* 6¼
FIELD MARKS: Rufous wing bars.

RANGE: S. United States, Mexico (Baja California to Tamaulipas and south to Chiapas; favors arid or semi-arid regions), and south to n.w. Costa Rica; in winter to w. Panama.

BLUE-BLACK GROSBEAK, *Cyanocompsa cyanoides.* 6 Plate 45
VOICE: The song is loud but mellow and somewhat plaintive; the move-
ment is slow. A phrase may be likened to *see say mar-ch to day*,
provided one uses a "sing-song" rhythm. This requires a total time
of three sec.; the *mar-ch* is a drawn-out, slurred figure. The pitch of
these figures varies about G^4 F^4sharp F^4-F^4sharp G^4 D^4. At times the
phrase as given is followed immediately by a hurried jumble of soft
figures. There is also a "whisper song" that is quite soft and hurried
but pitched about the same as the loud song. It goes on and on as a
continuous period; the structure may be shown by the words *You
cant-sing-like-I-can-do*. This requires only one and a half sec. but is
repeated immediately so that it goes on with only slight variations
here and there.
RANGE: Mexico (c. Veracruz and e. Oaxaca and south; lowlands up to
3000 ft.; in dense underbrush in humid woods) to Brazil and
Bolivia.

BLUE BUNTING, *Cyanocompsa parellina.* 4½ Plate 45
FIELD MARKS: Azure blue marks on forehead, cheeks, lesser wing-
coverts, and rump of male; female brown.
RANGE: Mexico (Sinaloa to Oaxaca; Nuevo León and Tamaulipas
south to Chiapas and Yucatán; favors shrubby underbrush), Guatemala, El Salvador, Honduras, and Nicaragua.

INDIGO BUNTING, *Passerina cyanea.* 4½
FIELD MARKS: In winter the male is largely brown but in spring migra-
tion may be blue. No azure marks.
RANGE: E. North America; winters south to Panama.

LAZULI BUNTING, *Passerina amoena.* 4½
(Considered a race of *P. cyanea* by some.)
FIELD MARKS: Two distinct white wing bars.
RANGE: W. North America to w. Mexico (Baja California to Chihuahua;
south and east in winter.)

VARIED BUNTING, *Passerina versicolor.* 4½
FIELD MARKS: The female lacks brown streaks on breast and has a
greenish brown rump (not blue).
RANGE: S.w. United States, Mexico (Baja California to Tamaulipas
and south to Guerrero, Puebla, and Veracruz; favors brushy areas
in arid and semi-arid regions; migratory in north), and Guatemala.

ROSITA BUNTING, *Passerina rositae.* 5 Plate 45
FIELD MARKS: Female is creamy buff below.
RANGE: Mexico (semi-arid Pacific slope of Oaxaca and Chiapas).

PAINTED BUNTING, *Passerina ciris.* 4½
RANGE: S. United States to n. Mexico (Chihuahua to Tamulipas); south in winter as far as Panama.

LECLANCHER BUNTING, *Passerina leclancherii.* 4½   Plate 45
FIELD MARKS: Female has eye ring and underparts clear yellow.
VOICE: The song phrase is made up of distinct motifs. A typical phrase may be shown as *cheet-weet a-weet-cheet a-chewit.* This requires two sec. Others are a bit shorter and some are longer, but all are quite similar in form. Pitch varies from F^4 to G^4.
RANGE: S.w. Mexico (Colima, Guerrero, w. Puebla, Oaxaca, and the Pacific slope of n. Chiapas; semi-arid brushy areas up to 3000 ft.).

LARK BUNTING, *Calamospiza melanocorys.* 6
FIELD MARKS: Winter birds may resemble a female Red-winged Black-bird.
RANGE: W.c. North America; winters to Mexico (Baja California to Tamaulipas and further south in the central plateau).

DICKCISSEL, *Spiza americana.* 6
FIELD MARKS: Female has only one dark moustache line at the side of the throat and no distinct brown line through the eye.
RANGE: C. North America; winters south as far as n. South America.

RED CROSSBILL, *Loxia curvirostra.* 5½
RANGE: Northern Hemisphere; in North America south to n. Nicaragua confined to mt. pine forests in Central America).

PURPLE FINCH, *Carpodacus purpureus.* 5½
RANGE: N. North America to mts. of Baja California.

CASSIN FINCH, *Carpodacus cassinii.* 6
FIELD MARKS: Male has no brown streaks on sides.
RANGE: Mts. of w. North America to n.w. Mexico (Baja California; in winter south to Zacatecas, Mexico, and Veracruz).

HOUSE FINCH, *Carpodacus mexicanus.* 5¼
FIELD MARKS: Males have forehead and stripe along side of crown red (occasionally yellow—possibly in birds in poor health); center of crown grayish brown or red; brown stripes on sides.
RANGE: W. North America to Mexico (Baja California to Nuevo León and Tamaulipas south to Oaxaca and Veracruz; largely in arid interior basins but also in pine woods in the mts.).

SAFFRON YELLOW-FINCH, *Sicalis flaveola.* 5   Plate 45
RANGE: South America; introduced into c. Panama where rare.

GRASSLAND YELLOW-FINCH, *Sicalis luteola.* 4½
FIELD MARKS: Head and rump olive-yellow; back brownish green,
streaked with black; wings dark brown; tail brownish black, usually
with white spot near end of outside feather; underparts yellow.
RANGE: Costa Rica to Argentina and Chile.

MEXICAN YELLOW-FINCH, *Sicalis chrysops.* 4½   Plate 45
(Considered a race of *S. luteola* by some.)
FIELD MARKS: Wings and tail dusky. At a distance in the rice fields
may easily be mistaken for a Yellow Warbler.
VOICE: One song phrase may be represented by *tseet-see-seee-seee-
seeeeee-seeeeeeet;* it lasts two sec.; pitch varies from G⁵ down to
C⁵ (the *tseet* slurs up from F⁵ to G⁵; the *seeee* starts at C⁵ but is
mostly at D⁵). Longer phrases may contain many *churr* figures.
Calls may be represented by *clipcheeup,* which takes a half sec. (it
is so fast it may sound more like *seeseelp*), and by *Suee ClipCheeup.*
RANGE: Mexico (Morelos to n.w. Puebla; s. Veracruz to Chiapas; mostly
in rice and sugar-cane fields in the west and grassy pastures in
the east) and Guatemala.

AMERICAN GOLDFINCH, *Spinus tristis.* 4¼
RANGE: North America to n.w. Baja California, Mexico; south in
winter as far as San Luis Potosí and Veracruz.

LESSER GOLDFINCH, *Spinus psaltria.* 4
RANGE: W. North America to Venezuela and Peru.

LAWRENCE GOLDFINCH, *Spinus lawrencei.* 4¼
RANGE: California and n. Baja California; winters to Sonora.

BLACK-HEADED SISKIN, *Spinus notatus.* 4¼   Plate 46
RANGE: Mexico (Sonora and Chihuahua south to Chiapas; s.w. Tamaulipas and e. San Luis Potosí to Veracruz; in pine, oak, and
cloud-forest areas; from 3000 to 8000 ft.; migratory in north),
Guatemala, south to Nicaragua.

GUATEMALAN SISKIN, *Spinus atriceps.* 4¼   Plate 46
RANGE: Mts. of Chiapas, Mexico, and Guatemala.

YELLOW-BELLIED SISKIN, *Spinus xanthogaster.* 4   Plate 46
RANGE: Costa Rica to w. Venezuela and Bolivia; pastures and meadows
in the mountains.

PINE SISKIN, *Spinus pinus.* 4¼
RANGE: North America to Mexico (high mts. of Michoacán to Chiapas;
also Mexico, Puebla, and Veracruz) and Guatemala.

BLUE-BLACK GRASQUIT, *Volitinia jacarina.*   4   Plate 46
FIELD MARKS: Male has a concealed white spot at the juncture of the
   wing and body that can be seen in display flights. Female and
   winter male are brown with darker streaks on breast. Immatures
   are variously intermediate between brown and black plumage.
VOICE: The song phrase is a thin, quick *kee-zeit.* It lasts only a half
   sec. The pitch of the last figure in the motif slurs down from G^5 to
   A^4. The bird springs into the air with three very quick wing beats
   to a height of one or two feet and bursts out with its song as he
   reaches the top of his flight and falls back to the perch.
RANGE: Mexico (s. Sonora to Chiapas; s. Tamaulipas and e. San
   Luis Potosí south to Chiapas; in grassy fields up to 8000 ft.) to
   Argentina and Chile.

OLIVE GRASQUIT, *Tiaris olivacea.*   4   Plate 46
FIELD MARKS: Most individuals are plain olive; adult male has black
   face with some gold markings.
RANGE: Mexico (s. Tamaulipas and e. San Luis Potosí to Chiapas and
   Yucatán; in weedy fields and pastures up to 6000 ft.; partly
   migratory, and flocks may seek hedge rows in winter) to Venezuela
   and Colombia.

YELLOW-BELLIED SEEDEATER, *Sporophila nigricollis.*   4
                                                            Plate 46
RANGE: S.w. Costa Rica to Brazil and Peru.

MINUTE SEEDEATER, *Sporophila minuta.*   3½   Plate 46
FIELD MARKS: Female has buffy white edging to wing coverts, but
   distinct wing bars are not formed.
VOICE: Shriller, thinner, and more varied than that of the Morellet
   Seedeater.
RANGE: Mexico (Pacific slope in Nayarit, Guerrero, Oaxaca, and
   Chiapas; up to 1000 ft. in semi-arid regions but favors marshy
   pastures), Guatemala, El Salvador, Nicaragua, Costa Rica (s.w.
   region), and w. Panama; also n.e. Argentina.

HICK'S SEEDEATER, *Sporophila aurita.*   4   Plate 46
   (Considered a race of *S. americana* by some.)
FIELD MARKS: Male has rump almost entirely black; throat either black
   or white (two color phases); belly partly white. Female belly white.
RANGE: W. Costa Rica to c. Panama.

BLACK SEEDEATER, *Sporophila corvina.*   4   Plate 46
   (Considered a race of *S. aurita* by some.)
FIELD MARKS: Male has a small white spot on wing at base of pri-

maries (frequently not visible); under wing-coverts white (show in flight); female has pale buff belly.

RANGE: Caribbean slope from s. Mexico (s. Veracruz and e. Oaxaca south) to n.w. Panama.

CINNAMON-RUMPED SEEDEATER, *Sporophila torqueola.* 4
Plate 46

FIELD MARKS: Male has a small white spot on wing near base of primaries; female has underparts yellowish buff.

RANGE: Pacific slope of Mexico (Sinaloa to Oaxaca).

MORELLET SEEDEATER, *Sporophila morelleti.* 4 Plate 46
(Considered a race of *S. torqueola* by some.)

FIELD MARKS: Male has white collar around neck; underparts white except for black band across chest; female has two buffy white wing bars.

VOICE: The song is somewhat Canary-like and although the phrases are varied may be recognized by the form *sweet-sweet-sweet-cheetacheeta.* The *sweet* figures are clear and distinct, but the other parts are weak and hurried.

RANGE: Mexico (Veracruz, e. Puebla, e. Oaxaca, and south to eastern and western slopes of Chiapas, and Yucatán; in weedy fields up to 6000 ft.) to Costa Rica and n.w. Panama.

SHARPE'S SEEDEATER, *Sporophila sharpei.* 4 Plate 46
(Considered a race of *S. torqueola* by some.)

FIELD MARKS: The adult male resembles the immature of the previous species (lacks a white collar around neck and has no distinct black band across the chest).

VOICE: The usual song phrase is a loud, clear *sweet-sweet-sweet-cheer-cheer-cheer*; sometimes the series of *sweet* figures is followed by a low and indistinct roll or jumble more after the fashion of the Morellet Seedeater.

RANGE: S. Texas and n.e. Mexico (Nuevo León, Tamaulipas, and e. San Luis Potosí).

SLATE-COLORED SEEDEATER, *Sporophila schistacea.* 4
Plate 46

RANGE: S.w. Costa Rica to Brazil and Bolivia; favors dense underbrush in openings or shrubby thickets in edge.

GUERRERO SEEDEATER, *Amaurospiza relicta.* 5 Plate 46
(Considered a race of *A. concolor* by some.)

FIELD MARKS: Dull slate blue; female dull olive-brown.

RANGE: Mexico (Guerrero; very rare).

BLUE SEEDEATER, *Amaurospiza concolor.* 4½   Plate 46
FIELD MARKS: Dull indigo (dull black in some light); female brown.
RANGE: Mexico (s.w. Chiapas) to Ecuador; wet subtropics.

THICK-BILLED SEEDEATER, *Oryzoborus funereus.* 4   Plate 46
(Considered a race of *O. angolensis* by some.)
FIELD MARKS: Bill as deep as long. The black male has a white spot
on the wing at the base of the primaries, but this spot does not al-
ways show. The female is brown.
RANGE: Mexico (s. Veracruz and e. Oaxaca and south) and along
the Caribbean slope to Nicaragua; Costa Rica and Panama to
Ecuador.

NUTTING SEEDEATER, *Oryzoborus nuttingi.* 5½   Plate 46
(Considered a race of *O. crassirostris* by some.)
RANGE: Caribbean slope of Nicaragua and adjacent Costa Rica.

RUFOUS-CAPPED ATLAPETES, *Atlapetes pileatus.* 5   Plate 47
RANGE: Mexico (Chihuahua to Nuevo León and south to Oaxaca and
Veracruz; mostly in mt. oak regions, but down almost to sea level
locally; usually found near ground in patches of dense shrubbery
or weeds).

WHITE-NAPED ATLAPETES, *Atlapetes albinucha.* 6½   Plate 47
RANGE: E. Mexico (e. San Luis Potosí, e. Puebla, Veracruz, Oaxaca,
and Chiapas; mostly in underbrush of humid woods at 4000 to 8000
ft.) and Colombia; semi-open areas.

YELLOW-THROATED ATLAPETES, *Atlapetes gutturalis.* 6½
                                                Plate 47
RANGE: Mts. of s. Chiapas, Mexico, and south to Colombia.

CHESTNUT-CAPPED ATLAPETES, *Atlapetes brunneinucha.* 7
                                                Plate 47
RANGE: Mexico (Guerrero to Mexico and south to Oaxaca; e. San
Luis Potosí and south through e. Puebla and Veracruz to Chiapas;
3000 to 5000 ft. in cloud forests and humid woods or in cañons in
somewhat drier regions; dense underbrush) and south to Venezuela and Peru.

SAN MARTIN ATLAPETES, *Atlapetes apertus.* 7   Plate 47
(Considered a race of *A. brunneinucha* by some.)
RANGE: Confined to the cloud forest areas on Volcán San Martín and
nearby mts. of the Sierra de Tuxtla in s. Veracruz, Mexico.

GREEN-STRIPED ATLAPETES, *Atlapetes virenticeps.* 7 Plate 47
(Considered a race of *A. torquatus* by some.)
FIELD MARKS: Stripe through middle of crown yellowish olive.
RANGE: Mexico (s. Sinaloa and Durango south to Morelos and Puebla;
s. Tamaulipas to e. San Luis Potosí; favors underbrush in oak-pine
woods at 3000 to 8000 ft.).

GRAY-STRIPED ATLAPETES, *Atlapetes assimilis.* 7 Plate 47
(Considered a race of *A. torquatus* by some.)
RANGE: Costa Rica to Venezuela and Peru; favors second-growth
thickets outside the forest.

BLACK-HEADED ATLAPETES, *Atlapetes atricapillus.* 8 Plate 47
RANGE: E. Panama and Colombia; rare.

GREEN-TAILED TOWHEE, *Chlorura chlorura.* 6¼
FIELD MARKS: Gray chest band.
RANGE: W. United States; winters to c. Mexico (Michoacán and San
Luis Potosí).

COLLARED TOWHEE, *Pipilo ocai.* 8 Plate 47
FIELD MARKS: Line through center of black forehead, line over eye,
throat, and belly white.
RANGE: Mexico (three well-isolated groups: c. Guerrero, extreme e.
Puebla and adjacent Veracruz, and c. Oaxaca; in pine-oak and pine-
fir forests mostly from 7000 to 11000 ft.; favors shrubby cover in
partly cleared woods).

OLIVE-BACKED TOWHEE, *Pipilo ocai* x *maculatus.* 8 Plate 47
FIELD MARKS: Variously intermediate between the Collared Towhee
and the Spotted Towhee. In central Mexico there is an area over
four hundred miles long and on the average about fifty miles wide
that stretches from c. Jalisco to the mts. forming the boundary of
the states of Mexico and Puebla in which this hybrid species is found.
In the extreme west, most individuals appear much like Collared
Towhees but lack the white line through the center of the forehead
and have a restricted superciliary. In the extreme east, all individuals
look very much like Spotted Towhees but have olive, instead of
black, backs, and the amount of white spotting on the back and
wing is restricted. In the area between the extremes, numerous
different degrees of hybridization are found; nowhere in the whole
region, however, are there any birds of the "pure" type of either of
the supposed parent strains. While it may be said that in general
there is less white on the throat and less rufous on the crown in
birds as one proceeds from west to east and less spotting on the back
and wings as one progresses from east to west, there is no smooth

gradient either way; pockets may be found where one factor or another is more or less prominent. There is a spot in n. Morelos where many birds have white throats and a place far out in Jalisco where birds with completely black throats may be found.

RANGE: From c. Jalisco east through Michoacán, Mexico, and Morelos to the volcanoes on the Mexico-Puebla boundary; mostly from 7000 to 11000 ft. in pine-oak forests.

SPOTTED TOWHEE, *Pipilo maculatus.* 7¼ Plate 47
(Considered a race of *P. erythrophthalmus* by some.)
FIELD MARKS: Wing bars and spots on shoulder of wing white; no white on head or throat. Sexes similar.
RANGE: W. United States to Mexico (mts. of Baja California across to Nuevo León and s.w. Tamaulipas and south to Nayarit and Veracruz; s. Oaxaca and Chiapas; 5000 to 8000 ft.) and Guatemala.

RED-EYED TOWHEE, *Pipilo erythrophthalmus.* 7¼
FIELD MARKS: No white spots on back or wings; sexes not alike.
RANGE: E. North America to c. Texas and Florida; in winter a rare visitor to n.e. Tamaulipas, Mexico.

CANON TOWHEE, *Pipilo fuscus.* 7¼ Plate 47
FIELD MARKS: Median breast and belly white; back grayish brown; crown frequently rufous-tinted, contrasting with back.
RANGE: W. United States and Mexico (Sonora to Tamaulipas and south to n. Guerrero, n. Puebla, and w. Veracruz; except in the northwest, mostly in high interior basins and arid mt. regions.)

CALIFORNIA TOWHEE, *Pipilo crissalis.* 7½ Plate 47
(Considered a race of *P. fuscus* by some.)
RANGE: Pacific coast of United States (California) and Baja California (northern and central part).

SAN LUCAS TOWHEE, *Pipilo albigula.* 7 Plate 47
(Considered a race of *P. fuscus* by some.)
FIELD MARKS: Lower one-third of throat white, in contrast with the buff upper portion; chest brownish gray; belly white.
RANGE: Cape district of Baja California, Mexico.

WHITE-THROATED TOWHEE, *Pipilo albicollis.* 7 Plate 47
FIELD MARKS: Similar to Cañon Towhee, but throat white. There is usually a dull yellowish buff band across the lower throat that is more or less set off from the white by some narrow, dusky lines. Wing-coverts sometimes edged with dull white; this may form an indistinct bar.
RANGE: Mexico (e. Guerrero, s.w. Puebla, w. and s. Oaxaca; high semi-desert basins and arid mts.).

ABERT TOWHEE, *Pipilo aberti.* 8
RANGE: S.w. United States and n.w. Mexico (n. Baja California and n.w. Sonora).

KIENER GROUND-SPARROW, *Melozone kieneri.* 6   Plate 47
FIELD MARKS: A rufous bar across grayish olive face; black spot in center of white breast.
RANGE: Mexico (s. Sonora and Chihuahua through Nayarit and Morelos to Guerrero, Oaxaca, and w. Puebla; in foothill cañons in the north and in areas of rather dense tree growth either in highlands or in lowlands further south; favors dense thickets in woods from near sea level up to 5000 ft. in subhumid regions).

PREVOST'S GROUND-SPARROW, *Melozone biarcuatum.* 5½
Plate 47
(Considered a race of *M. kieneri* by some.)
FIELD MARKS: Face white; bar at side of head almost black; no black spot in center of chest.
RANGE: Mexico (highlands of s.w. Chiapas; occasionally down almost to sea level near Pacific coast), Guatemala, and El Salvador.

CABANIS GROUND-SPARROW, *Melozone cabanisi.* 5½   Plate 47
(Considered a race of *M. biarcuatum* by some and of *M. kieneri* by others.)
RANGE: Highlands of c. Costa Rica; favors open shrubby areas.

WHITE-EARED GROUND-SPARROW, *Melozone leucotis.* 6
Plate 47
RANGE: Highlands of Nicaragua and Costa Rica; tends to range a bit above the previous species.

SALVIN'S GROUND-SPARROW, *Melozone occipitalis.* 7
Plate 47
(Considered a race of *M. leucotis* by some.)
FIELD MARKS: A gray stripe through center of crown; a yellow stripe above the ear.
RANGE: Highlands of extreme s. Mexico (s. Chiapas), Guatemala, and El Salvador.

SLATE-COLORED SPARROW, *Spodiornis rusticus.* 5   Plate 47
RANGE: Has been collected near Jalapa, Veracruz, and on Volcán Tacaná in Chiapas, Mexico; very rare.

PEG-BILLED SPARROW, *Acanthidops bairdi.* 5½   Plate 47
RANGE: High mts. of c. Costa Rica.

BIG-FOOTED SPARROW, *Pezopetes capitalis.* 7½   Plate 47
FIELD MARKS: Forehead and sides of crown black; center stripe of crown and most of face gray.
RANGE: Mts. of Costa Rica and w. Panama; grassy areas and edge at or near timber line.

YELLOW-THIGHED SPARROW, *Pselliophorus tibialis.* 7
                                                                       Plate 47
RANGE: Highlands of Costa Rica and w. Panama; from timber line down to about 4000 ft.

YELLOW-GREEN SPARROW, *Pselliophorus luteoviridis.* 7
                                                                       Plate 47
RANGE: W. Panama (e. Chiriqui).

BARRANCA SPARROW, *Lysurus crassirostris.* 5½   Plate 47
FIELD MARKS: Crown chestnut; throat dusky gray; belly yellow.
RANGE: Costa Rica and w. Panama; humid subtropics.

ORANGE-BILLED SPARROW, *Arremon aurantiirostris.* 6
                                                                       Plate 47
RANGE: Mexico (s. Veracruz and e. Oaxaca and south; wet tropical forest) and south to Peru.

TEXAS SPARROW, *Arremonops rufivirgatus.* 5½   Plate 48
FIELD MARKS: Pale, dull brown stripes at side of crown that are not sharply defined and set off from the median stripe.
RANGE: S. Texas and n.e. Mexico (Nuevo León and Tamaulipas to e. Puebla, Veracruz, and e. Oaxaca; underbrush in semi-arid regions).

SCHOTT'S SPARROW, *Arremonops verticalis.* 5½   Plate 48
   (Considered a race of *A. rufivirgatus* by some.)
FIELD MARKS: Lateral crown stripes streaked with black; throat almost white.
RANGE: Mexico (semi-arid regions of n. Campeche and Yucatán).

GREEN-BACKED SPARROW, *Arremonops chloronotus.* 5½
                                                                       Plate 48
   (Considered a race of *A. conirostris* by some.)
FIELD MARKS: Very similar to previous species, but lateral crown stripes blacker and back bright olive-green instead of grayish or brownish olive-green; chest darker gray, making the throat seem whiter.
RANGE: Mexico (underbrush in humid woods in Tabasco, e. Chiapas, Campeche, e. Yucatán, and Quintana Roo), British Honduras, e. Guatemala, and n.e. Honduras.

RICHMOND SPARROW, *Arremonops richmondi.* 6   Plate 48
(Considered a race of *A. conirostris* by some.)
RANGE: S. Honduras to w. Panama; humid region edge.

BLACK-STRIPED SPARROW, *Arremonops striaticeps.* 6   Plate 48
(Considered a race of *A. conirostris* by some.)
RANGE: E. Panama (from Canal Zone) to Pacific Colombia and n.w
Ecuador.

CHESTNUT-STRIPED SPARROW, *Arremonops superciliosa.* 5
Plate 48
(Considered a race of *A. rufivirgatus* by some.)
FIELD MARKS: Similar to Acapulco Sparrow, but darker.
RANGE: N.w. Costa Rica.

ACAPULCO SPARROW, *Arremonops sumichrasti.* 6   Plate 48
(Considered a race of *A. rufivirgatus* by some.)
FIELD MARKS: Lateral crown stripes light chestnut; chest light buffy
gray.
RANGE: Mexico (Sinaloa to w. Chiapas; semi-arid Pacific lowlands).

STRIPED SPARROW, *Oriturus superciliosus.* 6   Plate 48
VOICE: The song is rather similar to that of the Cañon Towhee.
RANGE: Mexico (highland basins and grassy places in pine forests
from s.e. Sonora and Chihuahua to Puebla and Veracruz; mostly
from 7000 to 10000 ft.; avoids "deserts").

SAVANNA SPARROW, *Passerculus sandwichensis.* 4½   Plate 48
FIELD MARKS: A distinct buffy white stripe through center of crown;
distinct line over eye white or partly yellow; breast and sides marked
with short, narrow streaks.
RANGE: North America to Mexico (Durango and Chihuahua south to
Puebla; in winter Baja California to Tamaulipas and south to Oaxaca,
Veracruz, and Yucatán); in winter south to El Salvador and Cuba.

BELDING SPARROW, *Passerculus beldingi.* 4½   Plate 48
(Considered a race of *P. sandwichensis* by some.)
FIELD MARKS: Stripe through center of crown indistinct; line over eye
indistinct; crown and back olive streaked with black; breast and
sides broadly streaked.
RANGE: Pacific coastal marshes of c. California south to western coast
of c. Baja California.

LARGE-BILLED SPARROW, *Passerculus rostratus.* 5   Plate 48
(Considered a race of *P. sandwichensis* by some.)
FIELD MARKS: Above light grayish brown, indistinctly streaked with

darker brown; line over eye pale buffy gray; breast and sides streaked with dark brown.

RANGE: Mexico (both coasts of s. Baja California; delta of Colorado River and coastal marshes of Sonora to c. Sinaloa; winters to southern tip of Baja California).

GRASSHOPPER SPARROW, *Ammodramus savannarum*.   4½
RANGE: North America to Mexico (savannas in Mexico, Oaxaca, Veracruz, and Chiapas; more widespread in north during winter) and south to w. Ecuador; locally.

BAIRD SPARROW, *Ammodramus bairdii*.   4½
FIELD MARKS: Above rather like a Grasshopper Sparrow and below like a Savanna Sparrow.
RANGE: C. North America; winters to n. Mexico.

BAILEY SPARROW, *Xenospiza baileyi*.   5   Plate 48
FIELD MARKS: A short-winged, long-tailed sparrow resembling the Lincoln Sparrow above and the Savanna Sparrow below.
RANGE: Mts. of w. Mexico (Durango, Jalisco, Mexico, and Morelos; in bunch grass areas in pine woods); rare.

VESPER SPARROW, *Pooecetes gramineus*.   5½
RANGE: North America; winters to Mexico and Guatemala.

LARK SPARROW, *Chondestes grammacus*.   6
RANGE: C. and w. North America to Mexico (Chihuahua to Tamaulipas; quite widespread in winter); winters to Guatemala and El Salvador.

FIVE-STRIPED SPARROW, *Aimophila quinquestriata*.   5¼
                                                                       Plate 48
RANGE: W. Mexico (s. Sonora, Chihuahua, Sinaloa, Durango, and Jalisco; mostly in foothills and lowlands).

BRIDLED SPARROW, *Aimophila mystacalis*.   5½   Plate 48
VOICE: The songs are high pitched, thin, and fast. One phrase consists of two introductory figures followed by a rattle; it may be indicated as *weechip weeche*, followed by twelve *che* figures. This requires a total of only one and a half sec. The pitch of the *weechip* is about F^5 (slurs up to G^5 on the *wee* and the *chip* is F^5); the final rattle is about the same pitch. There is also a somewhat slower *chip-at-it chip-chip-chip-chip-chip-chip*, which requires one and a quarter sec.
RANGE: S. Mexico (semi-desert plateaus in Puebla, Veracruz, and Oaxaca; mostly for 4000 to 7000 ft.).

BELTED SPARROW, *Aimophila humeralis*. 5½ Plate 48

VOICE: The song is a series of short, shrill, identical motifs, rapidly repeated and so accented that it seems to be a gallop. A motif may be represented by *jerk-ya-feet*. This motif may be repeated twelve times in five and a half sec. The pitch varies from G^5 down about five tones, but the main tones are F^5, C^5 sharp, G^5.

RANGE: W.c. Mexico (Michoacán, Colima, Guerrero, Morelos, w. Puebla, and n. Oaxaca; foothills and brushy cañons in the plateau region).

RUFOUS-TAILED SPARROW, *Aimophila ruficauda*. 6¼
Plate 48

FIELD MARKS: Head black with a broad white line over the eye and a narrower one through the center of the crown.

VOICE: Calls may be sharply accented, *Chedk,* or a fast series, *checpchec-chec-chec.* The song is a rapid repetition of a motif. Although there are a number of different ones, the motifs are of the same style and about the same pitch and tempo. One may be given as *check-yo-credit,* repeated five times in two sec.; the pitch varies from E^3 down about three tones (this motif being D^3-E^3-D^3 E^3). Most often the male and female sing duets. One may sing something like *Can-she-jump-up-SheWill* five times in four sec., while the other will sing a shorter motif, such as *BachUp* sixteen times in the same four sec. Such duets sound like a very complex jumble.

RANGE: W. Mexico (Nayarit south to Chiapas; favors subhumid, brushy savannas up to about 2000 ft.) to n.w. Costa Rica.

RUFOUS-WINGED SPARROW, *Aimophila carpalis*. 5 Plate 48

FIELD MARKS: Whisker line black; rounded tail grayish brown.

RANGE: S. Arizona and n.w. Mexico (Sonora and Sinaloa; arid mesquite-cactus regions with bunch grass).

SUMICHRAST SPARROW, *Aimophila sumichrasti*. 6 Plate 48

FIELD MARKS: A double whisker line at each side of throat; tail rufous brown.

VOICE: These birds answer high-pitched rattles, at least during the breeding season, and hence are constantly squeaking loudly from roadside bushes at cars or trucks that pass through their territory. This squeaking is a rapid and confused jumble of high-pitched figures and is usually produced by two birds singing a duet. The songs are somewhat varied and may consist of an introductory figure followed by a fast rattle (*chip che-he-he-he-he*), a similar, but slightly slower, *let le-che-che-che-che*, or more frequently a longer, more elaborate phrase, such as *see-yet Keep-it-up yet Keep-it-up,* which requires one and a quarter sec. The *Keep* is always strongly accented and is pitched about B^4. There may be a longer introductory motif, as in *Keep-keep-cheeah weet-weet-Cheet Keep-it-up Keep-it-up Keep-it-up*, which requires a total time of three sec. One bird, presumably the female, may do a long and very fast series of *tit* figures while the other sings a rapid *keep-it-up* series; it is this duet which at the roadside sounds like confused squeaking. At the proper stage of the breeding cycle the male also sings a dawn song.

RANGE: Mexico (arid brushlands of Pacific slope in Oaxaca; sea level up to 2000 ft. or more).

OAXACA SPARROW, *Aimophila notosticta.*   6   Plate 48

FIELD MARKS: Very similar to Rusty Sparrow, but whole bill is black, and tail is light brown instead of rufous chestnut.

RANGE: Mexico (mts. of c. Oaxaca).

RUSTY SPARROW, *Aimophila rufescens.*   6½   Plate 48

FIELD MARKS: In n.w. Mexico, where this species appears grayer above than in other parts of the range and where it does not have the black edging to the cap, it may be difficult to distinguish it from the following species unless one uses care.

VOICE: There are several rather similar songs; all are loud and clear and quite simple in form. The pitch of the main tones varies from D^4 up to G^4. A phrase requiring one and a half sec. may be represented as *chep-chep chee-chee-chee-cheebur*. Some lasting one sec. are *chuwee chep-chep* and *cheep-chep-chep-chep*.

RANGE: Mexico (Sonora and Chihuahua, south to Oaxaca and Chiapas; s.w. Tamaulipas and e. San Luis Potosí, south to Veracruz and Chiapas; from 2000 to 6000 ft. in semi-arid regions, brushy oak woods, and second-growth cloud forest areas) to n.w. Costa Rica.

RUFOUS-CROWNED SPARROW, *Aimophila ruficeps.*   5¼

Plate 48

FIELD MARKS: Bill dark brown (upper one not black); rump brownish gray contrasting somewhat with the brown tail.

RANGE: S.w. United States and Mexico (Baja California and Sonora across to Tamaulipas and south to Oaxaca and Veracruz; in grassy, shrubby areas in rather dry oak woods).

BOTTERI SPARROW, *Aimophila botterii.*   5½   Plate 48

FIELD MARKS: Throat cream-colored; tail when spread shows areas noticeably browner than the back; a small spot of yellow at the bend of the wing may not always be visible. In humid areas the birds are darker, more richly colored, and have a larger yellow patch at the bend of the wing.

VOICE: The song period begins with a series of thin calls given in a halting manner; eventually there are two loud, clear calls (a couplet of identical figures) followed by a series of figures that begin slowly, speed up quickly, and end in a rattle that sounds very much like that of the Texas Sparrow. Although the individual figures vary considerably, the form of the song phrase remains the same. Phrases may be represented by *wit wit cheeup cheeup Cheer-Cheer chee chee che che-che-che-che-che-che-che* and *wit chee-ee chee-ee chip chip ip ip Chee-Chee wit wit wit-wit-wi-wi-wi-wi-wi-wi-wi*. At times the preliminary calls are continued for a much longer time and then stopped without the addition of the song phrase.

RANGE: S.w. border of United States and Mexico (Sinaloa south to Chiapas; Coahuila, Nuevo León, and Tamaulipas south through San Luis Potosí to Campeche; in grassy savannas from sea level up to 5000 ft. or more; favors areas where there are thickets of shrubbery and scattered small trees; migratory, at least in north) to n.w. Costa Rica.

CASSIN SPARROW, *Aimophila cassinii.* 5½

FIELD MARKS: Throat dull white; tail not browner than back.

VOICE: The song phrase, which lasts about two sec., is thin but clear and sweet. The intonation and structure may be indicated by *I I sing for thee* (the *sing* is a high-pitched vibrato figure that takes up about half the total time of the phrase).

RANGE: S.w. United States and Mexico (Coahuila to n.e. Tamaulipas; in winter in other border states and further south).

BLACK-THROATED SPARROW, *Amphispiza bilineata.* 4½

RANGE: S.w. United States and n. Mexico (Baja California and Sonora across to Tamaulipas and south to Sinaloa, Durango, Hidalgo, and San Luis Potosí; in semi-desert regions; from sea level up to about 6000 ft.).

BELL SPARROW, *Amphispiza belli.* 5

RANGE: W. United States and Baja California; winters to Sonora and Chihuahua.

CHIPPING SPARROW, *Spizella passerina.* 5

RANGE: North America, Mexico (n. Baja California across to Chihuahua and south to Chiapas and Veracruz; pine-oak woods in mts. and high savannas; mostly above 5000 ft.; elsewhere in winter), and south to Nicaragua.

CLAY-COLORED SPARROW, *Spizella pallida.* 4½

RANGE: C. North America; winters south as far as Guatemala.

BREWER'S SPARROW, *Spizella breweri.* 4½

RANGE: W. North America; winters to Baja California, Jalisco, and San Luis Potosí.

FIELD SPARROW, *Spizella pusilla.*   5
RANGE: E. North America; winters to n.e. Mexico.

WORTHEN SPARROW, *Spizella wortheni.*   5   Plate 48
(Considered a race of S. *pusilla* by some.)
FIELD MARKS: Similar to Field Sparrow but paler and grayer; white
eye ring more conspicuous; no brown line back of eye.
RANGE: Arid uplands of Mexico (Chihuahua across to Tamaulipas and
south to Zacatecas; winters to Puebla and Veracruz).

BLACK-CHINNED SPARROW, *Spizella atrogularis.*   5¼
RANGE: S.w. United States and Mexico (Baja California across to Coahuila and south to Guerrero, Puebla, and Hidalgo; in semi-desert
basins and arid mts.).

WHITE-CROWNED SPARROW, *Zonotrichia leucophrys.*   6
RANGE: W. North America; winters to c. Mexico.

WHITE-THROATED SPARROW, *Zonotrichia albicollis.*   6
RANGE: N.e. United States; winters to n. Mexico.

GOLDEN-CROWNED SPARROW, *Zonotrichia atricapilla.*   6¼
RANGE: N.w. North America; winters south to Baja California.

RUFOUS-COLLARED SPARROW, *Zonotrichia capensis.*   5
                                                                Plate 48
VOICE: The song is high pitched and liquid (piccolo-like); it may be
represented by *che-eep cheo-cheo-cheo.* This requires about two sec.
The first part, although shown in two parts, is really a drawn-out,
slurred figure; the last part is much faster, but the figures are distinct.
RANGE: S. Mexico (pine woods and mt. meadows in s.c. Chiapas;
6000 to 8000 ft.; replaces House Sparrow in the towns) to Tierra
del Fuego.

FOX SPARROW, *Passerella iliaca.*   6¼
RANGE: N. North America to mts. of California; winters to n. Baja
California.

LINCOLN SPARROW, *Melospiza lincolnii.*   55
RANGE: N. North America; winters south to Panama.

SONG SPARROW, *Melospiza melodia.*   5½
RANGE: North America to c. Mexico (Baja California, Sonora, and Chihuahua south to Mexico and Puebla; mostly from 4000 to 8000 ft.;
in northwest descends to sea level; in marshy areas; more widespread
in winter).

SWAMP SPARROW, *Melospiza georgiana.*   5
RANGE: E. North America; winters to n.e. Mexico.

WEDGE-TAILED SPARROW, *Emberizoides herbicola.*   7½
                                         Plate 47
RANGE: S.w. Costa Rica to Argentina and Bolivia; tropical savannas;
    favors tangled bushy and grassy areas, such as used by Grasquits.

VOLCANO JUNCO, *Junco vulcani.*   6¼   Plate 48
RANGE: Costa Rica and w. Panama; high mts. near timber line.

MEXICAN JUNCO, *Junco phaeonotus.*   5½   Plate 48
FIELD MARKS: Iris yellow; lower bill pale yellow; back rufous brown,
    contrasting sharply with the gray head and olive-gray rump; breast
    gray, blending smoothly into the grayish brown sides.
VOICE: The song usually begins with a series of *chee* figures, as in
    the phrase *chee-chee-chebur-chee-chee-chee.* Frequently the last
    part of the phrase is a series of *chip* figures delivered faster and
    faster until it becomes a rattle.
RANGE: S. Arizona and Mexico north of the Isthmus of Tehuantepec
    (n.w. Sonora and Chihuahua south to Oaxaca; Coahuila, Nuevo
    León, and w. Tamaulipas south to Veracruz; in pine and fir forests;
    mostly from 9000 to 10000 ft. but down to 3000 ft. locally in the
    north).

BAIRD JUNCO, *Junco bairdi.*   5¼   Plate 48
    (Considered a race of *J. phaeonotus* by some.)
FIELD MARKS: The cinnamon-brown back blends gradually into a buffy
    brown rump; the black of the lores does not extend into a narrow area
    around eye; the sides are cinnamon.
RANGE: Victoria Mts. in cape district of Baja California.

CHIAPAS JUNCO, *Junco fulvescens.*   5½   Plate 48
    (Considered a race of *J. phaeonotus* by some.)
FIELD MARKS: Similar to Mexican Junco, but back is browner (less
    rufous) and the color blends into that of the olive-brown rump in-
    stead of being sharply cut off; sides brown.
VOICE: The song phrase is usually in two motifs, as *cher-cher-cher-chip-*
    chip-chip.
RANGES Mts. of c. Chiapas; pine-oak-madroño association; 5000 to 9000
    ft.

GUATEMALAN JUNCO, *Junco alticola.*   6   Plate 48
    (Considered a race of *J. phaeonotus* by some.)
FIELD MARKS: Similar to last species but larger and much darker.
RANGE: Mexico (humid mts. near Pacific coast of extreme s. Chiapas;
    8000 to 11000 ft.) and w. Guatemala.

SLATE-COLORED JUNCO, *Junco hyemalis.* 5¼
RANGE: W. North America; winters casually to n. Mexico.

OREGON JUNCO, *Junco oreganus.* 5¼
RANGE: W. North America; winters to n. Mexico.

PINK-SIDED JUNCO, *Junco mearnsi.* 5¼
 (Considered a race of *J. oreganus* by some.)
FIELD MARKS: Head and breast gray (not black).
RANGE: W. United States to mts. of n. Baja California; winters to n.
 Mexico.

GRAY-HEADED JUNCO, *Junco caniceps.* 5½
FIELD MARKS: Whole bill light (pinkish white).
RANGE: W. United States; winters to n. Mexico.

RED-BACKED JUNCO, *Junco dorsalis.* 5½
 (Considered a race of *J. caniceps* by some.)
FIELD MARKS: Upper bill dark; lower bill light.
RANGE: S.w. United States; winters to n. Mexico.

McCOWN LONGSPUR, *Rhynchophanes mccownii.* 5¼
RANGE: C. North America; winters south to Durango, Mexico.

CHESTNUT-COLLARED LONGSPUR, *Calcarius ornatus.* 5
RANGE: C. North America; winters south to Sonora, Chihuahua, and
 Veracruz.

INDEX